Competitive Strategy Dynamics

Competitive Strategy Dynamics

Kim Warren

London Business School

JOHN WILEY & SONS, LTD

Copyright © 2002   John Wiley & Sons Ltd, The Atrium, Southern Gate, Chichester, West Sussex PO19 8SQ, England

Telephone   (+44) 1243 779777

Email (for orders and customer service enquiries): cs-books@wiley.co.uk
Visit our Home Page on www.wileyeurope.com or www.wiley.co.uk

Reprinted March 2003

Other Wiley Editorial Offices

John Wiley & Sons Inc., 111 River Street, Hoboken, NJ 07030, USA

Jossey-Bass, 989 Market Street, San Francisco, CA 94103-1741, USA

Wiley-VCH Verlag GmbH, Boschstr. 12, D-69469 Weinheim, Germany

John Wiley & Sons Australia Ltd, 33 Park Road, Milton, Queensland 4064, Australia

John Wiley & Sons (Asia) Pte Ltd, 2 Clementi Loop #02-01, Jin Xing Distripark, Singapore 129809

John Wiley & Sons Canada Ltd, 22 Worcester Road, Etobicoke, Ontario, Canada M9W 1L1

British Library Cataloguing in Publication Data

A catalogue record for this book is available from the British Library

ISBN 0-471-89949-6

Project management by Originator, Gt Yarmouth, Norfolk (typeset in 10/12pt Palatino)
Printed and bound in Great Britain by TJ International, Padstow, Cornwall
This book is printed on acid-free paper responsibly manufactured from sustainable forestry in which at least two trees are planted for each one used for paper production.

Contents

To Christina

Preface

The Strategic Management field is in a somewhat sorry state today, as compared with the confidence it exhibited in the 1970s and 1980s. Strategy as "planning" was in its heyday, and the field was given new confidence by Michael Porter's seminal work on industry forces, which seemed to provide a powerful explanation for how the competitive environment constrained opportunities for profit (Porter, 1980, 1985). Managers could identify the forces ranged against them, by customers, suppliers, and rivals, and work out how to manage those forces to improve their earnings. Analyzing the cost and value drivers within the business and among others up and down the supply chain provided more clues as to where changes could be made to further uprate performance. Even today, derivations of this concept form the foundation for much of the work of top strategy consulting firms.

The 1990s saw monumental upheavals in the social, economic, political, and technological backdrop faced by firms and industries. The established methods of strategy analysis, being largely static, seemed to offer little guidance in these turbulent times, and were increasingly ignored by management. Regular surveys by consultants, Bain & Co., of the management approaches employed in business show that the use of most formal strategy techniques has been in steady decline for many years (Bain & Co., 2001).

Disillusion with "planning" is understandable, given the frequent failure in practise of formulaic approaches to strategy—forecasts have been unfulfilled, orchestrated action plans are rarely implemented, and, even if they are, fail to deliver the expected outcomes. Mintzberg was quick to point out that, even during that era, strategy as actually practised was a far more messy business than the "planners" would have liked to believe (Mintzberg and Quinn, 1997). He and others pointed to the importance of the strategy "process"—*how* strategy comes about, and is communicated and enacted.

It is sometimes implied, then, that analysis and planning *can't* work, but paying attention solely to the strategy process does not free managers from the importance of discovering choices of action that might help build strong and sustained business performance. The achievements of strategic managers with long-established credibility and track records show that sustained strategic success does not come from process alone, nor from simple checklists or isolated initiatives. Rather, it depends on a deep and thoughtful understanding of exactly how their firm functions, and interacts through time with the industry in which it operates. If strategy methods are to be of any value, then, they must help managers understand and steer this complex system into the future, with some indicators of scale and speed of progress.

Concern with the limited use of theory from the strategy field to help management encouraged partners at McKinsey & Co. to undertake in the late 1990s the "Strategy Theory Initiative"—an extensive review of the most promising writings about strategy in recent decades—in an effort to discover whether something powerful and reliable might have been missed (Huyett and Roxburgh, 2000). The result was less than encouraging. There was little more to help managers choose *where* to compete than Porter's work from 1980. Though this approach remains a sound starting point for identifying opportunities, consultants and managers struggle to extract from it more than the broadest guidance, expecially in situations of rapid change. On the question of *how* to compete, the study identified some general principles to follow—build and sustain strategic resources, concentrate on core competencies, and so on—but little that was practical or analytically reliable.

This need for strategy tools to help managers with the complex, unfolding pattern of critical decisions they have to make for strategic success provides a further motive for this book. In our dynamically complex world, strategic choices and decision making based on intuitive judgment are more likely to be wrong than right. The result is an often tragic record of business failure—the high mortality rate of new businesses, the catalog of failed diversifications and international ventures across many industries, and the continuing disappointment with acquisitions, mergers, joint ventures, and other strategic big throws.

The financial waste of such failure is bad enough—destruction of shareholder value is undoubtedly regrettable. But, it is often forgotten that people are involved here! Every failed new venture, every downsizing exercise, every ill-conceived reorganization or diversification, and every disastrous attempt to break into new markets or pull off that glittering acquisition is a battle in which ordinary folk are the cannon fodder. While no single contribution can hope to make a large difference to this problem, just a small swing in favor of the probability that strategic management will succeed rather than fail would be worthwhile.

Who will find this book useful?

A primary target for this work is the business student population, through the medium of business school courses. Its frameworks are intended, not to replace executives' judgment, but to offer a means for capturing their wisdom, as a resource for the emerging generation of managers. Discussion of common business situations that should be familiar to most readers ground the principles in practical realities, and these examples may be integrated into conventional case-based teaching. There also exists an increasing variety of simulation-based learning materials that provide the opportunity for direct experiential learning of the frameworks described here.[1]

The aspiration, though, is to reach much further than the current population of business school students. This book is meant to be useful and relevant to practising managers, whether in large or small firms, manufacturing or service sectors, public service or not-for-profit contexts. Many who have understood its frameworks at an early stage in their managerial career have found them to be helpful for setting out their thinking, and communicating it persuasively to senior managers whose support and commitment they need. It is hoped that senior management will find the approach powerful and practical for working with colleagues to create robust and actionable strategic development programs, though they may prefer to pass on to support staff the detail of populating the frameworks with the accurate information needed.

Outside the organization itself, professional advisors (such as legal, accounting, marketing, and others) may find the language helpful for communicating with their clients. It offers a way to understand the dynamics of the firms and industries they are advising, and to appreciate the particular role that their service and support can provide. Those concerned with financing and investing in firms should also be able to achieve a better understanding of the current health and future prospects of their clients, enabling them to make better-informed investment decisions. Finally, many in the management consulting community have found that the methods outlined here can help build an understanding of the challenges facing their clients more quickly and confidently than alternative approaches. In addition, they seem to find the frameworks helpful in focusing and controlling the often extensive analysis that is needed.

Scope and organization of the book

It is often helpful to split the topic of Strategy into two levels of complexity:

- the single-activity business unit, whether an independent trading entity, or a division within a larger organization; and
- the multibusiness firm, whether diversity arises from operating several *types* of business, or from operating in different geographical markets.

The strategy topic is so extensive that it would not be practical to attempt to cover both these levels of concern in a single work. Consequently, this volume focuses on the first level—strategic management of the single-activity business unit. Nevertheless, managers and advisors to more complex enterprises will also find significant benefits. Not only must such organizations have some means of appraising and directing the business units of which they consist, but it should be readily apparent how many of the principles discussed in this

---

[1] See, for example, the products from Global Strategy Dynamics Ltd., designed by the author and others to complement this book (www.strategydynamics.com).

volume can be leveraged through the relationships that exist in multibusiness firms.

Within the business unit context, however, the aim is to offer extensive coverage—from the detailed attention given to how individual resources and capabilities behave, up to the competitive interactions between firms, and the scenarios of industry evolution that arise.

A final comment concerns the analytical leaning that will be apparent throughout this book. While the messy, ambiguous, and qualitative nature of the strategic management challenge is not denied, the strategy field has, in my view, swung way too far from a concern with the quantitative facts of the factors that drive business performance. Fundamentally, investors in commercial firms are concerned with the earnings that the organization can deliver into the future, and those earnings depend on the *quantities* of resource that are available. It is essential, then, to show that the policy choices by senior management that constitute its strategic management enhance these quantities. In this effort to demonstrate this contribution, many readers will feel that this book (particularly, later chapters) pursues an excessive and unreasonable concern for quantification and analysis. However, this excess is a quite determined attempt to "reset" the expectations that the business community should have of those of us who presume to offer advice on strategy.

Figure A illustrates how various chapters map onto both the range of focus (from narrow to broad) and degree of clarity (from precisely quantifiable, to ambiguous and qualitative). We start in Chapter 1 with a focus on performance

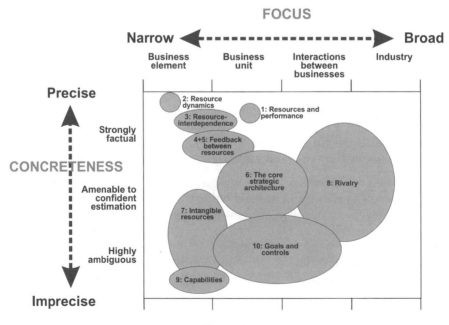

Figure A

itself, principally the financial performance of commercial firms, although other performance metrics can be dealt with for charitable and other not-for-profit organizations. Chapters 2 to 6 build up from an understanding of how individual resources behave through time, through the mechanisms by which they interact, to a coherent approach to identifying the core "strategic architecture" that lies at the heart of any organization. The second half of the book starts by adding to this core a means of dealing with critical intangible factors, such as reputation and staff skills, then offers formal means for quantifying the dynamics of competitive interactions. Finally, we look at the subtle development and influence of organizational capabilities and the tricky issue of how management sets goals for the enterprise, and controls its progress through time.

We won't solve our problems with the same kind of thinking that we used when we created them

Albert Einstein

Acknowledgments

My main thanks must go to Professor Jay Forrester, formerly of MIT, for codifying the dynamics of social systems as long ago as the 1950s. I remain mystified as to why these essentially simple mechanisms that constitute the processes of change in all social systems (as well as many physical ones) have lain largely ignored for four decades. I am also most grateful to my colleague Prof. John Morecroft, for both introducing me to these ideas and for encouraging my efforts to develop their application to the strategy field. Finally, I would like to thank the huge number of colleagues, both academics and executives, who have added their encouragement and contributions, as well as my students in recent years for stimulating development of these ideas as they took form.

Part I

Getting Started

1

The Critical Path—the Meaning of "Dynamics"

Key issues

❑ Clarifying the issue of "dynamics"—explaining the time-path of strategic performance

❑ Strategic resources drive performance

❑ Existing understanding of what determines "performance"

It is important, before setting out to tackle the issues of strategy dynamics, to give some clarity to the critical questions raised in the Preface, namely:

- *Why* has the historical performance of my business followed the time-path that it has?
- *Where* will the path of future performance take us if we carry on as we are?
- *How* can we alter that future for the better?

The first question may not be relevant in every case—a new venture start-up has no history. However, for most firms, their strategic history is highly relevant to the likely *trajectory* of future performance, at least in the short to medium term. To see why all three questions may be important, and what exactly we mean by each, consider the following three situations, all simplified from real cases:

- *Case A*—A leading retail bank faces the challenge of rationalizing its branch network in the face of customer losses and declining transaction volumes. Like traditional branch-network banks in many countries, this firm is losing business to new banking services offered through the Internet, telephone, and post.
- *Case B*—A pharmaceuticals supplier faces an attack on its major product market by the dominant rival, who is about to launch a near-identical product. The General Manager of this $300m business unit, appointed in early April 1997, was greeted with the news that he had just four weeks to prepare for this competitive onslaught.
- *Case C*—The BBC has one of the best libraries of high-quality TV programming in the world, and wishes to build a strong market for this material

among cable broadcasters in South America. The programming has been built up over many years, and is known to be popular with high-value viewer segments in many countries. This is attractive to cable companies as it stimulates strong advertising revenues.

All three situations raise deep concerns for the management teams involved: What are the prospects for their firm under current policies, what can they do to improve those prospects, and what lessons and resources can be brought to bear on the problem from their past experience? But the three examples also illustrate why robust tools for understanding and directing the dynamics of competitive strategy are so desperately needed.

In each case, there is a substantial *scale* of problem or opportunity to be addressed, and the difference between success and failure is considerable. The bank will lose hundreds of thousands of customers and tens of millions of Euros in revenue. The new executive heading the pharmaceuticals business faced losing the majority of his revenues and profits, and with these his market reputation and the commitment of a highly motivated salesforce. If this were to happen, the rest of his business would face collapse. The opportunity facing the BBC is extremely valuable, not only in South America but in burgeoning broadcasting markets throughout the world. Getting this early initiative right will build its confidence and credibility as it seeks to take more such opportunities.

In each case, there is also a *timescale* over which the strategic issue will evolve, and achieving sufficient speed of progress is vital. The pharmaceuticals firm will win or lose its battle over a few weeks, and the BBC has little time to establish a successful platform for its future in international markets. Even though the bank expects its core business to contract over some 4–5 years, its *immediate* decisions on branch closures, development of alternative channels and staff redeployment will all have substantial consequences over that timescale.

Finally, each case exhibits a *time-path* of progress—the firm's situation will not just start and end at specific points, but evolve at a varying rate as its future unfolds:

- The bank may at first lose few customers, then suffer increasingly rapid losses as its branches are closed and attractive new types of service become available. If it closes branches too slowly, it will be left with un-competitive cost levels. If it closes branches too fast (as it may already have started doing), it will bring about the very problem that is driving it to rationalize in the first place. Similar tricky judgments have to be made about transferring, and reskilling staff, while sustaining adequate, but not excessive service support in the remaining branches.
- The pharmaceuticals firm can expect the rival's salesforce to target the best customers first and to attack very fast, following which there may be a slower rate of attrition as they find later customers more difficult to capture and have to accept increasingly unattractive business. It will have to choose carefully whether to react on price, and if so by how much and when, and whether to undertake marketing efforts to head off the rival's attempt to build interest in the new product. Again, when to act, how, and how much

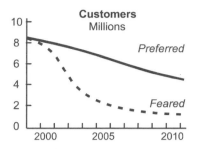

Figure 1.1   Time-chart of implications for branch rationalization in retail banking.

are difficult questions that continue throughout what will be a painful strategic episode.

- The BBC will want to see a positive initial uptake of its high-quality programming, but will soon need to consolidate its growth to avoid a boom-and-bust. If it pushes out its high-quality content too fast, it will win considerable interest from audiences, and enthusiastic support from cable channels and their advertizers. However, it will also raise expectations at the same time as depleting the very resource that is driving the opportunity, so may put itself in a position of having driven up activity to a rate that it cannot sustain. On the other hand, if it is too cautious in releasing content onto the market, audiences, broadcasters, and advertizers may not take sufficient notice to develop continuing demand. In addition, the window of opportunity will be left open for rival program suppliers to take a strong position, leaving the BBC squeezed out.

These verbal descriptions of the strategic issues confronting these firms are succinct and nicely focused on the heart of the issue, whether a problem or opportunity. However, since we are concerned with the *scale* and *timing* of performance, they are not enough—we must express them numerically and dynamically if we are truly to understand them and steer performance into the future.

The challenge facing the bank is depicted in Figure 1.1, which illustrates three critical characteristics of a well-defined dynamic issue:

- a clear numerical scale (customers);
- a timescale over which the dynamic is expected to play out (12 years, from 1999); and
- the *time-path* (how far and how fast the situation changes over that timescale).

This is a highly simplified summary of the key numbers. For example, it ignores the important issue of the *size* of customer accounts lost or retained (there is a world of difference between losing a profitable business account and a low-income consumer). Nevertheless, it provides a focus for the problem, and additional considerations can be added at a later stage. The chart also avoids some common problems in management debate about strategic performance. It focuses on the critical *resource* at stake—customers—rather than on indirect financial

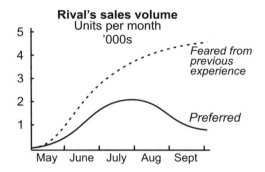

Figure 1.2 Rival's attack on the leading position of a pharmaceuticals supplier.

implications (e.g., revenues or profitability). It also focuses on the *absolute* numbers, rather than ratios like market share. This is important, since the firm's responses will act upon the resource itself (customers again), not on some derived arithmetical ratio.

This retail bank case also illustrates why it can be vital to understand the time-path of history—firms frequently have inside or around them the conditions that are *already* driving their trajectory into the future. The branch rationalization has already caused many customers to desert—even many loyal account-holders who had been with this bank, often with a single branch, for decades. Even if the firm *immediately* ceases its branch closures, customer losses will continue, driven not only by competitors' new offerings, but by decisions that the bank took some time ago.

It is important to appreciate that such time-paths as Figure 1.1 are *not* forecasts, and there is little to be gained by devoting analytical effort to getting them "right". Rather, they are an expression of what *might* emerge. They come from careful and open debate among the management team, informed by whatever experience they can draw upon—examples from other countries or other indus-tries, consideration of which customers might migrate and how fast, and so on. The two time-paths shown also signal an important idea—that an unattractive future might turn into disaster if the firm doesn't respond well, and that a better response may make a significant but realistic improvement to that future.

The time-chart description for the pharmaceuticals firm's rival is shown in Figure 1.2. Once again, both the preferred and feared outcomes are shown. If the new general manager does not react quickly and correctly, the competitor could build up a sales volume and installed base that will create further advan-tages for them to use against him in future. Note, by the way, that this issue plays out over just a few weeks—no five-year plans here, and no conceptual debate about "Vision" or process! This executive *must* make the right decisions about the scale and timing of his marketing efforts, salesforce bonus scheme, pricing, and so on. And he must make them quickly against a rapidly evolving situation.

We will not get into semantic debate about the meaning of "Strategy", but adopt a simple position—strategy is the set of policies that an organization

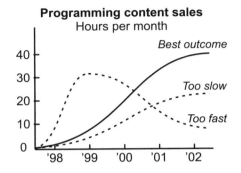

Figure 1.3 The BBC's expected sales of high-quality programming into South American cable channels.

adopts in pursuit of medium to long-term performance objectives (whether those policies are explicit or implicit), and an issue is strategic if it has a significant impact on that likely performance. On this criterion, the pharmaceuticals incident is most certainly of strategic importance. This division provides a substantial share of the corporation's cash flows, and this one product makes up a substantial share of that contribution. Loss of even a small piece of this market not only impacts those cash flows but threatens the morale and performance of the salesforce, not just on this product but on others in the division. The potential gains to the competitor will enhance *its* cash flows and salesforce performance, and boost its reputation in the sector, all of which will enable it to build further products, sales, and cash flows. This one event could, in fact, reduce the division's contribution to shareholder value by over a half.

The BBC's initiative in South America is illustrated in Figure 1.3. Note again the three critical features—a well-specified scale for the strategic issue (programming content sales), a timescale for the dynamic to play out (4 years), and the time-path (again, both preferred and feared outcomes are shown).

Establishing such a clear specification of the dynamic issue may appear simple, and it is tempting quickly to sketch out a chart that appears to fulfill the need. However, it is rarely so simple in practice. Often, even the *history* is poorly documented, in which case it is important to collect and test managers' best recollections of what has happened. This initial step deserves the efforts of the top team and a wide-ranging and open discussion of alternative views.

Strategic resources and performance

So, now that the nature, scale, and time-path of the threat or opportunity is clearly described, what explanations might exist for the eventual outcome, and what might we be able to do to alter it for the better? Industry analysis has traditionally been a popular tool for developing strategy, but it will not help much to address the critical challenges in any of these cases.

The limited relevance of industry conditions to the bank has already been noted, and the disaster waiting to happen in this case will result from internal errors of judgment about the pace of branch closure, product offerings, and service levels offered to remaining customers.

The pharmaceuticals firm *will* lose customers—the rival already exists, so barriers to entry are irrelevant. We could perhaps use game theory and consider retaliatory options that may be feasible. But this will tell us little about the scale or speed of attrition we will face or how to affect the speed of that process. The rival is going to have to market its competing product, motivate its salesforce, and ensure reliable supply and customer support. It is the *time-path* of this process that must be understood if there is to be any chance of influencing the future.

The BBC, too, will learn little from industry analysis. The customers and cable channels already exist and are continuing to develop. The BBC itself is already involved and may wish to erect barriers to entry against new rivals, but, in practice, competitors can easily make the same thrust, and the end-market and broadcasting channels for reaching it are already understood and available to many firms. Assessing the drivers of cost and value in the industry may help somewhat, and certainly gives a clear picture of break-even revenues and economies of scale that may help determine the company's pricing flexibility. But this is going to help little to explain the time-path in Figure 1.2. Typically, such considerations would focus around questions like: "How many hours of programming do we think we could sell at a price of x if rivals' prices are y?" But this question already makes many assumptions; for example, that awareness of the BBC brand is high, that its reputation among potential viewers is strong, and that cable channels are both taking the programming and managing well its place in the broadcast schedule.

These discussions of the three mini-cases hint at a possible start-point for attacking the problem—a consideration of the *strategic resources* involved, either for the firm itself or for its rivals. Table 1.1 lists some of the resources relevant to each case.

Note that the lists in Table 1.1, as well as including many simple, tangible items (staff, customers, capacity) also feature several intangible factors—items that are tricky to define, let alone measure or touch. Such "soft" issues often arouse

Table 1.1   Examples of strategic resources for three illustrative firms.

Bank rationalization	Pharmaceuticals attack	BBC programming
Customers	Salesforce	Program library
Branch network	Existing customers	Quality of the library
Customer-service staff	Production capacity	Cable customers
Savings and lending products	Reputation in the medical	Viewers
Reputation for service	community	Reputation among potential
	Salesforce morale	advertizers

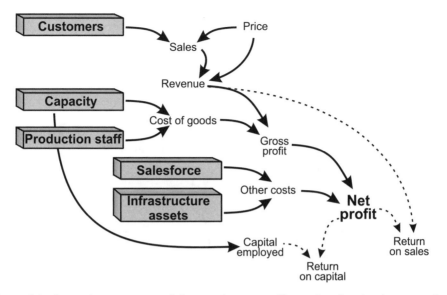

Figure 1.4 Strategic resources and firm performance: illustrating the simple connection.

skepticism among those devoted to fact-based analysis, but managers *know* that their product's functionality, their service reputation, investor support, and staff morale make a substantial difference to performance. So, to dismiss these items as unobservable and unmanageable is unhelpful. Furthermore, firms increasingly take the trouble to research and track exactly such soft issues, so the second criticism—that even if they matter, they are not practically observable—is also inaccurate.

We'll get into a deeper consideration of strategic resources shortly, but, first, we need to clarify the very direct link between these items and firm performance. This link has long been clear to strategy writers, but if we are not careful, it risks becoming a somewhat banal observation. Given that we know what resources the firm has *right now,* our accountants can tell us the firm's performance with almost total precision. Indeed, they have performed exactly that task for hundreds of years! This direct link between firm resources and profitability is illustrated in Figure 1.4.

But here's a puzzle. This simple picture explains firm performance precisely, even though it includes only a few of the resources, mostly tangible, discussed thus far. We know that intangibles are important, but they don't appear to be needed. Indeed, we don't need anything else at all. This implies that attempts to correlate firm performance at a moment in time with any other observations is pointless—you can't improve on a complete explanation!

The solution to this puzzle lies in the fact that this is merely a snapshot at a moment in time. Sure, these few tangible resources *today* explain precisely our profitability *today.* Similarly, the state of those same items *tomorrow* will explain

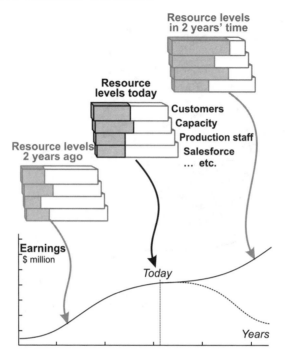

Figure 1.5 Strategic resource levels determine performance—past, present, and future.

precisely our profitability at that time too. But what we cannot yet do is explain how those resources get to change from today's level to tomorrow's (Figure 1.5). That explanation lies at the heart of the framework for strategic performance that follows in later chapters.

Doing it right!

"Word-and-arrow" diagrams like Figure 1.4 feature widely in contemporary management writing, but the items and connections used convey a wide variety of meanings.

In contrast, each element in the figures in this book has a specific meaning. The boxes simply denote resources, which will be defined more precisely in the next chapter. The curved arrows do not mean merely that there is some vague relationship between two items, they state that one item can be immediately calculated or estimated from another, just like a formula in a spreadsheet cell.

The problem of valuing businesses and their strategies

The valuation of firms starts from understanding the motives of investors, who are primarily interested in the likely future stream of earnings. Strictly, the best indicator is free cash flow—the cash that will be generated, after reinvesting what is needed to deliver that growth. Current free cash flow, therefore, is:

Operating income

+ Depreciation

− Tax payments

+ Non-operating income

− Net investment in current assets

− Net investments in fixed assets

Since we will devote our attention throughout this book to the time-path of cash flows, newcomers to the issue are well advised to familiarize themselves with the essentials of valuation. Copeland *et al.* (2000) is one example of many sound texts, the early chapters of which provide an accessible introduction to the topic. The principles of valuation have been further extended to provide the foundation for "value based management"—a means for setting performance and rewarding managers and other staff (Martin and Petty, 2000). Note that the purely financial view implied by this approach to valuing firms can be entirely consistent with other objectives, and with concerns for wider issues like social responsibility. Later chapters will make clear that lack of respect for such interests will likely lead to losses of key resources, notably staff and customers, which ultimately damage long-term sales and earnings.

Having computed *today*'s free cash flow, valuation requires a forecast of *future* free cash flows. These will be discounted by the firm's cost of capital, to arrive at a value for the firm. This task is typically built on some variation of the following approach (Martin and Petty [2000, chapter 4]; Copeland *et al.* [2000, chapter 11]):

- estimate growth in sales turnover;
- project operating profit margins (operating profit divided by sales);
- forecast the ratio of operating assets to sales (net working capital, and fixed assets divided by sales);
- project the rate of tax;

... from which the free cash flow calculation is repeated for each year of the forecast period.

But this forecast is precisely the step where financial evaluations typically lose connection with the firm's strategy. These ratios and projections are made on the basis of estimating the impact of competitive conditions the firm will face, and efficiencies that management can be expected to make in its operating ratios. These forecasts, in turn, are developed by estimating future market size, market share, prices, staffing, wage rates, inventory, and so on.

The problem is that, while we have detailed and rigorous analytical methods for computing value from estimates of future free cash flows, the firm's cost of capital, and the resulting shareholder value, this model is then populated with highly speculative estimates for sales, costs, and margins. The exactitude of the value calculation thus becomes largely spurious.

Industry factors and firm performance

Analysis of industry-level competitive conditions has dominated fact-based efforts to understand and forecast firm performance for the last 20 years. This dominance arises from the centrality of the Structure–Conduct–Performance paradigm (SCP) within industrial economics (Figure 1.6). This view asserts that managerial conduct of firm strategy (entry, differentiation, pricing, etc.) is heavily constrained by industry conditions, and therefore limits any firm's ability to perform significantly differently than the average for its sector. The industry conditions in question relate largely to the barriers that obstruct firms who wish to enter or leave the industry, or switch between rival suppliers and substitute products. These barriers may be financial (e.g., the cost of constructing capacity, gaining market access, developing competitive products) or strategic (fear of retaliation by rivals, customers' reluctance to switch from trusted suppliers).

The implications of the SCP view for strategic management are somewhat depressing. If industry conditions dominate your likely performance, then all you can do is pick an "attractive industry" and your destiny is determined, at least as regards profitability. There is no further role for management. This view is supported by the fact that firms fail to outperform the industry average for any sustained time—excess profitability gets competed away.

However, two observations provide more optimism that management does have a role to play in determining the strategic performance of their firms. First, the strategy field itself acknowledges that industry conditions are a poor predictor of performance. McGahan and Porter (1997), responding to analysis by Rumelt (1991) that suggested that industry conditions only explained 15% of the variance in profitability among a large sample of firms, discovered that this was

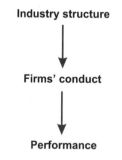

Figure 1.6   The Structure–Conduct–Performance paradigm.

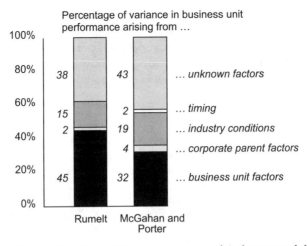

Figure 1.7 Two estimates for the relative importance of industry and business-unit factors in explaining performance.

indeed an underestimate (Figure 1.7)—they could account for 19% of profitability variance by industry conditions! This analysis offers three observations:

- industry factors provide a desperately poor explanation for business performance;
- management does, indeed, matter—since business unit factors and corporate parent effects both cover issues under managerial control;
- taken together, these factors still give us a pretty poor understanding, overall, of why some firms are more profitable than others.

Furthermore, the failure of firms sustainably to outperform their industry does not prove that industry conditions dominate. These conditions are not the only factors that change through time—management changes too—so it is likely that business unit factors also feature in the failure of firms to sustain an advantage.

The second reason to be more optimistic about the opportunity for strategic management to make a difference is the wide variance that exists among the performances achieved by firms within any given sector. Firms differ widely in both the revenue growth and return on capital that they achieve. Indeed, such differences *must* exist if underperformers are to drag themselves up from the bottom and leaders are to fall from their pinnacle, thereby causing the low rate of sustained outperformance noted above.

The failure of industry factors to explain firm performance calls into question the value of the SCP paradigm as a basis for identifying strategic opportunities or advising management on how best to take those opportunities. In fairness, developments of that view, which are beyond the scope of this book, have recognized the influence of management, not just in determining the firm's own performance but also, thereby, changing the very industry conditions that were thought to dominate.

The key, for our purpose, is to recognize that the world is the way it is today because Bill Gates, Rupert Murdoch, Jack Welch, and a host of others have made it like this! All of us contribute in some degree, be it large or small, to shaping the future, and the challenge we will address is how to design that path for your enterprise to stand the best chance of bringing about *your* preferred future.

Summary

The challenge and responsibility facing strategic managers is to understand and direct the *time-path* of performance for their enterprise (whether stated in terms of financial or other objectives). It is vital to understand that time-path, not just qualitatively but including the specifics of scale and timing as well.

Dynamic issues of strategic importance to the firm may consist of either opportunities to be exploited or damage to be limited. They may be largely driven by forces internal to the firm, or by rivalry and other external pressures. Many such challenges will concern the business at large, but others may be largely centered upon particular functions within the organization. The timescale over which the issue will play out may range from many years down to just a few weeks or months in especially fast-moving sectors.

It has long been understood that current performance is a direct function of the strategic resources that the enterprise either owns or has reasonably reliable access to, at this moment in time. The same is true at all times in the past, and will be true in the future, so if the time-path of performance is to be understood and managed, the management team needs the means to understand how resource levels change through time and how that process can be controlled.

2

Strategic Resources—the Fuel of Firm Performance

Key issues

❏   Identifying and defining strategic resources

❏   How resources support sustained performance

❏   Understanding how resources accumulate and deplete over time

❏   Some simple, but critical, arithmetic

Most managers understand the importance of building and conserving the resources of their business, both tangible items such as staff and customers and intangibles such as staff morale and investor support. They also know that resources are interdependent—good product quality is of little value if delivery performance damages reputation with customers, and a highly motivated sales-force can do little with a poor range of products. "Ranking" resources in order of importance is thus pointless—if *any* resource is in bad shape, the whole business is endangered. Similarly, efforts to determine "value drivers" in the business are doomed to failure—the best customer service in the world will contribute nothing to the price customers will pay if the product constantly fails or deliveries frequently miss critical deadlines.

Before worrying about interdependence, though, a sound framework is needed to understand *how* resources develop, working first with familiar, tangible examples.

A sharper focus on strategic resources

Before we go on to describe the firm's strategic architecture and show how it can be applied, some definitions need clarifying. Many definitions for "strategic resource" have been offered, and it will be unhelpful here to embark on a semantic debate. Rather, we need a practical way of identifying resources. Let's start from the idea that a resource is anything to which the firm *has access*

Table 2.1 Illustrative listing of tangible resources and corresponding intangible items.

Tangibles	Corresponding intangibles	Possible measures
Customers	Customer quality	Average sales per customer
Staff	Staff skill	Years of experience
Production capacity	Production efficiency	Yield of salable product
Distribution facilities	Delivery performance	Delivery lead time—days
Products	Product quality	Fraction of warranty claims

that might be useful to it in some way. This suggests a few places to start looking for strategic resources.

First, the firm's balance sheet may include tangible resources, such as plant capacity, information systems, or cash. That doesn't mean we want to express them in financial terms, just that they will at least be listed there. To these we can then add items that the firm might think of as similar to balance sheet assets such as staff and patents. Third, we can look *outside* the firm, remembering that we don't have to own a resource, only have somewhat reliable access to it. This brings in items such as customers, distributors, suppliers, and partners.

This has largely covered the more tangible items, but a final check should be made to ensure that the list adequately covers both supply-side and demand-side issues. Does it include the firm's products and services themselves, everything needed to create them, and everything needed to get those products and services to market? Then, does it include customers, distributors, and any others in the market who we may need to make our product or service usable?

The end result of this search for tangible resources sometimes creates some surprises. For example, we would normally expect the list to include our *staff*, as well as some measure of our *capacity* to deliver products and services. In service industries, however, "capacity" often consists of the staff themselves. You might also expect that *customers* would always feature, but some firms may not have distinctly identifiable "customers". This arises when products are supplied to true commodity markets, such as in oil and some agricultural products.

Next, we should look for important intangibles. A tip here is that this category of "soft" resources often includes items closely associated with a tangible already on the list. Such items can be thought of as some quality or characteristic that the tangible item possesses. Table 2.1 gives some examples, and also suggests the type of measure that might be appropriate.

Measuring such items often relies on a survey of some kind, either within the firm's operations or among customers or staff. This suggests another possible category of intangible factors that may be particularly difficult to control, namely those that are to do with how people *feel* about things (e.g., staff morale, customer satisfaction, investor support, and supplier commitment). These items too may be identified through surveys.

A final tip for getting the resource list right is to be clear about certain items it must *not* include. First in this list of exclusions is any item that can be classed as a capability or competence of the firm. Capabilities are clearly important, and we will see how to work with them later, but they are different from resources, so exclude them for now. A simple rule here is that a capability is something that the enterprise, or a part of it, *is good at doing*, whereas a resource is something useful *to which the firm has access*. So, your list of resources should probably not include any words ending in "-ing" or "-ment" (e.g., marketing, product development, recruitment, selling, etc.).

A second exclusion from the list of resources would be any *process* carried out in a part of the business (e.g., cost reduction, production engineering, order processing). This category may overlap with the capability list, which is not surprising, as it's another listing of things that the enterprise *does* rather than *has*. Other exclusions are items that appear in the firm's profit and loss or cash flow statements. Such items describe the *rate* at which something financial is happening ($ per annum), not the *amount* of something that the firm has at any time.

These tips may seem tricky to work with right now, but they should become clearer by the time some examples have been developed in the coming chapters.

What is already known about resources and sustained performance

A managerial discussion of how resources contribute to competitive advantage— the so-called "resource-based view" of strategy (RBV)—can be found in many strategy texts (e.g., Grant [2001, chapter 5]). A more extensive treatment of the concepts, including comprehensive coverage of the supporting literature, can be found in Barney (2001, chapter 5). Although recent interest in the topic was awakened in the mid-1980s (Wernerfelt, 1984), the fundamental importance of firm resources can in fact be traced back over 40 years (Penrose, 1959).

It may seem self-evident that resources are important to sustaining performance over time, rather than simply explaining performance right now. However, it is not immediately obvious how this dependency operates in any specific case, how to quantify the influence that each resource has on profitability, nor what to do about it. These issues are generally addressed by considering the following questions:

- *How **durable** is the resource?* A resource that decays, deteriorates, or becomes obsolete quickly is not likely to provide sustainable advantage. Plant wears out, staff skills may decline, and investors' enthusiasm to fund an enterprise may fade away. Even if the resource itself doesn't change (e.g., efficiency of production facilities or standards of service in retailing), it may effectively be non-durable because of the progress of technology or rising customer expectations.
- *How **mobile** or **tradable** is the resource?* Many resources, while important to effective operation of the business, are so easily acquired or moved between

firms that they provide little sustainable advantage. Resources are particularly mobile if they can be bought and sold (i.e., if they are "tradable"). Equipment suppliers may be keen to sell the latest technology to your rivals as well as yourselves, customer lists may be purchased, and staff may be attracted by better salaries. Resources move between firms for other reasons than price. Staff move for a better lifestyle or environment, and suppliers of important items may favor rivals who operate in more attractive end markets.

- *How **replicable** is the resource?* Many resources can be easily copied by rivals, and thus offer little scope for competitive advantage. A firm can add new items to its product range, and boost its market share for a short time, but if the product is easily copied (e.g., a new mortgage product offered by a retail bank), the benefit will be short lived.
- *Can the resource be **substituted**?* Even if your business cannot buy or copy its competitors' resources, you may still be able to challenge them by using a different resource that fulfills a similar purpose. A common example is the use of alternative distribution channels (e.g., telephone ordering or Websites) to overcome lack of access to retailers.
- *Are the resources **complementary** (i.e., do they work well together)?* Strong awareness for a brand is of little value without the distribution channels to generate sales, a technologically advanced product will not penetrate a market without cost-effective production capacity, and so on. It will be seen later that this question of complementarity between resources is crucial to capturing firms' strategic progress through time.

Much of what is understood about the role of strategic resources builds on these questions. In particular, they are often taken to explain whether access to any particular resource constitutes a "barrier to entry". This notion implies that you *must* have the resource if you are to participate in an industry at all. Without it you are excluded, but with it you are in. However, in spite of the intuitive appeal of the criteria above, they expose three fundamental weaknesses in this approach to understanding the resource basis of competitive performance:

- First, the characteristics listed are rarely black and white in nature. Very few resources are totally durable, absolutely nontradable, or totally impossible to copy or substitute. Examples that come close to these ideal criteria include natural resources like a bauxite mine for producing aluminum, "natural monopolies" like gas-transmission networks, or fundamentally limited facilities like British Airways' take-off slots at Heathrow airport. Yet even these are not absolutely immune—rivals find other mineral resources, regulators impose open access to supply networks, and rivals develop services from nearby airports. Thus, each of the resource characteristics above applies, not absolutely, but *to some greater or lesser degree.*
- The second issue, central to the story we will develop in the next chapter, is that the ability to maintain, remove, copy, or substitute resources is an inherently *dynamic* issue. With the possible exception of tradable resources, none can be simply switched on or off at an instant in time. Instead, there is

always the problem of *how fast* a resource can be built or may decay. Without a means of measuring and representing rates of change in resource levels, progress in understanding the scale and variation in a firm's overall competitive advantage will be difficult.

• Third, while managers and researchers alike recognize the importance of interdependence between resources, some means is needed to capture the mechanisms by which resources actually *work together* through time.

The first two of these issues together point to serious weaknesses in the "barriers to entry" concept. A moment's thought shows this to be a desperately poor description of reality. Firms participate in many industries with just *a little* of each strategic resource, compete more strongly with *more* of each, and build competitive advantage if they can *grow* them. Strategic resources are therefore not so much barriers to entry as "hills" of varying height and steepness, up which firms try to climb and from which they can compete to a greater or lesser degree, depending on how high they have managed to climb.

In spite of these limitations of static resource analysis, a review of relevant resources is an important early task for understanding competitive strategy dynamics. It is at least an improvement on the common "strengths and weaknesses" approach, which can confuse the firm's resources with competencies and processes, and lead to ambiguous lists that are impossible to action.

SWOT analysis—a poor basis for sound strategy

Before sophisticated strategy professionals throw up their hands in horror at the sight of such a naive framework appearing in a serious Strategy text, it should be pointed out that SWOT is *still* what most ordinary managers think of first when asked how they would go about assessing their strategy. It is therefore appropriate to explain how a resource appraisal lends clarity to any assessment of a firm's SWOT. This four-part checklist splits naturally into two halves:

• Opportunities and Threats are features of *the external environment*, mostly competitors and other external pressures. These external factors are more properly dealt with by two formal methods that will be discussed in Chapter 8, namely industry forces and analysis of political, economic, social and technological factors.
• Strengths and Weaknesses are features of *the firm itself*, relative to existing and potential competitors and other external forces.

Since this second pair of topics focuses on the firm itself, then, these are the key topics that have the closest connection with the resource-based view. Strengths and weaknesses are evaluated in terms of the resources and capabilities that the firm has, or needs, for its system to work, in the context of the external conditions in which it is participating (Table 2.2).

A more rigorous approach to assessing strengths and weaknesses, then, is to carry out the quantified, fact-based analysis of resources introduced earlier in

Table 2.2 Strengths and weaknesses as the presence or absence of resources and capabilities.

Strengths	Weaknesses
Resource and capabilities to which the firm has access, with one or more of the following characteristics:	Resource and capabilities to which the firm has access, with one or more of the following characteristics:
a. greater quantity	a. smaller quantity
b. greater quality	b. lower quality
c. slower rate or lower risk of loss	c. faster rate or higher risk of loss
d. faster rate of acquisition	d. slower rate of acquisition
e. support for the acquisition and retention of other resources	e. lack of support for other resources
. . . compared with actual or potential rivals.	. . . compared with actual or potential rivals.

this chapter and developed throughout the remainder of this book, notably in Chapter 7, which deals with intangible factors. Capabilities are dealt with in Chapter 9. Even if management decides not to take on this approach in full, a sound appraisal of a firm's strengths and weaknesses can only be arrived at from a rigorous, factual and quantified appraisal of resources and capabilities.

Resource analysis will discover a wide variety of relevant items. This complexity can be dealt with by grouping resources into different categories (e.g., financial, physical, human, or technological). Such groupings can help to organize and simplify the otherwise daunting lists of relevant resources, and may provide a useful checklist to ensure that no potentially important resources have been left out. One categorization that is often used is the distinction between tangible and intangible resources, discussed above and illustrated in Table 2.3 for a retail bank.

This illustrative list may seem surprisingly short. Surely, we need to split out all the different types of customer, groups of product, geographic regions, and so on. Such distinctions rapidly give rise to what is known as "detail complexity"—the notion that firm performance is difficult to understand simply because there are so many specific items to worry about. And, as the assessment of dynamic performance develops, it may indeed become necessary to consider such detail. However, a key message here is that management judgment is more often confounded by *dynamic complexity*—the surprising and counter-intuitive behavior of the whole system over time. It will become apparent that much of this uncertainty, illustrated in the three mini-cases at the start of this chapter, can be explained by a high-level understanding of the key resources and their interactions. For this purpose, therefore, a compact list of the critical items is an adequate start-point.

We now need to set out the basic framework for understanding how resources build and decay and how their interdependence operates.

Table 2.3 Illustrative listing of tangible and intangible strategic resources—retail banking.

	Examples	Typical measures
Tangible resources	Retail branches	Number of sites
	Customer-service staff	Number of people
	Products	Number of items, by type (savings, lending, and others)
	Customer base	Account-holders
	Information systems capacity	Technical definitions
	Cash	$ millions
Intangible resources	Quality of retail branches	Customers per branch, revenue per branch
	Staff skills	Fraction of required skill levels
	Customer-base quality	Average deposits/borrowings, added-value per account-holder
	Product features	Measures of customer value such as interest rates offered or charged, flexibility, etc.
	Information systems quality	Reliability, ease of use, ability to provide required information

Winning and keeping resources

Since firms' performances derive directly from the strategic resources that are available at any time, the challenge managers must address is *how to build and maintain the level or stock* of each resource. To help understand this problem, a resource can be thought of as being held in a tank where it accumulates. Resources are built by boosting the *flow* of new resource into the stock, so for example winning customers *adds to* a customer-base; recruiting new people *increases* our employee resource; promoting our products and services *raises* market awareness; training our staff *enhances* their level of skill.

At the same time, though, we lose resources through misfortune, mistakes, or the actions of others: customers are *lost* to competitors, resignations *deplete* our employee base, consumers' loss of interest *cuts* overall market awareness, and technological advancement *reduces* the appropriateness of current staff skills. Such losses can be thought of as resources flowing out of the tank in which they are held.

This defining characteristic of resources—that they build and deplete over time, so-called "asset-stock accumulation"—is well known to be critical to strategic performance (Dierickx and Cool, 1989). This idea is captured for our staff resource in Figure 2.1. The "tank" in the middle holds the number of staff

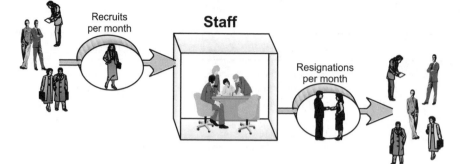

Figure 2.1 Building, and losing, the staff resource.

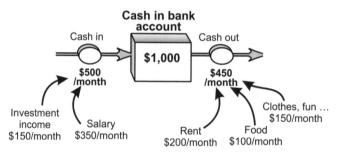

Figure 2.2 Drivers of flows into and out of your bank account.

we have right now. To the left is the outside world, where there are many people, some of whom might become future staff. The big "pipe" flowing into the tank has a pump on it that drives *how fast* that stock of staff is being added to. On the right, another pump on a pipe flowing out of the stock determines how fast we are losing staff, and again you can see people in the outside world who include our former employees.

This picture begins to show why the firm's history may be critically important. The level of resource we have today is on a trajectory through time that reflects how well we have been building it (and holding on to it!) in the past. This not only explains why the business is in its present state, but also determines its current trajectory into the immediate future.

The behavior of this process (known mathematically as "integration") is intuitively tricky to estimate over time, but is in fact quite familiar. You probably have a bank account and know roughly what was in it at the end of last month. You know roughly how much will be added to it during this month, whether from salary, investment income, or other sources, and you have some idea how much you will have to pay out of it. You therefore have a good idea of what will be left at the end of the month.

Figure 2.2 shows this idea, and the numbers illustrate another valuable point. If the inflows and outflows differ then you know exactly how *fast* the resource is changing—if the numbers in Figure 2.2 continue through time, you will have $1,050 at the end of next month, $1,100 at the end of the month after, and so on. It doesn't take rocket science either to work out what will happen if your rent goes up from $200/month to $300/month. If this illustration makes sense to you, it seems you already know how to "integrate" resources over time, even if you didn't realize it!

Doing it right!

The simple principle captured in Figures 2.1 and 2.2 has a deeply fundamental implication—*that the amount of each resource we have right now is the sum of everything we ever gained, minus everything ever lost.* This is not a matter of opinion, nor the result of surveys, research, or statistical analysis—it is mathematically unavoidable. There is *no* other explanation for the amount of cash in your account besides the historical sum of payments in and out.

Similarly, the number of customers you have today is precisely equal to the sum of all those you ever won, minus all those ever lost. Consequently, today's customer base cannot be correlated with your marketing spend, pricing, number of rivals, or any other factor. A customer won last week is (all else being equal) no more or less important to you than another that you won last month, last year, or a decade ago. So, it is the *winning and losing* of customers that is driven by marketing, pricing, and other conditions, not the current number at any point in time.

This is the defining characteristic of "asset stocks" of which resources and capabilities are examples.

To show how the same principles apply to resources in a business or any other kind of enterprise, Figure 2.3 shows a firm's customer base. This figure introduces two absolute rules:

- Whatever the measure of resource in the stock, the inflows and outflows are *always* measured in the same units *per time period*. There is never any exception to this.
- The *only* way the resource can change is by something flowing in or out. The curved arrow in Figure 2.4 is thus meaningless, and forbidden.

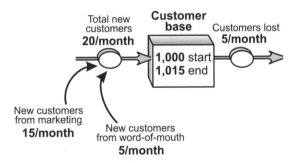

Figure 2.3 Stock-and-flow basics—winning and losing customers.

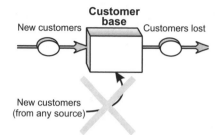

Figure 2.4 Resource stocks can only be changed *via* the flows.

It is most important that these principles be understood and complied with, since they apply to *all* resources, whether tangible or intangible. If we get anything wrong at this stage, the remainder of the dynamic framework will break down.

Doing it right!

As explained in Chapter 1, the curved arrows in these diagrams mean that you can immediately calculate one item from those connected to it (and only from those items). In Figure 2.3, therefore ...

Total new customers (during this month)
  = (this month's average rate of)
    new customers from marketing
  + (this month's average rate of)
    new customers from word of mouth

So ... + 15/month + 5/month = + 20/month

This is quite different from the thick flow arrows, which can be thought of as the actual flow of material into or out of the "tank". In other words:

Customer base (end of this month)
  = Customer base
    (start of this month)
  + Customers won or lost
    (during this month)

So ... 1,000 + 20 − 5 = 1,015

This sets up next month, which will start with 1,015 customers.

In the remaining chapters, it will become clear that the math of this asset-stock accumulation is deeply fundamental to all business situations (as well as to all social systems and many natural ones). No adequate explanation for the current state, at any moment, of such systems can be arrived at without the explicit, quantitative formulation of this phenomenon (see the Appendix for a summarized theoretical discussion of the main frameworks developed here).

Defining and measuring resources and their flows

Table 2.4 illustrates a few of the wide variety of resources that may arise in different contexts. It also provides examples of:

- the units of measure that may apply to each resource;
- the nature of the inflows and outflows that accumulate and deplete each resource;
- the units of measure for those flows; and
- typical factors that may drive such flows.

These examples raise some further important points about resource levels, changes, and measures.

*It may not be easy to estimate numerically what **rate** of change results from the factors that drive it* (e.g., what difference a 10% salary differential makes to the rate at which we can hire staff). This difficulty may cause skepticism and resistance. However, such uncertainties simply have to be addressed—*managers make judgments on such assumptions every day; all we are doing here is asking them to make those assumptions explicit.* This is not in order to attack them for any apparent foolishness, but to understand how they see the world. Without such shared clarity, there is little hope of understanding how the whole enterprise operates.

Tricky cases arise when a resource itself includes time. An example in Table 2.4 is production capacity, measured in

Table 2.4 Inflow and outflow drivers for various tangible and intangible resources.

	Units of resource	Inflows and outflows	Units of inflows and outflows	Typical drivers
Tangible resources				
Cash	$	Cash received	$/month	Sales
		Cash spent		Salaries, new capacity, raw materials
Staff	People	Recruitment	People/month	Number of staff on hiring, attractiveness of salaries
		Resignations		Pressure of work
		Dismissals		Performance failures, shortage of work
Customers	Firms	New customers won	Firms/year	Salesforce size, price vs. rivals
		Customers ceasing to trade with us		Delivery performance, quality, price vs. rivals
Plant capacity	Tons/week	New plant purchases, debottlenecking	"Tons/week" per quarter	Investment, production-engineering effort
		Plant closures		Poor utilization
Intangible resources				
Product quality	Reject fraction	Reduction in rejects	± Reject fraction/month	Process improvement effort
		Increase in rejects		Change in raw material quality
Delivery performance	Days' lead-time	Lead-time reduction	± days per quarter	Outsourcing logistics to dedicated provider
Morale	Index	Increase in morale	± Index/month	Salary increase, sales successes

"tons/week". If we *change* capacity (e.g., by adding new equipment or closing a factory), the result is an inflow or outflow of a certain number of "tons/week this quarter" (this is a special one-off inflow that will be dealt with shortly). Delivery lead time poses a similar risk of confusion—it is measured in "days", but any improvement we make during a quarter means that the *change* in delivery lead time has units of "change in delivery lead-time days this quarter". Fortunately, there are few such examples to worry about.

Choose a time period that is appropriate to both the timescale of the issue you are trying to address, and to the rate at which changes are actually occurring in the resource. Referring back to the three cases from Chapter 1, the bank is losing customers at a rate of many thousands per quarter; a rate that may well vary considerably, and be amenable to our countermoves, from month to month. Choosing a time period of years will lose this dynamic, whereas a timescale of weeks may include too much noise, or random fluctuations, to be useful. In contrast, for the pharmaceuticals firm, the feared loss of sales will reflect some very rapid events—in this particular case, the manager had his team monitor customer losses on a *daily* basis, and watched the overall trajectory of the situation as it emerged week by week.

Intangibles often create measurement difficulties. The best tip here is "if there's a sound measurement available, use it", but choose the measure that really matters. For product quality, for example, is reject fraction most important or mean time to failure? The first may be an important driver of unit cost, while the second may drive customer-loss rate. Similarly, customer losses may depend on delivery performance, but which measure or mix of measures *really* make customers give up—"delivery lead time (days)", "fraction of on-time deliveries", or "fraction of complete deliveries"?

A change in one resource may drive a change in another (e.g., an increase in capacity drives a cash outflow). This is one example of *interdependence* between resources that will be central to seeing the firm as an integrated system.

Always identify inflows and outflows separately if possible. This does not simply mean "when we have the data". You may not happen to have separate numbers for the rates at which you are winning and losing customers, but these two separate numbers are critically important, each is driven by different forces, and you *must* find out what is going on. A good estimate is better than simply ignoring this distinction.

Doing it right—focus on *your* situation!

Although many common structures and relationships arise in applying these ideas, every situation has its own unique characteristics. Consequently, while there is much to learn from others' experiences, *your* issues are unique to *your* enterprise. This observation is both alarming and liberating. It may be demoralizing to realize, contrary to the impression given by many commentators, that there are no "standard" answers to pull from the shelf. On the other hand, we hope it is reassuring to know that you can take control of a situation that is entirely your own.

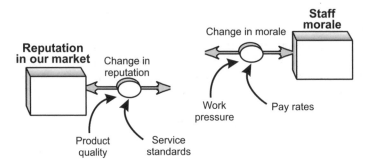

Figure 2.5 Resources where inflows and outflows cannot be easily split.

Separating inflows and outflows for some intangibles is both difficult and unnecessary. Staff morale, for example, may either rise or fall in response to work pressure. More pressure may lead to falling morale, less pressure may raise morale—or, of course, morale may actually *improve* with pressure, if your people thrive on being busy.

Figure 2.5 gives two examples of how the simple resource-building framework is adapted when separating gains and losses is difficult. Dealing with the numbers in such intangible cases is tricky, and will be dealt with in Chapter 7.

It might be wondered why the "stock and flow" structure is needed here at all—surely staff morale simply depends directly on work pressure, pay rates, and so on, and reputation depends directly on product quality and service? Unfortunately, though life would be much simpler if this were the case, it is never so. Staff may continue to be highly motivated for some time after workloads rise, but continued pressure will start to *deplete* morale. Similarly, reputation can stay depressed in spite of long periods of high quality and good service, but these will eventually cause a progressive *increase* in reputation.

Summary

The first step in building the resources needed for future performance is to define them properly, both tangible and intangible items, and identify those that apply to *your* enterprise (whether to pursue current objectives or alternative opportunities). It is also vital to identify clear *measures* for strategic resources, and sources for this information.

Resources provide advantage if they are durable and not easy for rivals to buy, copy, or substitute with alternatives. However, these are neither black-and-white nor static criteria—performance over time depends on *how much* of the necessary resources one has, and at what rate they are being accumulated. Consequently, viewing resource ownership as a "barrier to entry" is of little value.

Resources must also be *complementary* (i.e., work well together, both to build upon each other and to deliver performance). So, for managers to use resources to build performance over time, some mechanism for understanding complementarity is vital.

Although firms possess a rich array of strategic resources, those that directly determine current performance are largely tangible items. The key challenge for management is therefore to identify, win, and keep these resources. Resources share common characteristics—they accumulate and deplete over time, so the *level* of resource at any moment depends on the total of all historic gains and losses.

To understand resource changes properly, they must be clearly *defined* and *measured*. Their rate of change is *always* defined in the same units "per time period". Since rates of gain and loss are critical to future resource levels, the drivers of these gains and losses for each resource must be identified and the strength of their influence understood. These drivers will include issues under management's control, other factors internal to the firm, and external forces.

3

Getting Specific—Quantifying Change

Key issues

❏   Calculating resource changes from rates of gain and loss

❏   Using time charts to show the dynamics of change

❏   Developing and exploiting potential resources

❏   Developing resources throughout the business—and beyond

Having defined resources properly and put reliable measurements on each, it is now possible to quantify how they develop over time.

Get quantitative!—the importance of scale, rates of change, and time charts

This task starts from the fundamental point made in Chapter 2, that today's resource level is the sum of everything ever gained minus everything ever lost. To deal with this reality requires moving on from a current snapshot to capturing the history and future of gains and losses. The "stock-and-flow" idea introduced in Chapter 2 therefore needs extending to deal with how resource levels change *through time*, whether our particular problem concerns building them, sustaining them, or reducing an excess.

To illustrate the importance of this question, imagine that our two firms are competitors. It is clearly an important difference between us if we have a different size of customer base. Yet, even if we have the *same* number of customers at a certain instant—say, 1,000 each—our two firms may still enjoy very different degress of competitive advantage. For example, you may feel you are in a stronger position if you are winning 100 new customers per month while I am only winning 20.

But this may not be the end of the story. Are you still so confident if each month I lose only 20 customers (at the same time as winning 20) while you lose 100 as well as winning 100? Winning customers is costly, so you will suffer

The most unfortunate example I have come across of resources, gains, and losses concerned a security services firm, who told me that their annual numbers for all three items were *the same*. Each year, they won a hundred customers, had a hundred on their books, and lost a hundred!

While this situation may seem bizarre, the process by which it came about is hardly unusual. One month, the firm loses a key customer, so revenues and profits are down. Head Office calls and demands that "something be done!" (i.e., cut costs and replace the customer).

The manager concerned gears up the sales effort and manages to replace the lost customer. He cuts staff to reduce costs and bring profits back on target. With the new client coming on board, these staff cuts damage service quality, so next month two customers leave ... so revenues and profits are down again, and the phone call from Head Office comes through once more—"Do something about sales and costs!" ... so the manager seeks more new customers and cuts some more staff.

Eventually, client turnover reaches very high rates, and both sales and service staff are working frantically to keep the business going at all. The solution in this case was to *stop* selling business! Switching management and staff effort onto service delivery rebuilt quality for remaining clients and stopped the high rates of client churn.

higher costs, and you might well be worried that you keep losing 10% of your customers every month, while I lose only 2%.

Follow through a similar thought experiment for the staff resource of our two firms. We each have 100 employees, but each year you both recruit and lose 50, while I recruit and lose 10. Our respective staff resources will again differ considerably. Not only will I incur much lower costs of recruitment and training, but my people will also have an average of 10 years' experience, while yours have only 2 years.

What happens if the rates of gain and loss for a resource are themselves changing? Consider the difficulties that arise, say, if your recruitment rate falls below the normal rate of staff losses, or if you start to lose customers faster than you win them. Capturing these evolving interactions between a resource level and its flows requires repeating the arithmetic explained in Figure 2.3 for each period.

Figure 3.1 shows this process applied to a firm's staff base—recruitment continues at a steady, apparently satisfactory rate of 15 per month. Initially, attrition is only 11 per month, though starting to rise. The number of employees seems at first to progress quite satisfactorily. Even by mid-year, there seems little cause for concern—hiring is still sustaining a strong group of staff. However, whatever has caused the attrition to grow seems to continue, so that it progressively overwhelms the firm's hiring rate. This information from Figure 3.1 is readily shown as a time chart (Figure 3.2).

Such charts have important messages for managers. In this case, for example:

- Recruitment is not the real problem—rather, it is staff losses.
- Simply stabilizing the rate of staff losses will not be enough. Attrition will then continue to run ahead of recruitment, so that all we will achieve is to fix the downward slope of the staff population. In another 12 months, there will be no one left.
- Having the right information is vital to understanding what is happening through time. A regular report on staff numbers is useful, but a report sep-

Staff

Month	New staff	Staff (end)	Staff lost
		100 start	
January	+15 per month	104 (end)	-11 per month
February	+15	107	-12
March	+15	109	-13
April	+15	110	-14
May	+15	110	-15
June	+15	109	-16
July	+15	107	-17
August	+15	104	-18
September	+15	100	-19
October	+15	95	-20
November	+15	89	-21
December	+15	82	-22

Figure 3.1 Calculating the level of a resource through time.

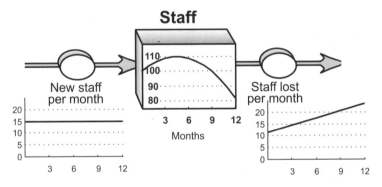

Figure 3.2 Time charts show how resource levels evolve as inflows and outflows change.

arating gains and losses is much more valuable (in the sense of indicating where action is needed). A *time chart* of losses is better still, since changes in direction will warn of impending danger or confirm that the resource is under control.

Surprisingly few firms seem to report such "rates of change" data or use them for continually informing their decisions. Management information systems often report numbers of staff (or other resources) and occasionally go further in recording net changes (e.g. "our staff fell by seven people last month"). But, since different forces may be driving inflows and outflows, it is essential to separate these two items. Furthermore, the evolution of these change processes make it essential to watch the time-path of these flows, not simply report their current values.

Whole industries can get resource flows wrong

Late in 2000, major firms in IT and telecoms ... Cisco, Lucent, Nortel, and others ... found themselves in trouble from the technology sector downturn. They had spent the previous 5 years frantically trying to hire enough smart technologists, salespeople, and so on to meet the demands of a burgeoning economy. This challenge was especially tough because the war for this talent had become so fierce that attrition rates had reached 20–30% per year.

Then, the bursting bubble in e-commerce did catastrophic damage to sales rates, forcing these firms to slam on the brakes in a desperate effort to stay profitable. Not only was hiring almost frozen but existing staff had to be laid off too. These firms assessed their short to medium-term staffing needs, and announced lay-off programs to bring staffing to the new target levels. All were determined to get it right and, though painful, go through just one round of major lay-offs, rather than have their staff suffer continuing insecurity.

Unfortunately, their projections assumed continuing high rates of natural staff turnover. In just a few months, fears of job insecurity became so great that underlying turnover dropped to well under 10% per year. Consequently, by Spring 2001, these firms and many others had to announce a second, major round of lay-offs.

Could this have been better managed? Scenario approaches to strategic planning have been well understood since the early 1980s. It was always inconceivable that these industries would continue, indefinitely, the astonishing growth of the late 1990s. So, they should, for some time, have been asking: "How will a slowdown affect us, and how should we prepare for it?" The first signs of a decline in the net formation rate for new technology-based enterprises were evident many months before the staffing challenges became apparent, and should have alerted management to the need to revise HR strategies.

The story has a sorry postscript. Investment banks and strategy consultants, too, were suffering staff losses to technology-based start-ups during the late 1990s, at just the time when they were experiencing unprecedented demand from client firms. In a desperate attempt to keep at least some access to future professional staff capacity, many offered their departing talent guaranteed return tickets ... "Sorry you are leaving us, and we'd really like to have you back, so if this new venture doesn't work out for you, there will be a job for you." When did these leavers exercise their option to return? At exactly the time when demand for strategy consulting and investment banking services collapsed.

It may seem puzzling that such simple information is rarely available, but the central importance of resource flows has only recently become clear. Even if a firm understands the importance of tracking gains and losses of resources, very real difficulties arise. A consumer products company, for example, may know how many consumers are interested in a brand, and from this they can work out the net change from month to month. But, how do you split out the gains of consumers remembering your latest advertizement from the losses you have suffered as others lose interest? A retail bank might be expected to know how many customers it has (number of accounts, adjusted for multi-account holders), but this is not a reliable measure of *active* customers. Account-holders may simply stop doing any business through an account, while leaving small amounts of money in it.

Adding "lumps" of resource

Growing resources in the continuous manner implied thus far may not always be sufficient—firms often make step shifts in resource levels, either to correct some imbalance in the system or to initiate other changes. Examples intended to increase resource levels quickly include raising finance or launching a range of new products. In other cases, resource may be *lost* quickly,

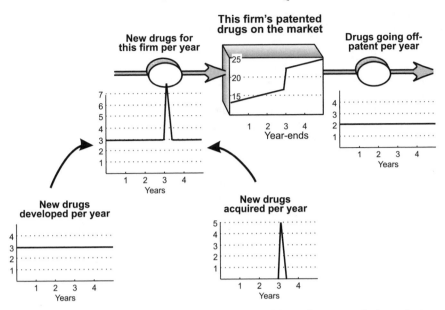

Figure 3.3 Adding a "lump" of resource—acquiring pharmaceutical products.

either by accident (e.g., when a whole team of staff leave at once) or deliberately (e.g., when a firm closes a whole group of unattractive customer accounts). Such changes are captured with the same stock-and-flow structure, but show up as a *pulse* on the inflow, which causes a *step* in the stock.

Take a pharmaceuticals firm, developing new drugs at the rate of three new patented products each year, while its stock of drugs on the market is going off-patent at the rate of two per year. Its rivals have stronger product portfolios and are also developing new products more rapidly.

The firm's product portfolio is falling behind that of its competitors. Filling this competitive shortfall of patented drugs with new development (i.e., trying to boost the flow of new products into its current stock) will take many years. The company therefore acquires a rival whose product portfolio complements its own. The level in the product-resource stock, which was previously growing at a steady but slow rate, receives a one-off surge in its inflow, creating a step in its level at the moment the acquisition is made (Figure 3.3).

Representing this in the stock and flow framework *still* requires the basic rules to be fulfilled—the stock of resource can only be increased *via* an inflow. Figure 3.3 shows how such a *one-off* acquisition is added to the *continuous* flows of product increases and losses to quantify how the resource level changes from the start of each year to the end. (*Note that Figure 3.3 defines items quite precisely. The stock is of **this firm's** patented drugs on the market, not **all** drugs—to signify that no total increase in drugs arises from the acquisition. Similarly, the inflow is new drugs on the market for this firm, to be clear that it includes both those emerging from its own development process and others acquired.*)

Important observation—whole numbers!

A careful look at Figure 3.3 shows that the time chart for the stock of products is a continuously sloping line (apart from the year when it jumps). This suggests that at various times during each year there are fractions of a product on the market. This is clearly nonsense, and to examine what is happening in detail within a shorter time period, management would wish to know when each new product arrives and each old product goes off-patent. The result would be a timeline with a series of small steps. To understand the revenue and margin implications, the exact contribution of each product would also need to be represented.

However, Figure 3.3 is designed to portray the shape of this firm's future product range. So, provided that the issue of concern is adequately covered by this broad pattern, there is no need to track whole numbers. The same applies to the time charts of customers, staff and other resources developed throughout this chapter—if the whole numbers are important to the issue being tackled, show them; if not, the smooth timeline is sufficient.

This approach to the capture or loss of "pulses" of resource shows that acquisitions, mergers, and joint ventures are simply ways to make step increases to a number of resources simultaneously. A complication may arise, however, because step changes across the entire business can upset whatever balance existed previously. This kind of upset may be deliberate or accidental:

- Deliberate upset may be caused because the acquiring or merging firms see an opportunity to follow the deal with an immediate rationalization of surplus resources (typically, staff or fixed assets).
- In accidental cases, the firms fully intend to sustain the combination of two pools of some critical resource such as staff, distributors, or customers. However, since people are involved in these resources, unintended flows may arise of their own accord immediately after the intended shifts arising from the acquisition or merger itself.

Examples of both deliberate and accidental resource changes arise in mergers of professional service firms. These are commonly predicated on the assumption that bringing two independent staff groups together will enhance the service portfolio that each could offer alone, and hence boost client win rates and business volume. Frequently, however, tensions between the two staff groups result in a post-merger increase in staff attrition rates. Further damage may then follow, as clients leave too, either because they associate more with the staff personalities than with the firm itself or because the now-depleted staff cannot maintain high service standards. Whether deliberate or accidental, such episodes of expansion and subsequent resource losses should be dealt with as shown in Figure 3.4.

Stimulating and exploiting potential resources

Figure 2.1, which started the discussion on building and depleting resources, made an important assumption—that the right people exist in the outside

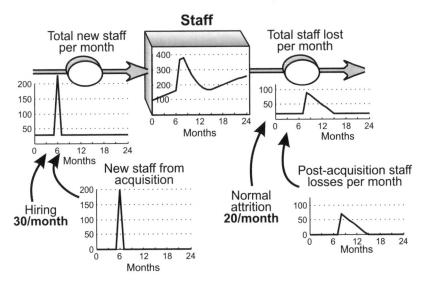

Figure 3.4 Resource step and subsequent decline in mergers and acquisitions.

world for us to hire and turn into actual employees. In reality, suitable staff may be scarce and, in extreme cases, our hiring targets for specialist individuals may represent a large fraction of *all* the people who may be suitable.

Scarcity may arise for many tangible resources, so we need to deal with such limits in assessing our ability to build performance. This task involves the following steps:

- identify the limited scale of availability for important resources;
- assess the rate at which the potential pool of resource is growing or declining;
- incorporate the known scarcity in any estimates for the rate at which the firm might capture resources for itself;
- seek ways to accelerate the exploitation of potential resources;
- evaluate means to stimulate growth of the potential resource.

This process can be illustrated with the example of a cable TV company. The early success of such companies depended upon achieving a rapid take-up of their service by consumers. Only consumers whose homes are passed by the cable are able to subscribe, and, even then, the company has to persuade those consumers to do so, by offering popular programming at an attractive price. Additional services such as low-cost telephone calls and Internet access may further increase the appeal to consumers of taking up a vsubscription.

To perform strongly, a cable company must both create the *potential* consumer base (by installing cable) and the *actual* consumer base (by marketing its services). Both activities are costly, and there is a trade-off between spending money on network expansion vs. exploiting localities that have already been cabled. Both investments face diminishing returns—as the network expands,

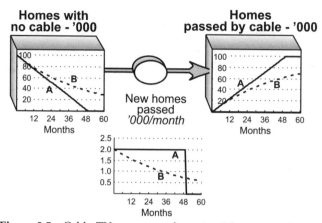

Figure 3.5 Cable TV coverage of a potential customer base.

the geographically compact region becomes exploited, leaving only less densely populated areas that are costly to reach. Similarly, after the most enthusiastic consumers have been signed up to the cable company's service, only the more reluctant consumers remain to be won.

How do these interacting issues play out over time? First, let us deal with the rate at which cabling of streets develops the potential market.

Consider a single, cable TV firm serving a town with 100,000 homes, in which the densest population areas make it possible to install cabling that passes 2,000 homes per month. If this rate were to continue, cabling could be available to all homes within about 4 years. However, after the most densely populated areas are covered, coverage will inevitably slow down, not in terms of the number of metres laid, but in terms of homes reached. One way to consider this process is for the rate of development to slow to a maximum *fraction* of remaining homes per month.

The implications of the decreasing rate of coverage are shown in Figure 3.5. If we followed the initial assumption that we can simply continue passing 2,000 homes each month, we end up with the rather unreal time-path shown by line A. Line B, on the other hand, shows the progressive slowdown in coverage, if we instead assume we can only add 2% of remaining homes each month. Initially, 2% of 100,000 is the same as the desired rate of 2,000/month. However, as coverage increases, "2%" becomes a progressively smaller number, until, by the end of 3 years, it corresponds to just under 1,000/month (2% of about 48,000).

Naturally, the actual numbers for any such case depend upon the specifics of the potential catchment population, the size of the cabling installation team (which may change over time), the particular density distribution of housing, and so on. Reflecting such factors accurately requires line B in the bottom chart for "new homes passed" to be laid out exactly as management believe the *actual* cabling rate will progress. The time charts for homes with and without cable can then be calculated.

The cable TV example illustrates a common difficulty in resource development—*early stimulation of potential resources is often easy and fast, but progress can slow down as an increasing fraction of the opportunity is taken.* While this observation may look rather obvious stated in this stark manner, it is surprising how often it takes executives by surprise. Many discussions with managers, especially in new ventures, start from an enthusiastic description of how quickly their enterprise grew during early months or quarters, only to move on to puzzled descriptions of increasingly difficult progress. Frequently, it becomes clear that the firm was "picking the low-hanging fruit" in the early success period, and now finds the remaining fruit to be neither so ripe, nor so reachable! It is essential in such cases to look forward beyond the early, easy phase and consider just how quickly it will become harder to sustain growth.

Returning to the cable TV example, this firm can now move on to estimate the rate at which *actual* subscribers might be captured. Once again, we would probably experience diminishing returns, this time for our marketing efforts. We can see the implications of this if we assume, for example, that we manage each month to sell to just 10% of those homes who have access to cable, but who do not currently subscribe (Figure 3.6).

At first sight, some elements of Figure 3.6 may be puzzling:

- Why, for example, does the middle resource stock stay nearly empty—what happened to all those homes in Figure 3.5 that were passed by our cable? Quite simply, they have been "moved along" into the pool of homes with *both* cable *and* a subscription. The total of homes reached at any time is the sum of these two numbers, shown in the time chart at top right.

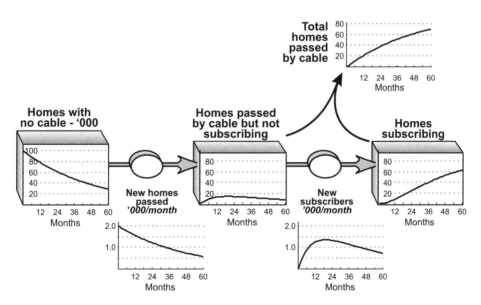

Figure 3.6 Take-up of cable TV by households as coverage and marketing continue.

Neglecting the constraints of potential resource pools can be costly

By 2000, the cable TV industry in the US was well developed, with a large fraction of homes within reach of cable, and over 80% of those homes actually connected. Thinking that a similar opportunity was available in all developed economies, a host of operators piled in to developing cable in other countries too. In the UK, NTL borrowed heavily to buy up these fledgling operators, amassing a £12b debt in the process. Unfortunately, competitive conditions for cable were somewhat different than in the US, due to the already strong presence of satellite broadcasting. Consequently, although NTL could reach 11 million homes, only 3 million were connected. Its only hope was that more of these households would switch to cable, for the additional services made possible by its high-speed, bi-directional services. But a large fraction of those households, especially those housing older, less affluent consumers, were never likely to be interested in such advanced services.

- Next, how come our winning of "10% of homes passed" each month actually translates into a quick boom in uptake, followed by a slow decline, as in the right-hand lower chart? This number is easily explained too—by definition, it is 10% of the *potential* new subscribers remaining in the middle stock at any moment.

Again, for any real case, we can use better estimates for the rate at which our company could actually expect to develop potential homes into paying subscribers. It may be, for example, that early months would see a rapid percentage of newly served homes developed as "early adopters" sign up, followed by a more rapid reduction in the rate of new subscriptions as the most resistant people are gradually won over. In this case, the number of homes passed, but not subscribing (the middle stock in Figure 3.6), would continue to rise, while the number of homes subscribing would succumb to earlier "limits to growth".

Whatever the specifics of the case, though, the principles of Figure 3.6 apply:

- you can only build an *actual* customer base from the *potential* customers available;
- the number of those potential customers may itself be subject to growth;
- as you capture of them, you (and your rivals!) deplete the pool of those who remain;
- ... so, further gains become increasingly difficult to achieve.

Neither the incremental activity from month to month nor the resulting evolution of your customer base (and hence revenues) are intuitively obvious:

- *the only way to get good estimates of the time-path of performance, when that performance relies on developing potential resources (as is always the case) is to do the math!*

Now that our cable TV company has a robust framework for capturing the time-path of customer development, it is possible to evaluate some alternatives. One policy dilemma for the cable TV firm, for example, is whether to drive harder to extend cabling across the whole locality, or to focus more effort on winning over more of those homes they pass.

Doing it right!—conserving resources

The sequence of resource stocks in Figure 3.6 introduces a further important principle of our method. If resources flow from stock to stock, they must be "conserved" along the chain. In other words, we can't gain or lose resources overall. This is why the middle stock in the figure is named "homes passed by cable but not subscribing" rather than, as in Figure 3.5, "homes passed by cable". By introducing a further place for them to move to (homes subscribing), we have had to let them flow out of the middle stock.

There is an easy way to check we are doing this right—the sum of all these connected stocks must equal the total population available. In this case, the three stocks always add up to the total of 100,000 households. The only way this could not be the case would be if there were inflows from the outside world or outflows to it (e.g., new housing construction). Even then, it is still possible to check we are doing it right, by working out what should be happening to the total across all the stocks.

Say the cabling rate was halved, to a rate of 1% of remaining homes each month, rather than 2%, but the marketing success rate doubled (winning 20% of non-subscribers each month rather than 10%). Surely, these two numbers should more or less balance out, but this is where the understimulation of the potential market really starts to hurt. The slower cabling rate creates a much smaller pool for the marketing efforts to exploit. Consequently, the population of *homes passed but not subscribing* remains almost empty, and the population of subscribers captured fails to match the scale of the first mix of policies (Figure 3.7).

The small test of alternative policies in Figure 3.7 creates a somewhat surprising divergence between the two cases. This is indicative of one of the most powerful benefits arising from the strategy dynamics approach:

- *The right choices of **what** to do **when** and **how much** is often not obvious and can only be found by working out how the dynamics of the situation may actually play out.*

This will become a still more important message when we look at how resources interact with each other in the next three chapters.

Developing resources within the business

Having developed resources from the external environment, and brought them into the firm's system, management must often continue their development. The most common resource to which this challenge applies is staff, though similar considerations apply to other resources such as products or customers. Another simplified example, this time for professional staff, will help clarify how this process can be captured.

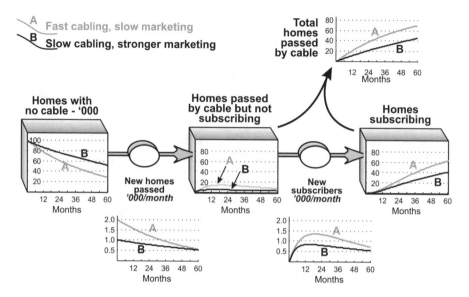

Figure 3.7 Take-up of cable TV by households—slower coverage and more successful marketing.

Professional service business such as law firms, advertizing agencies and consultants rely more than most on sustaining a strong and growing population of skilled staff—for these firms, staff *are* their production capacity. They compete to attract the best young graduates from the professional training sources (law schools, universities, or business schools), then develop them quickly into productive capacity to serve the demand from clients.

Within a few years, the best staff develop to take on client-management and project-management responsibilities. Others either remain as "foot soldiers" or move on to other firms—sometimes as a consequence of a deliberate policy of "up-or-out" by the firm. Eventually, the best managers may be promoted to the position of partner, where they have broader responsibility for developing and maintaining strong client relationships, for building the firm's staff, and for strengthening and extending the services it offers.

Similar staff development issues arise in many other types of firm. Companies' internal Information Systems groups must hire and train competent staff, develop managers to look after projects, and select leaders to build their reputation and demand from the business units who constitute their "customers". Manufacturing companies often have to build a force of service staff to support their installed base of equipment. Multiple-retailers have to build a structure of departmental, store-level and chain-wide managers. Since staffing is such a widely shared problem, it will be valuable to look at how hiring, promotion, and attrition interact to make the time-path of employee development so tricky.

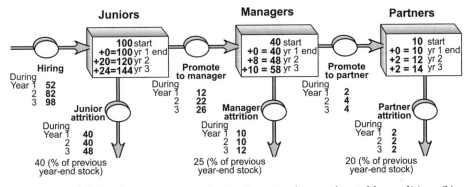

Figure 3.8 Staff development in a professional service firm under stable conditions (Year 1) and 20% growth (Years 2–3).

Consider a professional firm starting with 100 juniors, 40 managers, and 10 partners. Each year, this firm expects to lose 40% of its juniors, 25% of its managers, and 20% of its partners, and needs to know how many staff to hire and promote to stay as it is. If we try to work out the answer to this question by starting with the juniors, we soon get into difficulties—hiring has to replace both losses of juniors and promotions to managers, but we don't yet know what that promotion number needs to be. So, we had better start at the other end—with the flow of partners:

- losing 20% of the 10 partners means that 2 leave, so 2 managers must be promoted;
- losing 25% of 40 managers means that 10 leave, and the 2 promoted to partner must also be replaced, so 12 juniors have to be promoted. 40 juniors leave (40% of 100), so 52 new hires are needed to replace them.

This may seem a rather high hiring rate, but is a simple consequence of needing to replace attrition. However, consider what happens if this firm tries to grow at 20% per year. Figure 3.8 works the numbers through for each year, with Year 1 being the stable year, and Years 2–3 being years of 20% growth. The apparently modest growth rate seems to require promotion and hiring rates to be doubled!

But this scenario makes some bold and rather generous assumptions:

- First, it assumes that there are enough suitable managers to double the rate of promotion from 2 to 4 people. It happens that the base promotion rate of 5% in the first year (2 out of 40) is rather modest, so this is unlikely to be a problem in practice. However, if only 5% *were* suitable, the stock of managers would need to be *80* for us to find 4 suitable promotion candidates.
- Similarly, it seems about 12% of juniors are suitable for promotion to manager (12 out of 100 in Year 1). So, to provide 22 new managers in Year 2, our stock of juniors would need to be *183*, rather than 100.

The problem gets worse!

- If our stock of managers needs to be 80 rather than 40, the 25% attrition rate means we will lose 20 managers in Year 2 rather than 10. We therefore need to promote 10 more juniors—32 rather than 22.
- If there are still only 12% of juniors suitable for promotion, having 183 juniors will not be enough, we actually need *267*!

Doing it right!—changing flow rates within a longer time period

Chapter 2 explained the importance of choosing a time period for your assessment of strategy that is appropriate for the issue you are concerned with. Resource flows can always change *during* the time step you choose, and, if that time step is too long, this can lead to serious errors in your estimation of resource levels at the end of each period.

In Figure 3.8, we make the simplifying assumption that attrition during a year is a certain fraction of the number of staff at the *start* of each year. For example, in Year 3, we lose 40% of 120 juniors or 48 people. A more realistic assumption is that we *continually* lose people at the rate of 40% per year. Since the number of juniors rises from 120 to 144 *during* Year 3, the loss rate rises from 48 per year in January to 57 per year by December—which means of course that we would not in fact end up with 144.

We seem, then, to have chosen too long a time step in recalculating each year. To reduce the error to insiginificant levels, quarterly calculations would have been preferable. Reducing the time step to 1 month would improve estimates a little more, but there would be little point—we would be worrying about differences that are much smaller than the other uncertainties in the case.

Using time charts to estimate resource development

Although the precise arithmetic of the staff development chain is somewhat tricky, it is possible to estimate its behavior by working with the time charts. Figure 3.9 shows how this is done, just working with the juniors.

There are just a few points to be careful about with these estimates:

- *Be precise about exactly **when** the estimate is being made*—note that this chart specifies where the year ends are.
- *It's helpful where possible if the charts on the inflows and outflows are on equivalent scales.* That way, you can "eyeball" the likely trends. Here, hiring starts much lower than promotion-plus-attrition, so it makes sense that the stock of juniors is falling. But hiring is growing much faster than promotion, attrition, or the sum of the two. So, again, it makes sense that depletion of juniors slows down, then reverses. (Although it is helpful to use common scales in this way, it is not always practical to do so—when we put the three staff groups together, the hiring and promotion rates have to be on different scales so we can see the data for each.)
- *Adding and subtracting the rates of gain and loss gives the **slope** of the stock*, from

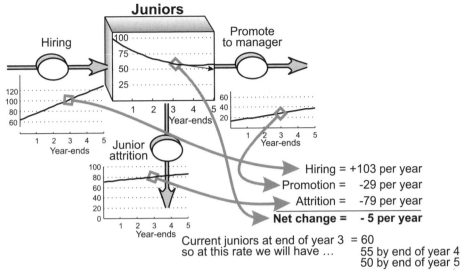

Figure 3.9 Getting approximate time-paths from gains and losses.

which you can see where it will end up at any time in the future, assuming current rates continue (the small arrow in the stock).

An illustrative scenario for staff development

There are clearly many scenarios for how this firm's staff resources could develop over these 5 years, so we will just look at a few possible stories, illustrated in Figure 3.10:

- *The firm starts in balance*, with hiring and promotion *to* each grade exactly balancing promotion *from* that grade, plus attrition. This is the same as the first year of Figure 3.8, but looks set to continue for 5 years (line A).
- *The firm's partners decide to pursue growth (line B)*, aiming to double the size of the firm in 5 years. They raise hiring from 62/year by a further 13 each year. Promotions to manager are also increased from the base rate of 12/year by an additional 5 each year, so that by Year 5 they expect to be bringing in 37 new managers per year. Similarly, promotion to partner rises from 2/year to 7/ year by Year 5. Unfortunately, they neglect to plan for fractional attrition rates eroding their growth plans. By Year 5, juniors will have only grown to about 150, managers to 73, and partners to 19.
- *One year into the plan, a group of 6 partners leave to set up a firm of their own*, foreseeing the inadequacy of the strategy (early phase of line C). They manage to take with them 20 managers, leaving the firm seriously depleted in the senior grades. The remaining partners decide that, to get the business back on its feet, they will have to adjust hiring and promotion

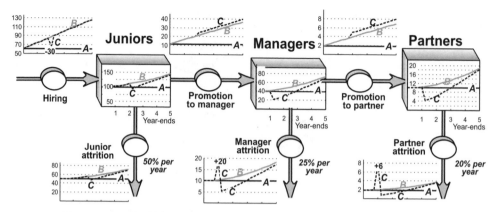

Figure 3.10 Staff development scenarios in a professional service firm.

policies (later part of line C). They lift the rate of promotion from the junior level. Doing this too quickly will deplete the junior staff too much, as well as bringing inexperienced people into senior grades. They therefore increase promotions to manager by a further 3 each year (on top of the steady increase already planned). Promotions to partner are also increased by 1 each year. Losing their colleagues has put the firm badly out of balance—with about half the number of managers and partners, there is not sufficient work to keep all the juniors busy. So, in Year 2, they drop hiring by 30 people, but only for the one year. These policies combine to put the firm gradually back on track, and, by Year 5, it is nearly back to the original objective.

*(Note in this example that the steady **fractional** attrition rates result in actual losses of people **dropping** when there are fewer staff in any grade to be lost.)*

The example in Figure 3.10 not only shows how resource-development structures can result in time-path outcomes that are dynamically tricky, but also illustrates how to work systematically through to resolve the complexity.

Developing resources beyond the firm

Not only do resources develop into and within the firm, they may also continue to develop even when they have moved on, yet still have a powerful impact on the immediate and long-term performance of the firms themselves, in spite of being well beyond management's direct control:

- Manufacturers of many kinds continue to benefit from the installed base of products sold in the past, often many years previously. Elevator manufacturers continue to sell maintenance services on old installations, printer manufacturers' sales of ink cartridges reflect the cumulative total of unit sales to date, and so on.

- Business schools, universities, and other educational institutions make considerable efforts to build and sustain the population of alumni by keeping in touch with former students. This resource can be immensely powerful, with institutions such as major business schools receiving considerable financial resources from their alumni. Moreover, such advocates can pull more good students through the system, by hiring its graduates. This further enhances the institution's ability to attract the best incoming students, which sets up the same mechanism for future years.

- Educational institutions are not alone in leveraging such alumni groups— many professional service firms actively use their up-or-out staff development process to breed a distributed population of former staff in key positions with client firms. Provided that the outplacement of such staff is handled positively, they will be favorably inclined to call on the services of their former employer when they find themselves in need of professional services. One of the strongest exponents of this mechanism is the strategy consulting firm McKinsey & Co. So successful was this network that a 1998 article in the UK's *Independent* newspaper, discussing the "Gentleman's club in St James Street" (the firm's London office), highlighted the key positions in business, banking, and politics occupied by former senior staff of the firm.

This chapter has shown how to quantify resource levels through time, how to portray these effects as time charts, and how to work with those time charts to understand wider implications, especially in the case of resource development. Chapters 4 to 6 will explain in detail how resources *depend upon each other* for their growth and depletion.

The failure of correlation methods to explain business performance

We end this chapter with a serious warning about efforts to understand profitability and other measures of business performance.

Chapter 2 explained the deeply fundamental nature and importance of the mathematical behavior of accumulating asset stocks. This process has devastating consequences. *The use of correlation methods to seek explanations for profitability and other performance measures is doomed to fail whenever an asset stock is involved that is accumulating or depleting which is the case in virtually all situations.* For example, a high rate of spend on marketing may eventually lead to an equilibrium where high customer win rates balance high loss rates around a large customer base. Lower marketing spend may, after customer losses have worked through, correspond to a smaller equilibrium customer base. Consequently, viewed over the long term and ignoring periods where the customer base is changing, a statistically significant relationship between marketing spend and customers may be found, but this says nothing useful about causality.

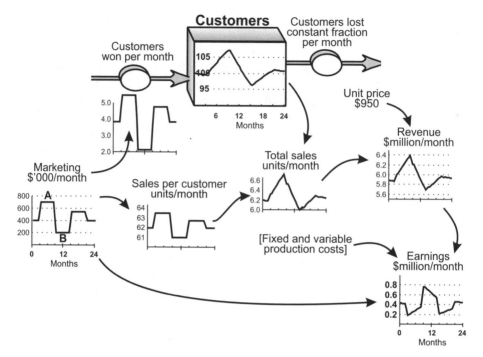

Figure 3.11   Revenue and earnings over time reflecting customer acquisition rates due to marketing only.

To illustrate the problem, consider a simple firm with the following characteristics:

- Customers are won, with no delay, by marketing spend—the more marketing, the faster they are won. The same marketing spend also encourages customers to buy more. A constant fraction of customers is lost each month.
- The firm's monthly revenue is calculated from the rate of units sold per month, multiplied by the unit price, and monthly earnings reflect this revenue, minus certain fixed and variable production costs and the marketing spend.

Figure 3.11 shows a specific performance scenario that arises when this firm follows a particular history of marketing spend. Figure 3.12 shows the plots of both revenue and earnings vs. marketing spend. Each × corresponds to a single month's results. These plots show why correlation will fail. For any new *static* rate of marketing spend, the firm's revenue and earnings will start *moving* along a new trajectory. Where that trajectory starts and ends will depend on both the original starting point and the period over which the new spending rate is continued.

During Period A (e.g., Months 3 to 9), the firm starts with low earnings—but earnings are only low because the historic marketing spend was already modest, *and* because spending has just been increased by $300,000/month. Earnings then start steadily increasing following path A, but, in Month 10, suddenly jump to a much higher rate, with much lower marketing, simply because the firm cuts its spending.

The apparent relationship between higher marketing and lower earnings, then, is entirely misleading. Had the firm continued the high marketing spend of period A, its earnings would, within a few months, have surpassed the earnings rate at the end of period B.

Correlation is equally impotent in identifying generalizable causal relationships among a large population of firms at a single moment in time (cross-sectional analysis). Every firm in such a sample will be on some trajectory through time, either due to choices it has made itself or actions taken by others. In general, *regression methods will be unreliable whenever an asset stock exists between a variable to be explained and any hypothetical cause.* To restate this in practical terms for management, be very careful whenever colleagues or consultants claim that "*x* is clearly caused by *y*", whether you are discussing the business itself, competitive activity, or industry conditions generally.

It should be noted, by the way, that the problems caused by asset stock accumulation and depletion are not restricted to the study of business

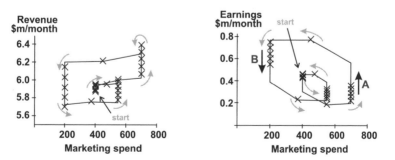

Figure 3.12 Example of how revenue and earnings reflect marketing spend when customers accumulate over time.

performance, but afflict research throughout the social sciences. For example, the number of people unemployed at any year end is the number out of work at the previous year end, plus any new people joining the workforce during the year, minus any finding work or leaving the workforce. This "asset stock" cannot, therefore, be usefully correlated with pay rates, taxation, or other hypothetical causes. Similarly, the number of terrorists in a country today is the sum of all those who ever took up terrorism, minus those who ever gave up or were killed. This asset stock too cannot, with any confidence, be correlated to rates of political or religious persecution, poverty, educational levels, and so on.

Summary

To be precise about resource levels at any future time, it is necessary to calculate gains and losses in each period, then add or subtract the net change from the current level. Repeating this process enables time charts of resource levels and flows to be created. These are a powerful means for communicating the evolution of resources, but care is needed to ensure accuracy.

Resources are frequently developed from *potential* resources existing in the outside world. Early in the firm's development, such potential resources may be plentiful, but the potential pool drains as it becomes exploited, slowing down further growth in captured resources.

Resource levels may be subject to a step change if there is a sudden acquisition or loss of a large "lump" of resource. Acquisitions and mergers are common mechanisms to achieve such step shifts in resource levels across the firm. However, care is needed to ensure that subsequent resource losses are as intended or expected.

Once captured by the firm, many resources "develop" through different stages—what is lost from one stage is transferred to the next. It is essential to ensure that the same type of item flows from stage to stage and is "conserved" in the process—every unit must be accounted for.

Furthermore, resources may continue to develop and have sustained impact on firm performance, even when the resource may be outside the firm's immediate ownership.

To have a good grasp of strategic performance requires constant awareness and *management* of all the flows of resource through such chains—from capturing potential resources initially, through their development within the firm, and on beyond the firm's direct control.

4

Building the Machine—Reinforcing Feedback between Resources

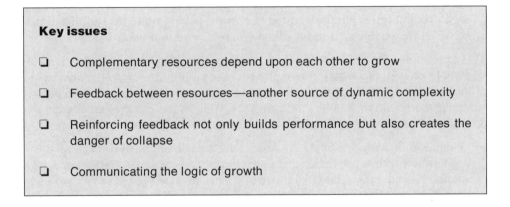

Key issues

❑ Complementary resources depend upon each other to grow

❑ Feedback between resources—another source of dynamic complexity

❑ Reinforcing feedback not only builds performance but also creates the danger of collapse

❑ Communicating the logic of growth

The first three chapters have provided the components needed to build an understanding of strategy dynamics: a clearly specified time-path of the strategic problem or opportunity, a robust specification of key resources, and a way of showing numerically how individual resources grow and decline. The next step is to define how exactly resources are "complementary" and capture quantitatively how this plays out over time.

Current approach to linkages within and beyond the business

The conventional approach to understanding the relationships between the firm's internal activities and profitability lies in analysis of cost drivers and value drivers. A formal framework for this task is the "value chain" popularized by Porter (1985), and widely adopted and developed since. Some version of value-chain analysis is commonly applied by strategy departments in many firms and by most strategy consulting firms at an early stage of client assignments. In addition to the obvious benefit of identifying where unnecessary costs may lie, value-chain analysis fulfills two main purposes regarding interrelationships between a firm's distinct activities:

- *Seeking sources of competitive advantage by **increasing** effort and cost at one stage of the firm so as to **save** costs elsewhere.* Examples include investing in production engineering efforts to reduce ongoing unit costs of production, devoting more effort to increase product quality and thus save on after-sales service, spending on inventory control to reduce costs of stockholding, and so on.

- *Identifying ways of differentiating the firm's offering to customers, by adding product or service factors.* This requires understanding how *customers and suppliers* make money, so analysis is extended to the value chains of these parties beyond the firm itself. If successful, such investigations may enable the firm to charge higher prices or win sales from rivals. Examples include spending on a product's development to make it cheaper for customers to use, or spending on advertizing to raise distributors' expected sales levels or achieved margins. Similarly, it may be worth paying more for supplies if this enables the business to reduce its own costs or obtain other benefits.

These principles can be extended throughout the industry supply chain, to make the whole process of serving the final customer more efficient, to the advantage of all firms in the chain. Although value-chain approaches have delivered considerable competitive benefits to firms, as well as efficiency benefits to the economy at large, they suffer three limitations:

- *First, it is difficult to capture dynamics with value-chain analysis.* The analysis generally produces a detailed description of the current situation, and lays alongside it the new state that the firm wishes to attain—*"our service engineers spend about 5 hours per year to support each item we sell and we need to get it down to 2 hours"* or *"our unit production costs are currently £80, and if we spend £5m we can get this down to £65"*. While this is useful information, it tells us little about the time-path of these changes. Do we expect to reduce our service cost progressively or, by changing our methods, do we bring it down in a step in 2 months' time? If we invest in production engineering, does nothing happen for 6 months while radical improvements are discovered and implemented or does the rate of cost reduction accelerate as we progressively discover mutually supporting savings? And, in each case, is this the end-point or will further improvements continue to arise?
- Such questions are relatively easy to answer for simple operational issues, but rather more problematic for the strategic challenges that affect several parts of the organization at once. *So, a second limitation to value-chain analysis arises in handling multifunctional problems* (rather than single-function issues). These may require simultaneous, progressive changes to product development, production, marketing, distribution, sales, staffing, finance, and so on. At this greater level of complexity, the firm will run into second-order effects: enhancing product reliability today reduces support costs, but sales volumes rise, putting pressure on distribution capacity and raising, rather than lowering, the demands on the service department, so that we have to recruit more people rather than downsizing, negating the original savings on support costs, and so on.
- Finally, *cost and value analysis cannot handle the crucial role of intangible elements of the firm's competitive advantage.* If the service department needs more people, the hiring rate can be increased, but people are under increasing pressure in the meantime, so morale takes a beating, which increases staff

losses, so product support is inadequate and the firm's reputation suffers, and so on.

What is needed, therefore, is a means of managing the time-path of strategic initiatives, extended to encompass all functions that may be involved in strategic developments. This will be dealt with in Chapters 4 to 6. The special features of intangible factors will be covered in more depth in Chapter 7.

"To he who hath shall be given"—the strength of complementary resources

To accomplish this integrated picture of a business, attention must switch away from cost drivers and back onto the firm's strategic resources discussed in Chapter 2. We must reflect a crucial reality of strategic management—*managers use resources they already have to develop others they need. This is not an expression of choice on the part of managers—it is an unavoidable reality. There is **no** way to build any resource without making use of others that already exist.* This principle even applies to new business ventures, where the entrepreneur appears to start with nothing, but in fact depends upon some vital intangible resources, like credibility with investors. Marketing staff cannot build a customer base without a credible product or service, salespeople cannot sell a product unless manufacturing has cost-effective production capacity, a firm cannot hire the people it needs if it has a poor reputation in the recruitment market, and so on.

None of this argument is meant to imply that the costs and margins identified by value-chain analysis are unimportant. The firm's resources are costly to obtain and to own, and product or service features may determine the price and hence value-added that can be obtained. However, the point being made here is that these cost and value features are *the financial consequences* of the firm's system of related resources—they do not *constitute* that system itself.

If the growth of any resource depends upon others already held, we need to look for those specific resources that are needed to grow each item in which we are interested. The simplest possible case of this interdependence arises when just a single resource creates its own growth. A common illustration of this phenomenon arises when happy *existing* customers encourage friends or colleagues to try our product or service and bring a further inflow of new customers. This is "word-of-mouth" feedback, common in very many markets. Though the most visible examples generally appear in customer-base growth, word-of-mouth effects are not restricted to this resource. Many firms are able to hire more effectively and at lower cost because existing employees recommend their friends and relatives to join the same firm.

Figure 4.1 shows how to quantify this word-of-mouth growth for a firm that starts with 1,000 customers. These customers discuss with others the fine service they are experiencing, to the extent that 20 new customers sign up each month for every 100 existing people the business is serving. This fractional growth rate—20% per month—defines quite precisely the power of the word-of-mouth effect

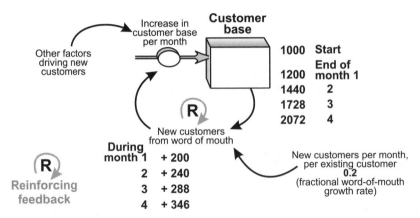

Figure 4.1 Reinforcing feedback grows a customer base.

and hence the *speed* at which the customer base will grow. The system shown in Figure 4.1 "reinforces" its own growth, as indicated by the R in the middle.

Provided that the word-of-mouth growth rate is positive, this self-reinforcing mechanism alone generates exponential growth—not merely a colloquial notion, but a mathematically precise mechanism. This is clearly a favorable situation for any company to create for itself. However, it comes with three warnings:

- *Self-reinforcing growth cannot continue indefinitely.* Sooner or later, the firm will come up against some limit, either external (e.g., no more customers to win) or internal (e.g., insufficient capacity to supply new customers). Nevertheless, the early years in the history of companies such as Nike or Microsoft, or of entire markets, like Japan's iMode phenomenon, demonstrate the considerable power of such mechanisms to drive very rapid growth and to continue up to extremely high limits.
- *Self-reinforcing growth does not come for free.* Something had to create the initial customer base of 1,000 people in the first place, probably marketing. Moreover, continuing this marketing effort can accelerate growth still further. Figure 4.2 shows what happens if this firm additionally attracts 100 customers per month with its marketing efforts. Not only do these extra users get added to the customer base each month, they also increase the size of the population on which the self-reinforcing growth can build (line B). This illustration offers an interesting observation—using marketing to bring in 100 new subscribers per month may not seem important in the context of what has become a firm with 12,500 customers. However, without it, there would have been fewer than 9,000—an increase of 3,500, although marketing only *directly* added 1,200 customers during the year.
- *Finally, note that self-reinforcing feedback has a dark side to its character*—it is equally capable of driving collapse. This issue will be examined shortly.

We will now move on to see how reinforcing feedback arises among a network of

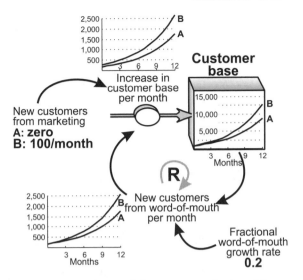

Figure 4.2 Reinforcing feedback leverages marketing-driven growth.

resources, and Chapter 5 will explain how "balancing" feedback acts to hold back the tendency of systems to grow or decline. This feedback view of business and social systems was popularized by Senge (1990)—a perspective that has become synonymous with "systems thinking" in management. Note, though, that many other system-based approaches to the social sciences exist (Richardson, 1999).

While management teams can benefit from sharing a qualitative understanding of feedback effects in their business and industry, management should exercise great caution. It should already be apparent from Chapters 2 and 3 that resource accumulation and depletion have important and nonobvious *quantitative* consequences for business performance through time. Consequently, discussion of feedback effects alone will not give rise to any useful insight as to the scale or timing of future cash flows or other outcomes. The more reliable foundation for a fact-based understanding of strategic performance dynamics, upon which we are building, originates with Forrester (1961).

Resource interdependence—an example of self-reinforcement in brand building

The ability for a single resource to drive its own growth is a special case of the general observation made earlier—that the firm can only build resources by using what it already has. More generally, then, it is necessary to identify which *other* resources are required and what impact they have on the *rate* of growth for the resource in which we are currently interested. The application of this principle will be illustrated with the challenge facing a consumer-goods

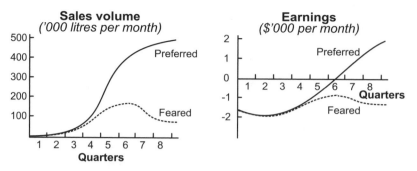

Figure 4.3 Time chart for sales and profits from a new product launch.

Table 4.1 Tangible resources needed to build a brand.

Tangible resources	Units of resource	Inflows and outflows	Units of inflows and outflows	Typical drivers
Consumers aware	People	New customers aware Consumers losing interest	'000 people per month	Advertizing, product availability Interest in other products
Stores stocking the brand	Stores	New stores stocking the brand Stores delisting the brand	Stores per month	Consumer demand, salesforce visits, price Better uses for shelf-space
Salesforce	People	New hires Resignations	People per month	Salaries, hiring effort Pressure of work, sales commission

firm that has developed a new brand of premium liqueur and wishes to create a profitable market.

From experience with comparable products, it is thought that about 5 million consumers might be made interested in the product, and about 50,000 stores may feasibly stock it in due course. Typical consumption is about 1 liter per person per month. Retail prices of about $11/liter are common in this sector, wholesale prices are around $8.50, and direct product costs are $7. The business needs a view of the time-path that it hopes this brand will follow and a clear statement of the strategic resources involved. Figure 4.3 illustrates two time charts for this launch that may provide top-level indicators of progress, and Table 4.1 defines just three key resources that will be involved: consumers, stores, and salesforce.

Since the firm has many other products, it can readily raise or lower the sales-

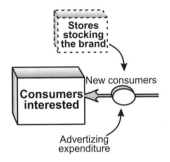

Figure 4.4 Drivers of growth in the number of consumers interested in the brand.

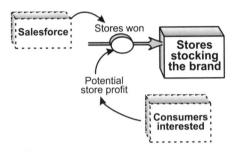

Figure 4.5 Drivers of growth for stores stocking the brand.

force effort on this brand by allocating people to or from these other products. Just two resources remain to be built—consumers and stores:

- Interested consumers are stimulated by advertizing expenditures, but are also won over to the product if they see it in stores. Figure 4.4 portrays these relationships. Note that the graphic elements follow the basic rules of resource accumulation—"consumers interested" can only be altered by "new consumers" arriving in the stock, and this flow itself can be estimated directly from the advertizing expenditure and the number of stores. (*Note that the process of building awareness, interest, and purchasing activity among customers is in reality a more involved, multi-stage process than this simple illustration implies—see Chapter 8.*)
- The rate of increase in the number of stores stocking the brand depends not only upon the size of the salesforce, but also upon the number of consumers who are interested in the brand—no consumer interest implies no retail sales, so no profit opportunity for stores. Again, the meaning of the graphic elements in Figure 4.5 precisely reflect the verbal description of how this piece of the business system operates.

Combining these two pictures creates an integrated view of the strategic architecture for the business (Figure 4.6). This is our first, simple picture of a business

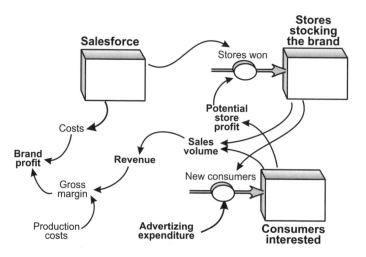

Figure 4.6 Interdependence of resources in building a brand.

as a system of interdependent resources—a dynamic resource system view (DRSV) of a firm's strategic architecture.

This structure shares certain characteristics with the word-of-mouth feedback around the ISP's single customer-base resource, discussed above:

- the system has the power to reinforce its own growth; but
- there are limits to this process (which will be discussed shortly).

As discussed in Chapter 2, the financial performance of this rudimentary business "hangs off the side" of the resource system. The revenues, costs, and profits reflect the resources that exist at any moment, and management can *only* alter underlying performance by actions and decisions that change these resource levels over time.

It is now possible to start estimating the time-path of performance for this business. Dealing first with awareness, the marketing vice president can be asked how quickly a certain advertizing expenditure will win consumers' interest. Initially, the rate of growth may be quite fast, since there is a whole population of people who will never have heard of the brand and can be made aware of it for the first time. As a larger fraction of the potential market gets to know of the brand, however, the pool of unaware people diminishes, and growth rates slow down, as shown in the upper-left part of Figure 4.7. *(For clarity, this figure hides some further effects that will be discussed later in this chapter.)*

As stores start to stock the brand, though, the second mechanism starts to operate—the brand's presence in stores also contributes to increased interest (upper-right part of Figure 4.7). As for advertising, though, store presence starts to "run out" of consumers to attract; so, after month 18, this rate too starts to diminish. Finally, the *total* rate of increase in consumers interested—

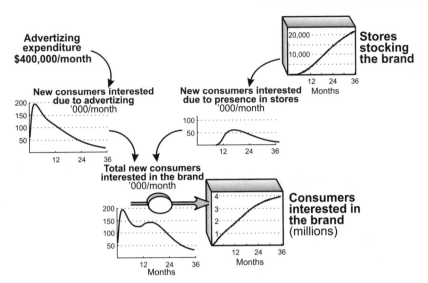

Figure 4.7 Consumer awareness driven by advertizing and availability.

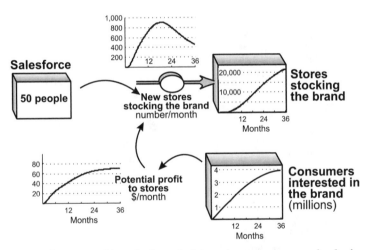

Figure 4.8 Stores stocking the brand, driven by awareness and salesforce.

the inflow to the stock at the bottom of Figure 4.7—is estimated by adding the expected effects of advertizing and store availability.

Turning to the stores, the same process can be used to estimate how rapidly stores will stock the brand, as a function of consumer interest and sales effort. The more consumers want the product, the greater the profit each store can expect to make from stocking it, so the faster they will agree to do so. However, they will still need to be called upon by sales people to be told of the opportunity. So the more salespeople are pushing this brand, the faster will be the uptake, up to the limits of salesforce effectiveness (Figure 4.8).

Getting things going can call for pretty big commitments

Not all cases of mutual reinforcement among resources involve committing just a few people or some thousands of Euros. Société Européenne des Satellites (SES) pioneered the direct to home (DTH) satellite TV business in Europe, seeking to capture revenues from renting satellite capacity to broadcasters.

The first satellite offered sufficient capacity for a limited number of programs for early-adopter broadcasters. This alone, though, was not enough. For broadcasters to justify renting this capacity, they needed to be confident that they would receive new revenues from advertizers. This, in turn, would only be possible if advertizers could expect consumers to watch the broadcasts, so households had to be won over to adopting the new service. Given the limited infrastructure at the time, this would only be possible if cable distribution networks were won over too.

Once this system started to run, growth could accelerate—the more and better programs were offered, the faster households could be won. The more households received the new service, the more attractive satellite transmission became for the broadcasters who could expect to increase their advertizing revenues ... all of which justified SES in its decision to launch additional satellites and raise capacity.

With the huge potential costs of kick-starting this system, SES chose its spending priorities carefully. They only ordered satellites for which firm commitments to take capacity had already been received or were highly likely. The company also pursued an aggressive end-consumer marketing campaign, even though they would receive no direct revenue from these end-consumers, as they realized that the creation of brand awareness would be important to create demand. They also committed early to providing an open and neutral platform, to avoid competing with their customers, the content providers.

Things could have been very different. Failure to build interest from households at the expected rate could all have delayed the point at which the entire system became self-sustaining. Poor-quality program content could have stimulated an outflow of viewers that held audiences below the level needed to sustain the confidence of broadcasters, advertizers, or cable channels. And marginally insufficient early commitment by any of these partner groups would have given the whole enterprise a rather short lifespan. All had to anticipate that future revenue streams would grow sufficiently fast to justify these substantial early costs.

I am grateful to Gilles Everling, formerly of SES, for providing this example.

The managerial judgment being made in Figure 4.8 is quite practical and is made up of three components:

- typical stores need to make at least \$20/month from this brand before they will be interested in stocking it, and the more margin stores stand to make beyond this threshold, the more rapidly will they take it on;
- the salesforce of 50 can make a maximum of about 1,000 sales calls per month, so this is the absolute maximum rate of stores growth;
- the salesforce rapidly approach this maximum success rate as consumer awareness (and hence potential store profits) climb, then become less successful again as the best stores are won over, leaving only the smaller stores for whom stocking the brand is of marginal benefit.

Finally, note an important difference between the growth of consumers and growth in stores:

- For consumers, the rate of increase was the *sum* of two separate sources—those made interested by advertizing and those won by the brand's presence in stores.
- For stores, the estimated relationship is fundamentally different—gains depend on *both* potential store profits *and* salesforce visits. If either of these is inadequate, no growth occurs, no matter how strong the other resource is.

These points emphasize an observation made previously—*do not assume* *that relationships from other cases apply to you ... exactly how each connection operates depends on the specifics of **your** situation.*

A challenge . . .

It is common at this stage to be challenged strongly on the practicality of making these estimates—*"How can anyone possibly know exactly how much impact these different effects are having?"*

The response is simple. Every single choice or decision made by a manager reflects implicit assumptions she is making about the nature and scale of these relationships. All we are asking is to make these assumptions explicit, so that the manager herself, and the team of which she is a part, can be clear about what they think *should* be happening. This provides several benefits.

First, the manager can check her assumptions against what is actually happening, and improve her judgment. Second, she can start taking measurements to learn more about critical relationships. Third, the team as a whole can build a better understanding about each part of the system, and thus make better-judged contributions in their own areas.

This last point mitigates one other difficulty. It can be very challenging to have to make explicit and justify judgments that have traditionally remained hidden. However, when it becomes clear that everyone faces a similar challenge, teams usually offer support rather than criticism!

Reinforcing feedback—the magic of exponential growth (but dangers of collapse)

Reinforcing feedback simply implies that the more of resource A we have, the faster we can grow resource B, and vice versa. The fact that the particular feedback structure in Figure 4.6 *reinforces* (rather than causing any other kind of behavior) can be checked by tracing the links around the system. The left-hand chart in Figure 4.9 extracts the feedback piece of the structure alone:

- start by asking what happens if "new consumers" arrive in the "consumers interested" stock (arrows 1 and 2);
- with more consumers interested, stores stocking the brand will make more profit (arrow 3);
- consequently, the *rate* of uptake by stores rises, so that the number of stores in the resource stock increases (arrows 4 and 5);
- crucially, this larger number of stores now makes the product more visible to consumers, so that the *rate of increase* in consumer interest is raised (arrow 6 matches arrow 1);
- next time around the loop, the same process repeats, and consumer numbers rise still faster (other things being equal).

This is the hallmark of reinforcing feedback—*an inflow of resource has consequences that drive a further inflow to the same resource.* The happy outcome of such

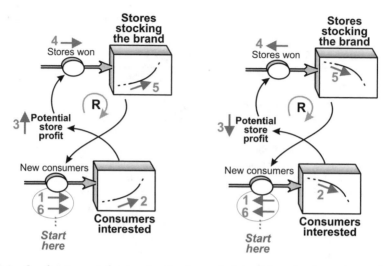

Figure 4.9 Confirming reinforcing feedback—an inflow drives further gains and an out-flow drives further losses.

reinforcing processes can be a pattern of exponential growth that can continue until other constraints intervene.

However, there is a dark side to this apparently happy feature—*reinforcing feedback is just as capable of driving exponential **collapse*** (right-hand chart in Figure 4.9). What happens, for example, if the number of consumers declines for any reason? The potential profit available to stores falls, causing some to delist the product. The brand is then less visible to consumers, and still more of them forget about it. Unless advertizing is constantly replenishing the stock of interested consumers, the brand can readily collapse, until both consumers and stores have forgotten it.

The risk of self-reinforcing collapse is common among systems of interdependent resources, but it can even arise for an isolated resource. For example, firms dependent on specialist staff departments, like information systems professionals, know it is critical to keep staff turnover within moderate limits. If attrition starts to grow, remaining staff can become overstretched and be still more inclined to leave, resulting in the initial "trickle" turning into a flood of resignations.

Tricky observation on reinforcing feedback

A true reinforcing process exhibits self-perpetuating behavior in both directions—an outflow from a resource has consequences that ultimately drive a further outflow, just as an initial inflow drives further inflows.

The word-of-mouth mechanism for the firm described in Figures 4.1 and 4.2 typically does *not* follow this rule—as fewer customers remain, there are fewer to be persuaded to leave, so the outflow slows down. This constitutes a hidden balancing mechanism, so word-of-mouth mechanisms are not, strictly speaking, pure reinforcing processes.

However, provided that managers focus on the practical consequences of inflows and outflows, this technical distinction should not cause problems.

Completing the resource-system in brands—adding limits to potential resources, resource losses, and management decisions

If reinforcing feedback is as powerful as Figure 4.9 suggests, why do the time charts in Figures 4.7 and 4.8 not exhibit the exponential growth curves just discussed—at least, not for long? The explanation for this constrained growth is that the reinforcing system in Figure 4.9 is not the complete picture. It is missing two elements, in particular:

- it does not reflect the limited *potential* of each resource—the estimated 5 million consumers and the total population of 50,000 stores;
- it does not show likely *outflows* from the stock of consumers or stores—consumers forgetting the brand or stores destocking it.

For consumers in particular, these two mechanisms interact to overwhelm the exponential growth. Early on, there are too few stores to provide enough product visibility, while later there is a diminishing pool of consumers to be won over. Also in later periods, more consumers have been made aware of the product, so more are available to forget it!

Figure 4.10 captures these mechanisms accurately for changes to the stock of aware consumers. The *net* gain of consumers (D) is the sum of gains from advertizing (A), gains from the brand's store presence (B), and losses due to consumers losing interest (C). This is why it was noted above that Figure 4.7 was not strictly accurate. The shape of lines A and B reflect the development of a resource from a potential pool (explained in Chapter 3), and the outflow of consumers losing interest (C) is simply calculated as a fraction of the current stock.

The final issue to add for a complete representation of the brand-building resource system is the role of *management decisions*. We have already seen one of these in action—advertizing spend. At least, two more important decisions are involved:

- First, the choice of *wholesale price* impacts on both sales volume and revenue. Higher wholesale prices are typically passed on by stores in higher retail prices. Stores thus enjoy higher margins per unit sold, but risk losing sales volume as consumer purchases reduce. The brand supplier too will suffer the lower sales volume, but will also enjoy higher unit margins.
- The second major decision is to change *the size of the salesforce*. This decision was simplified by assuming salespeople could be moved onto this brand from other products.

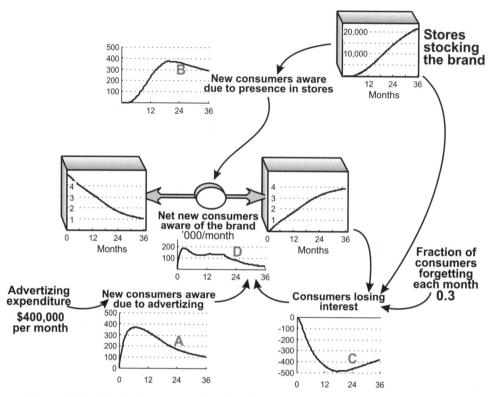

Figure 4.10 The limited potential and outflow of consumers limit brand building.

Although many other choices clearly arise in practice (consumer promotions, discounts to stores, and so on), these two decision items are sufficient to complete the core resource system in Figure 4.11. This figure contains more important features that arise in other situations:

- Incorporating management decisions in the framework has the effect of integrating the finances into the resource system structure. Now, rather than simply appearing as the "speedometer" for the machine, financial issues can also impact on the system's underlying performance over time.
- The picture distinguishes between costs that are purely discretionary at any time (e.g. advertizing in this case) and those to which the firm is committed for at least some period, due to the existence of a costly resource that cannot be instantly switched on or off (i.e., the salesforce). This distinction between immediately discretionary expenditures and "sticky" cost commitments is extremely common.
- A further effect of these financial connections is to increase the potential for reinforcing feedback. For example, more revenue enables higher advertizing spend, which boosts consumer awareness and drives revenue still higher.

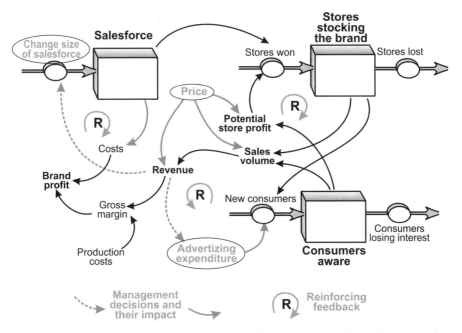

Figure 4.11 Adding management policy feedback to the brand-building example.

Higher revenues also allow management to argue for more salespeople, increasing store distribution and driving additional sales once again.

- Great care is needed, however—*only add feedback that involves management policy if these connections genuinely reflect the policy of the firm.* It is common for teams to draw a link from, for example, higher revenues to higher marketing spend when in reality no such policy exists.
- These policy links from revenues to spending may operate differently in the positive and negative directions. For example, it is common in retail businesses for labor costs to be *notionally* controlled to a target fraction of sales revenue—a policy that implicitly raises and lowers service capacity to match demand. However, it is rare for such firms to be so foolish as to keep cutting labor costs regardless of how far revenues fall.

Most resources need not be depleted to build others

This chapter has thus far concerned itself with how growth or decline of each resource depends upon others—but no attention has yet been paid to the fate of the resources that are being utilized. The reason is simple—*most (but not all) resources can drive growth in others without themselves being affected.* In Figure 4.11, none of the three resources is *depleted* to drive growth of the others: you don't have to lose stores to build consumer awareness, you don't have to lose

Where do markets come from?

Mutual reinforcement among resources accounts for the feasibility, potential scale, and speed of development for newly emerging markets. A market exists if there are sufficient buyers and sellers to cause a transaction rate that makes it worthwhile for both groups to continue participating. A perfectly feasible market may therefore fail to emerge, simply because either buyers or sellers accumulate too slowly to get over the critical switch point where transaction rates stimulate continuing participation growth.

During 1999–2001, MercadoLivre created an online auction service in Brazil alongside four rival services. All were anxious to build a strong business before the feared arrival of Ebay. Although promoted as consumer-to-consumer services, many entrepreneurial businesses saw them as cheap channels for reaching consumers. The strong supply-side volumes from these traders caused the auction sites to compete strongly for their attention. Strong seller reputation was critical, in order to build consumers trust and sustain growth in the demand side of the auction. As transactions accelerated, suppliers received ratings for their reliability that built their online reputations, so sites that achieved faster take-up by consumers won more attention from suppliers.

Given limited penetration of PCs and online access among Brazilian consumers, it was vital for MercadoLivre to capture potential buyers quickly and to retain them. It soon became apparent that general TV advertizing was hopelessly uneconomic in terms of cost per consumer won. Online advertizing and carefully selected magazine promotions proved much more effective, building the buyer community to more than 100,000 registered users in under 6 months. This ensured sufficient transaction rates to encourage sellers to favor MercadoLivre, and the strong policing of seller reputation ensured both that buyers stayed involved and that sellers continued to focus on this service in preference to rivals.

I am grateful to José Kalil for bringing this case to my attention.

consumers to win stores, and you don't have to lose salespeople for them to win stores.

In some special cases, however, a resource can only be used by being depleted. The most common example is cash. Money must be *spent* to build new capacity, to pay staff, or to fund the advertizing that will build awareness. Figure 4.12 illustrates this point for a company trying to boost its range of products. The illustration makes the simplifying assumption that cash expenditures result in an immediate and continuous increase in the rate of new product launches.

Until the end of Year 3, the rate of new product introductions is too slow to sustain its product range, given the rate at which obsolete products are discontinued. To increase its rate of new product introductions, the company has to spend more on R&D, which depletes the cash resource. Given the other cash flows (both income and expenditure), this temporarily stops the growth of the company's cash balances—though, in due course, sales of the new products would stimulate higher revenues and cash receipts.

Cash is by far the most common example of a strategic resource that can only be used by being depleted, though similar considerations apply to raw materials and other inventories.

Be clear where revenues and costs arise

We now return to the issue of cost drivers and value drivers with which this chapter started. First, it should be becoming apparent that any attempt to disaggregate the "value-added" by any single activity or resource within the integrated strategic architecture that constitutes a firm is doomed—customer

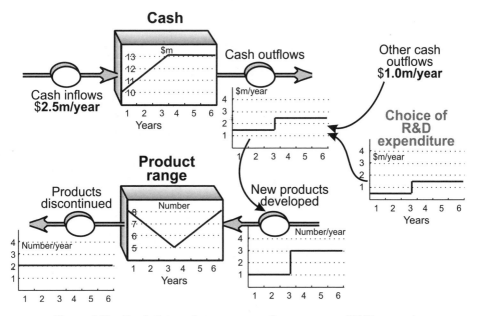

Figure 4.12 Depleting cash to grow another resource—R&D example.

gains and/or sales are a consequence of the *interrelated set* of resources. Remove, or reduce, any of these resources and the entire rationale that causes customers to take our offering falls apart. However, DRSV does bring into focus a key observation regarding the source of revenues—it is important to distinguish from where revenues arise—from new customers, from the customer base, or from both.

The brands example illustrates a case where revenues are largely driven by the *established base* of customers (both stores and consumers), which is typical for consumable products. In other situations, revenues may arise only from the event of winning a new customer. Sales of consumer durables, like washing machines, are a common example, but similar cases arise in many sectors. Firms in the elevator industry, for example, generate revenues from both new elevator sales and from maintenance. Since customers typically accept after-sales maintenance contracts from the original manufacturer, and these contracts continue for many years, the winning of a new customer is highly valued. Consequently, profitability on elevator sales is frequently poor, as rival manufacturers compete to win the installed base from which *future* revenues will arise.

The importance of distinguishing between revenue that arises from initial customer capture and that which arises from continuing customer ownership is clearly illustrated by the elevator industry. Figure 4.13 illustrates such a firm which, seeing slow sales of new elevators and a falling installed base of elevators under maintenance contracts, decides to cut the price of its new elevators. The price cut raises the rate of new sales and the installed base starts to grow, rather than decline. Revenues from new sales jump considerably, and maintenance

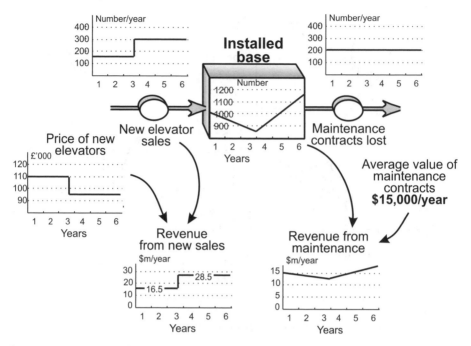

Figure 4.13 Distinguishing revenues from new customers and those from the installed base in elevators.

revenues start to recover. (Note, however, that the *profitability* of new sales probably declines badly, due to the high costs of the product itself and of installation.)

DRSV raises similar considerations in relation to *cost drivers*. It is important to distinguish where costs arise—from *capturing* the resource, from *having* the resource, or from *losing* it. A clear illustration of these distinctions arises in the case of the exploration and production facilities used in the oil industry. Here, *all three* items are exceedingly costly—constructing oil rigs, operating them, and ultimately disposing of obsolete units. In stock-and-flow terms, costs arise directly from the inflow, the outflow, and the resource stock itself. It is usually important to capture the dynamics of costs in any case where the financial outcomes are central to the issue of concern. It is therefore equally important that cost drivers be captured accurately in such cases. Fortunately, the stock-and-flow structure, together with the arithmetic needed to calculate costs, generally help to make these distinctions unavoidable.

Resource dynamics and value-chain analysis

The use of value-chain analysis starts from the simple observation that, to survive and prosper, a firm must be able to sell its goods and services for more than the sum of any bought-in costs plus its own operating costs. We must therefore be able to connect our view of resources as accumulating asset stocks with this important financial perspective.

Probing inside a single firm, the business costs are split out between two categories. First are the "primary activities"—those processes that act on the bought-in materials themselves, turn them into salable products, get them out to customers, and support those products once sold. A second group of "support activities" exist only to make the primary activities possible.

From these central concepts, many developments are possible. For example:

- The firm's cost build-up can be depicted diagrammatically, with each cost element shown in proportion to the firm's actual costs. This gives management a clear picture of where their major cost drivers lie. So, for example, a major manufacturer like Boeing would have a very large "operations" cost box, while a branded consumer-goods firm like Pepsi would exhibit a very large "marketing and sales" box.
- Each cost category can be further subdivided to pick apart in detail the sources of business costs.
- Costly activities can be compared with outsource alternatives; for example, product distribution can be contracted to a specialist distributor, removing this cost element from the firm's own value chain, but adding instead a further bought-in cost category.

Since its widespread adoption, value-chain analysis has provided considerable insight into firm strategy and performance. However, it remains a static, and financially oriented method, poorly connected with the substance of the business such as people, products, capacity, customers. The value chain's static nature gives rise to a particularly serious danger—*that cost savings are identified, which, while having no impact on today's ability to deliver customer value, both curtail the building of resources to enable future growth and even remove the minimum level of spending needed to sustain what is already in place.* A sound strategic architecture steers management away from this danger by making explicit the long-run undermining of the firm's substance by inappropriate attention to eliminating costs.

The resource-system perspective suggests a derivation of the value chain that differentiates four sources of cost:

- the costs of simply *possessing* resources (e.g., staff salaries, office rents);
- the costs of *retaining* resources (e.g., plant maintenance, customer support);
- the costs of *acquiring* resources (e.g., marketing, hiring);
- the costs of *developing* resources (e.g., training, product development).

Figure 4.14 illustrates the clarification that can arise from distinguishing just two of these elements—the sales cost incurred to win, and that to retain, customers. The firm in question starts with more than enough sales people to look after and retain its existing customers, so a surplus of full-time-equivalent staff is available to seek new customers. These extra customers not only drive increasing revenues but also demand more sales support.

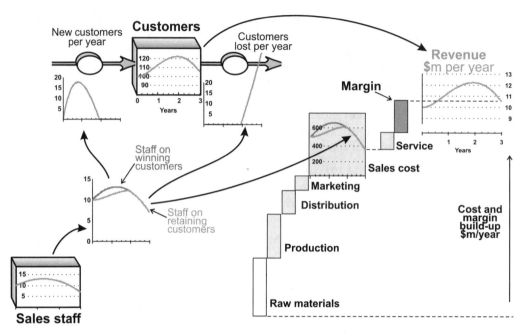

Figure 4.14 Splitting resource-building and resource-retaining costs for the sales element of the Value Chain.

Unfortunately, this occurs at the same time that the firm starts losing sales staff, so that the required support is not available. Consequently, from the end of the second year, customers start to be lost and revenues fall.

This clarification leads to an interesting observation. Figure 4.14, for example, treats the entire salary cost of the sales department as a cost of either retaining or acquiring customer resources. There is no remaining cost for simply *possessing* the sales resource. This implies that similar treatment of other cost drivers may also discover that most costs are incurred in acquiring, developing, and retaining resources, and very few are truly costs for being in existence. This treatment allows management and analysts alike to assess financially the true health of the firm's system, and make more realistic assessments of both the cost and timing of strategic commitments needed to drive revenues and earnings into the future.

A practical example—rejuvenating a knitwear brand

The following example illustrates how understanding the operation of reinforcing feedback can be used in practice to change a company's fortunes. A high-quality brand of knitwear had long been popular among affluent older adults, but was suffering declining sales. Management continued a long-held belief that

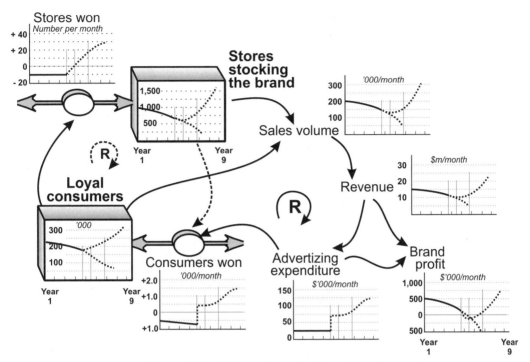

Figure 4.15 Rejuvenating a knitwear brand.

advertizing was prohibitively expensive for this niche product, and was not necessary, since it would "sell itself" once it was on retailers' shelves.

Figure 4.15 describes the problem for this declining product, with the solid time-paths up to Year 4 showing the company's historical performance under recent policies. The firm has poor information on the separate gains and losses of consumer interest in their products, which are difficult to separate in practice. The company had won very few stores in recent years, so recent net losses are a close indicator of *total* losses.

The historic declining timelines for sales volume, revenue, and profit are shown in the charts to the right. The only tricky part in these links is estimating how sales volume responds to the numbers of consumers and stores. Sales volume is dropping faster than the stock of loyal consumers, because not all of those people can find stores with the product they would *like* to buy! The solid line for the history of the *net flow* of consumers shows that there has been a slowly worsening rate of loss. The same decline is evident in the net outflow of stores. Note that the simple rule of accumulation and depletion applies—a constant *rate* of loss creates a steadily *decreasing* stock of stores.

The first thing to observe here is that the history of the charts (solid lines) is enough on its own to challenge the management's mental model. It is clear that the brand's presence in stores is *not* sufficient for the product to "sell itself". In addition, the firm's advertizing agency was able to tell them that rivals were spending upwards of $150,000 per month on advertizing—and winning consumers. This challenges the management's second assumption—that advertizing was too costly—a view clearly not held by rivals (and justifiably so, given what was known about their success).

Finding the place to look for fixing this problem relies on an unavoidable implication of the resource-system perspective—*management can **only** affect strategic performance by building resource levels, and this can only be achieved by actions or decisions that affect inflows or outflows.* Sure, we can kick profits upward next month by raising price or cutting the marketing budget, but both of these actions—and many other quick fixes—will damage the system by affecting the rate of gain and loss of customers (i.e., the *strategic* performance of the firm).

There are only two resources in this picture—stores and consumers, and since nothing could be done immediately to recapture stores, the fix depended on reversing the loss of loyal consumers. (The salesforce *could* have been a problem, but management's judgment was that their people were rather good—a view supported by rivals' efforts to hire them!)

To win back consumers, the company tripled its advertizing in Year 4—to a still-modest $75,000 per month, but it couldn't afford much more as its profitability was already in bad shape. This created a step shift in the *flow* of consumers from negative to positive. It may seem odd that consumer losses could be turned round with less advertizing than rivals. However, this was possible due to the large population of recently loyal consumers who could easily be recaptured. Rivals *had* to spend more, because their growth trajectory relied on reaching out to capture new groups of consumers through new advertizing channels.

The immediate effect of rebuilding consumer loyalty was limited to some extra sales volume through the stores, though total volume continued to decline because of further delisting. However, the *rate* at which stores delisted the brand was gradually stopped, aided by the salesforce pointing out to store-owners the recovering consumer base and rising sales in remaining stores. The rate of outflow of stores recovered to about zero over some 9 months, as stores discovered that the brand was not such a waste of shelf space after all.

From then on, sales efforts were successful in winning stores back to the brand, which, combined with recovering consumer loyalty, led to a sharp rate of growth in sales and an eventual turnround in profitability.

This example makes some important points about applying the dynamic resource-system approach:

- *Reliable, historical information is often not available, and must be searched out, created from what **is** known, and supplemented with management judgment.* This firm, like many others, had poor information on some of the critical data. It did not, for example, have historic data on consumer loyalty. How, then, could it even start on this analysis? Under such circumstances, there is no choice but to find out some current information fast, and use managerial judgment to fill in the unknowns. Consumer research in Year 4 provided data on loyalty at that point in time, but careful questioning offered estimates of how many consumers had *previously* been loyal buyers of the brand. This could be cross-checked with the time-path of unit sales through stores that were still stocking it, and by interviews with store-managers. The accounting records provided the number of stores over recent history. Note too that the company had no record of the *outflows* for either stores or consumers, but both charts are easily produced from data or estimates of the *levels* of each resource (outflow of stores = last month's number of store accounts minus this month's).

- *The strength of relationships driving rates of resource building need to be estimated.* It may be wondered how this firm could know that the outflow of loyal consumers might be reversed *to **that** extent with **that** scale of advertising?* This estimate also depended on consumer research, this time into magazine readership and advertizing spend and recall figures for similar brands. The firm's advertising agency played a key role here, working with management to estimate how just a little advertizing could reverse consumer losses.
- *It **is** possible to make confident estimates about the future time-path.* This brand was on a delicate knife-edge between recovery and closure, so it was crucial to anticipate and quantify the timing of its turnround. Understanding the accumulation and depletion of each critical resource was vital to building confidence in what could be achieved into the future.
- *Define performance measures, monitor progress, and use the information to increase confidence and refine the strategy.* The dynamic "hypothesis" about what might be possible, captured in Figure 4.15, clearly pointed to information the firm needed if it was to check that its revised strategy was working. Consumer research from the advertizing agency confirmed that the turnround in loyalty was indeed occurring at the expected rate. The firm itself checked with benchmark stores that this was translating into the expected recovery in sales. This confident information could then be used to reinforce the recovery by taking it to other stores, first to dissuade skeptical outlets to hold onto the brand, then to get the product back into other outlets that previously featured it.
- *Clearly communicate what is happening and build support.* This diagrammatic description of the strategy turnround had considerable communication value. Figure 4.15 could be taken to just about everyone involved—those within the firm, its advertizing agency, its retail stockists, even its investors—and the time-path of the recovery described. Everyone could see clearly what the plan was, offer further opportunities to improve it, and understand what part *they* could play in its delivery.

It is worth comparing this story with what might have been achieved by conventional analysis methods. Spreadsheet models would commonly encompass estimates of most of the items in the charts above, but would not make explicit *either* the vital distinction between resource stocks and flows *or* the implications of feedback. DRSV overcame these weaknesses, and consequently provided management with considerable confidence in their future prospects. They were able to test the realism of their assumptions about the impact of advertizing and consumer numbers on the rest of the system—similar to sensitivity testing in conventional planning, but more insightful, due to the interplay of gains and losses for the key resources.

An important consequence of the interdependence between resources in this case was that small changes could ultimately make a large difference to the outcome—a most valuable benefit, given the precarious state of the business. However, it is also important to note the *patience* that this recovery required, not only from the management itself but also from their staff and retailers.

This chapter has explained the important contribution of reinforcing feedback among complementary resources to driving business growth. In the process, it has also brought out important considerations in both the application of the dynamic resource-system method and process. It is now necessary to understand a second mechanism of interdependence between resources—when *balancing feedback* between resources constrains growth. It will then be possible to combine the two forms of complementarity (reinforcing and balancing feedback) to capture the entire strategic architecture for a business.

Summary

Linkages between activities, both within the business and with its suppliers and customers, are conventionally tackled with some form of value-chain analysis. However, since performance at any moment depends on current resource levels, the *dynamics* of performance make it necessary to understand how growth and decline arise from linkages between resources.

Managers can only build any resource by using others to which they already have access. Consequently, the more of any resource is in place at any moment, the faster others can be grown—provided that no balancing limit has been reached. Moreover, most resources can be used without being depleted themselves (the main exception being cash).

The self-reinforcing feedback that arises from these interdependencies among the firm's set of resources can cause exponential growth—or collapse. Some resources can even reinforce their own growth.

Financial outcomes arise from the firm's resource system; they also create the possibility for further reinforcement, as increasing revenues are deployed in the growth of those very resources that gave rise to those revenues in the first place. Management policy can be used deliberately to design-in such mechanisms.

Established approaches to laying out a firm's value chain can be adapted to portray its dynamics, by identifying separately the costs of building, holding, and retaining each resource. In addition, it is necessary to include the asset stock that drives revenues (i.e., customers) and to be clear about where revenues arise (i.e., from the inflow of customers or from the continuing customer base).

5

Removing the Brakes—Balancing Feedback Holds Back Growth

Key issues

❏   Resources can constrain, as well as enable, each other's growth

❏   There are dangers in pushing the business beyond its capacity

❏   Time delays make matters worse—causing overshoot and reversal

❏   Self-balancing effects arise in developing potential resources

Chapter 4 explained the interdependence between resources that arises from mutual reinforcement—the more of resource A you have, the faster resource B can grow. But, resources can be "complementary" in another sense—that *without* enough of resource A, resource B cannot grow. Such growth constraints arise from the need for *balance* between resources.

Recognizing balancing feedback

Balancing feedback arises in many contexts. Mobile phone operators, Internet service providers (ISPs), and games-console manufacturers, for example, need to build subscriber numbers fast, but those customers create demands on the firms' physical capacity (base stations, servers, and manufacturing plant, respectively). Unless this capacity is increased to meet these demands, the supply or service will deteriorate and customers will be lost. Constraints may arise from other resources too—many businesses rely on staff to provide the capacity they need to serve customers. One sector that has seen many high-profile cases of service delivery relying on staff capacity is the retail financial services industry such as insurance and banking (see Case example). Figure 5.1 shows how such a business might perform during the early months if marketing is the only source of new customers, bringing in 5,000 per month, and staff capacity is sufficient to deal with just 20,000 customers.

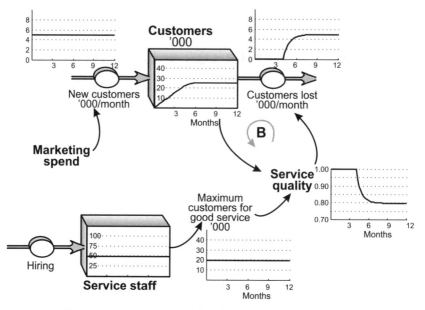

Figure 5.1 Resource balance for a direct savings bank.

The consequences are:

- after just 4 months, the staff become overloaded;
- service quality starts to deteriorate (rightmost chart);
- the worsening service starts to cause customers to leave (top-right chart);
- as customers continue to arrive, service quality drops still further; and
- by Month 7, service quality has dropped to 80% of ideal, sufficient to cause 5,000 customers to leave each month, which just balances the new customers attracted by marketing.

Case example—direct banking

In October 1998, Prudential PLC launched a direct banking service under the brand name "Egg", offering simple savings and loans at highly attractive interest rates. The company received 100,000 enquiries within 8 days, and 1.75m Internet hits. After 5 weeks, demand was so high that the company had to recruit 250 additional staff, and temporarily warned customers of a delay of up to 28 days before their applications could be processed.

Having resolved the staff constraint, Egg had, in less than 6 months, won 500,000 savings customers and £5bn ($6.5bn) in deposits.

(*Note:* Figure 5.1 makes a bold simplifying assumption—that workload arises solely from the *stock* of current customers, whereas in reality substantial work is caused by the processing of *new* customers. To reflect this accurately would therefore require service quality to be estimated from both the *stock* and the *inflow* of customers. See Chapter 4 for further discussion of this issue.)

The two stocks of customers and staff are certainly "complementary", but in a different sense than the reinforcing feedback discussed in Chapter 4. The stock of service staff now *constrains* the growth of customers. This form of interdependence is known as "balancing feedback"—hence the "B" in the middle—so-called (surprisingly enough) because it brings resources into balance. An inflow to the growing resource—customers—raises the stock to a level above the firm's service capacity and causes service quality to drop. Customer losses rise and reduce the customer base back toward a level nearer to the capacity limit.

A tricky observation ...

A careful look at Figure 5.1 suggests that there is actually no feedback at all—the connections go from *customers* to *service quality* to *customers lost*, but no further. The only connection from *customers lost* to *customers* appears to be the flow arrow, but this is going the wrong way! In fact, though, the *causality* implied by the flow arrow does go the right way, since any outflow causes a decrease in the resource stock—"customers to-day = customers last month minus customers lost (and plus customers gained)".

As noted in previous examples, the behavior of this system makes implicit assumptions about the nature and strength of each link. Figure 5.1 assumes, for example, that there is a simple relationship between customers, staff capacity, and service quality (service quality happens to be a simple ratio between customers and staff, whenever capacity is inadequate). There is also an assumed sensitivity to any imbalance—a close look at the data in Figure 5.1 will show that the *fractional* rate of customer losses happens to be equal to the fraction by which service quality is less than 1.0. When applying a Dynamic Resource System View (DRSV) and considering the strength of balancing effects, managers must think carefully about exactly how each such link operates.

Figure 5.1 illustrates some common features characteristic of balancing feedback:

- There is always some "control" item, in this case the capacity provided by the staff, toward which the resource tends to settle. For this reason, balancing feedback is said to exhibit "goal-seeking" behavior.
- If the resource level had happened to start well *above* the capacity constraint, the service quality would start low and be brought back toward the control level. (This might arise, for example, if one firm acquired another and simply transferred all the acquired customers onto its own systems.)
- It may seem odd that the system settles not *at* the capacity limit, but somewhat above it. This arises because there has to be some outflow of customers to match the inflow from marketing. If the flow of new customers were to stop, the outflow would gradually bring the customer stock into line exactly with capacity.

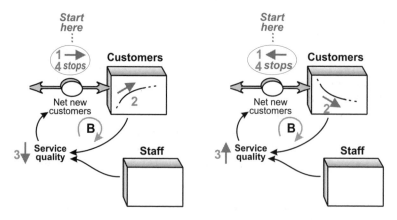

Figure 5.2   Confirming balancing feedback—inflows and outflows each cause events that lead to their own slowdown.

The character of a balancing feedback structure can be checked by thinking through the consequence of an initial change (Figure 5.2). Compared with diagnosis of the reinforcing feedback in Chapter 4 (Figure 4.9), there are two important points to note:

- Since balancing feedback arises from the interaction between gains and losses, it is necessary to look at the *net* effect of inflows and outflows (the two-way flow of customers in Figure 5.2).
- It is not so clear how the mechanism works when starting with an outflow (right-hand chart). This only operates when customers already exceed staff capacity and service quality is therefore poor. The outflow (arrow 1) reduces this imbalance, quality improves, and the outflow stops (item 4). *Balancing feedback does **not** imply that customer losses resulting from other causes (e.g., unattractive products) will be stopped.*

It may be thought that balancing feedback is ''bad'', in that it stops desirable growth from taking place. However, it has two positive benefits:

- First, *balancing feedback can prevent stresses becoming excessive.* For example, in the case of the bank in Figure 5.1, a large excess of customers over staff capacity would cause considerable strain for those employees, possibly leading to resignations and a further fall in capacity. Indeed, in many recent cases, businesses may have been more fortunate if customers had been *less* tolerant of poor service, so that remedies to the service quality problems could have been tackled under less stress.
- Second, *balancing feedback can act as a safety net when businesses are in danger of collapse.* Chapter 4 explained the mechanism of self-reinforcing collapse for professional service firms, when resignation of high-performing staff can trigger loss of key clients and lead to further staff losses. In such cases, the departure of high-grade staff can open up opportunities for ambitious

younger people, thus stemming the outflow of staff that started the collapse—a benign consequence of balancing feedback.

However, additional factors often intervene that cause balancing feedback to generate further difficulties.

Driving faster growth with unchanged constraints

First, what might happen here if the growth rate (inflow to the stock) is significantly different than expected?

- If growth is slow, our bank is simply left with costly staff who are underutilized, and if they cannot find ways to fill the customer resource quickly, financial losses may put them out of business.
- If growth is much more rapid, though, more interesting consequences arise. Figure 5.3 shows what happens if customer win rates are 5,000, 10,000, and 20,000 per month, respectively.

With faster win rates, the customer base not only grows more quickly but also grows to much higher levels, in spite of the system's capacity being unchanged. However, service quality is radically depressed at higher rates of growth. Indeed, this *must* arise in order for customer losses to happen fast enough to deplete the excess numbers being brought in. This may seem a somewhat ridiculous situation for a business to bring about, but is remarkably common (see Case example on page 76), and has occurred repeatedly in the financial services

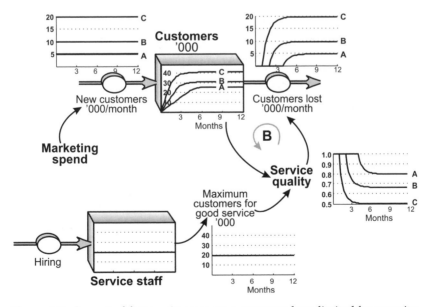

Figure 5.3 Impact of faster win rates on a customer base limited by capacity.

sector. It is not so surprising when one considers the difficulty, as in the case of Egg, of finding any reasonable estimate for the initial growth rate.

Adding perception time delays to balancing feedback

Problems frequently arise when *time delays* occur in situations of balancing feedback. It is common for customers, staff, and others to take some time to react to their experiences. If our bank were to accept more customers than it could serve, they may just assume for a while that poor service quality is normal, that it will eventually improve, or that the nuisance of switching to another provider will not be worth a possibly marginal improvement. Eventually, however, customers can become so annoyed with ever-worsening service that they depart in large numbers. Figure 5.4 shows how the system behaves with perception delays of zero (line A), 1 month (line B), and 3 months (line C). The dashed line from Month 9 in case C indicates that the scenario would not, in practice, continue—further changes would likely occur to customer reactions or management of the situation to cause further dynamics to emerge.

Perception delays allow the customer base to continue growing well beyond the point at which poor service starts to arise. With long delays, the overshoot can be substantial, and the firm builds a very large customer base. Optimism is premature, however, because customers eventually *do* respond to poor quality, and leave. Now, the delays become a real problem, because customers continue

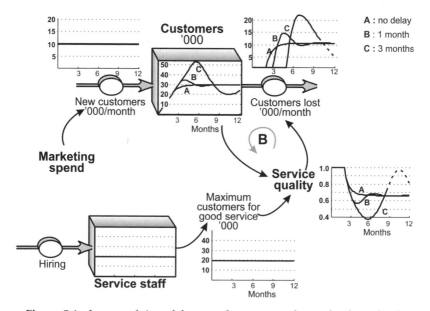

Figure 5.4 Impact of time delays on the customer base of a direct bank.

to act on their *perception* of poor service well after the system has in fact come into balance. In the case of a 3-month delay, customer losses are still continuing by Month 12, even though capacity was almost completely adequate in Month 10.

Figure 5.4 plays out the consequences of a rather simplified assumption regarding customer perceptions—that customers notice nothing at all for a fixed period of time, then suddenly become totally aware and motivated by their sudden discovery. In practice, of course, customers *do* notice poor service immediately, but may still not react until they have become increasingly annoyed by repeated problems. This is a further accumulation process, for a "negative" resource that we would rather have less of, and will be dealt with more fully in Chapter 7.

Increasing resource levels to remove balancing feedback

The final issue to consider is how management might respond to such situations. Clearly, it is in the interests of this bank to find ways to enable its customer base to grow without compromising quality. It is likely to have plans to add staff in order to relieve constraints. However, there may also be some delay between starting the hiring process and having the new staff fully functioning. Consider what happens if there is a 2-month delay, if management only tries to hire new staff when service quality actually deteriorates, and if they recruit the number of people they expect will be sufficient for 3 months' further growth.

Figure 5.5 plays out this scenario over a 2-year period, with a steady inflow of 10,000 customers per month. As might be expected, the business goes through short periods when growth is suppressed by staff constraints and management has to wait for new staff to arrive (line A).

The situation becomes more problematic if management also suffers delays in *discovering* the need to hire (line B). If there is a 1-month delay in obtaining research on customer-perceived quality, two distinct difficulties arise.

- First, the earliest decision to start hiring is taken in Month 3 rather than 2, so new staff will not come on stream until Month 5, and subsequent capacity increases become progressively delayed.
- Second, immediately after the decision to increase hiring, demand actually *falls* and quality starts to recover. When the new staff finally start to contribute in Month 5, the fall in customers from the now inaccurate perception of poor quality means that these staff are not fully utilized until Month 8. With customer growth now lagging well behind the original potential, a second tranche of new staff is not hired until Month 10, coming on-stream in Month 12.

The consequences of the delays in the system now become most serious. Not only is the firm losing the revenues it *could* have received, had it always had the right capacity in place, but its poor service has also lost it a total of nearly 120,000 customers—virtually the same number that it is eventually serving!

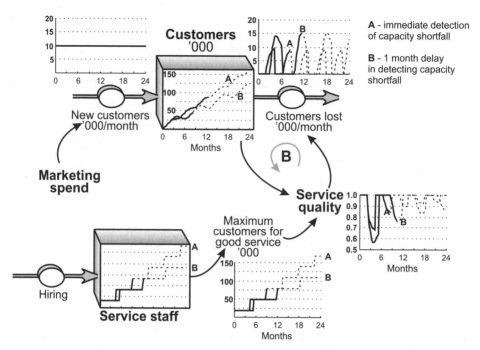

Figure 5.5 Effect on the customer base arising from delays in expanding capacity.

Once again, the dashed portion of the lines indicates that those involved in the system would not, in practice, continue to show such repeated behavior. Unfortunately, management's options include certain responses that, while apparently well justified by the situation, actually make matters worse. For example, the fall in demand could be interpreted as a reason to *cancel* hiring, or even to lay staff off, which would turn out to be unfortunate when customer growth resumes.

Further developments of the banking example

The framework of Figures 5.1 to 5.5 can be readily developed to illustrate further common features:

- First, there is the possibility of self-reinforcing growth through word of mouth, as discussed earlier in Chapter 4. Provided that current customers experience good quality, they will happily recommend the bank to friends and colleagues. This adds to the inflow from marketing, but also creates further uncertainty and risk in expanding capacity. This may lead to still greater swings in the balance between demand and capacity, and increase the danger of bad service and customer losses.

- Second, poor service quality would be expected eventually to damage the bank's reputation in the market as a whole—not only do current customers cease to recommend the bank to friends but they *and* former customers also warn their friends *not* to join. This implies that marketing expenditure starts to be less effective at winning new customers. (Reputation and other intangible resources will be examined in Chapter 7.)
- Naturally, banks and other firms do not in practice wait for bad news on service quality before adding capacity. It is common practice to plan capacity expansions ahead, and adopt guidelines for ratios between customer demand and capacity. To reflect this kind of policy, the framework above can be adapted to trigger capacity expansion according to some other rule than "when we hear of poor quality". The larger the excess of capacity over demand, the smaller is the frequency of quality problems and the smaller is the damage when problems do occur. However, this comes at the cost of holding excess capacity for larger fractions of time. To test this trade-off, alternative policies for capacity expansion might be tested (e.g., "add capacity when maximum workloads build to 80%, or 90%") and examine the consequences for growth, revenues, and quality.

Self-balancing resources

Chapter 4 explained how a single resource was able to accelerate through reinforcing its own growth, a process typified by word-of-mouth mechanisms. A similar observation applies to balancing mechanisms. Although there are many cases where one resource is limited by constraints caused by others, it is also possible, indeed common, for the growth of a single resource to constrain itself. This arises where *actual* resources must be developed from *potential* resources. This mechanism was implicit in the examples discussed in Chapter 3, but for completeness these balancing mechanisms can now be made explicit.

Returning to the case of cable TV, Chapter 3 simply noted that the larger the fraction of homes passed the less dense would be the remaining homes in the area. Consequently, the larger the fraction of homes passed the slower will be the network's coverage of remaining homes. The point may come where the cost and time to reach these potential subscribers is simply uneconomic, and development of this resource will cease. This balancing feedback is shown in Figure 5.6. The growing resource is the number of homes passed, and the constraining resource is the number of remaining homes.

Similar balancing feedback processes arising from practical limits to the development of potential resources are remarkably common, as the examples in Table 5.1 illustrate.

In such cases, there may be little point in attempting to push further development of the resource, and attention should be switched to creating or exploiting new potential resources. McDonald's, for example, has thrived for many years on developing, in country after country, its large market of families with young

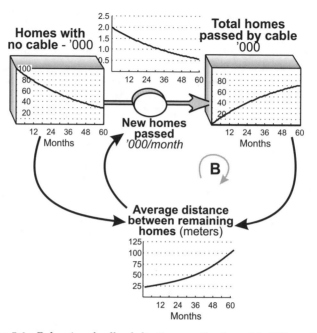

Figure 5.6 Balancing feedback limits growth of a cable TV service.

Table 5.1 Examples of balancing feedback arising from resource-development limits.

Actual resource	Potential resource	Typical resource-development efforts	Resource development limited by	Practical constraints
Consumers aware of a brand	People not yet aware	Advertizing	Increasing difficulty of reaching consumers still unaware	Advertizing budgets
Staff	Available recruits	Hiring	Success rate of hiring efforts	Affordable salaries
Staff skills	Remaining skills to be learned	Training	Limited value of further skills	Training time
Retail store locations	Localities not served by a store	Efforts of site-finding team	Declining size of communities without access to a store	Potential profitability of smaller stores

children, then retaining them as they grow older. Where penetration of this potential market reaches a limit, though, continued growth has become harder to sustain. In response to this declining potential, the company screens advertizements featuring an elderly person answering a knock on the door from

"Meals-on-Wheels" (a low-cost cooked food service for housebound people). On opening the door, the elderly person is greeted by a young man on roller skates, carrying a McDonald's meal. This marketing initiative serves to awaken a potentially substantial additional market for the company.

A note on spreadsheets, system dynamics, and simulation modeling

This chapter has explained the second form of interdependence between resources and the potential for balancing feedback to limit business development. Chapter 6 will move on to combine this mechanism with the mutual growth that can arise from reinforcing feedback to construct a complete strategic architecture for any enterprise.

It will have become apparent, though, that this rigorously fact-based approach to understanding the dynamics of business performance will quickly surface sets of interrelationships that are arithmetically complicated. Working through how the numbers will play out soon becomes tedious and prone to error, even for situations as simple as the drinks brand from Chapter 4 or the bank described above. It may be tempting to reach for our universal "hammer"—the spreadsheet—to hit this particular nail. But we are now dealing with a more sophisticated object, so need a more sophisticated tool for the job.

It is perfectly possible, if rather challenging, to work through the mathematical relationships in our resource systems by conventional use of a spreadsheet. For those who wish to try it, a reasonable routine is as follows:

- name some rows to match successive time periods such as Months 1 to 24;
- reserve early columns (B, C, etc.) to record constants like the fractional rate at which existing customers attract new customers for us, or decision inputs like monthly marketing spend;
- reserve the second range of columns to represent each resource (e.g., a column for "Customers at month end") and highlight these columns (remember that resources are critical);
- a third block of columns calculates any intermediate values that are calculated from the constants, decision values, and *last*-period's ending resource levels;
- the final set of columns calculates the *resource flows*—these being always the last items that can be calculated for the period (e.g., "new customers won during the current month");
- the final step is to calculate the closing resource level for *this* period, so that it can be used to estimate all the intermediate values and resource flows for the next period.

Now, all that is needed is to repeat this exercise for every resource in the system (including intangible factors such as morale and reputation), remembering to pick up the dependencies of every resource flow from the period-end levels of every other resource that might be involved in its accumulation or depletion!

This spreadsheet exercise may seem rather trivial, especially for those who routinely do such calculations for financial reporting, inventory management, and so on. However, it illustrates further, deeply fundamental features of reality that are both unavoidable and critical to any understanding of business or other systems:

- The state of the world at any moment in time is explained entirely by asset-stock levels and instantaneous consequences of those levels. Business examples include "customers" and "sales rate", "staff" and "current salary costs", "morale" and "staff productivity". Examples from other situations include "rabbits" and "grass consumption rate", "water level in lakes" and "supportable fish population", "consumer confidence" and "retail sales rate".

- The *last* items that depend, at that same moment in time, on current levels of asset stocks are the rates at which those same stocks, and others, are changing—customers won or lost per month, staff hired or resigning per year, increase or decrease in staff morale per week, rabbit births and deaths per day, rainfall and river flows (cubic meters per hour), increase or decrease in consumer confidence per quarter.

- It is these resource flows, *and these alone*, that determine the system's trajectory into the future, and the level of all asset stocks at the end of the next period.

- This storing of asset stocks from one time period to the next is the *only* means by which feedback can occur. (Your spreadsheet with a row for each period will complain about "circular references" if you try to portray instantaneous feedback without passing the resource level forward from row to row.)

Spreadsheet tools suffer a serious drawback for the purposes of capturing and portraying the dynamical systems that make up our world. As should by now be evident, the interdependencies between resources, their immediate consequences, and the resource flows that carry us into the future are made crystal clear by the graphical maps we have used to show the causalities involved. Spreadsheet tables and disconnected charts, no matter how elegantly drawn, do not come close to providing this clarity, since every person inspecting these data and charts will have their own implicit assumptions about how they depend upon each other.

The alternative is to turn to the system dynamics method developed by Forrester (1961), and available now in a number of relatively easy-to-use PC modeling packages. An exploration of these tools is beyond the scope of this book, as is the discipline required for using them to build reliable dynamic business models. Fortunately, Sterman (2000) offers encyclopedic coverage of the system dynamics method, together with good practise in its use and in model formulation. Readers will find, however, that this work, like virtually all others in system dynamics, tackles business issues from a systems-thinking start-point. Our view, however, is that this is a risky start-point, for reasons touched on earlier in this chapter. Consequently, we recommend that business challenges be tackled by the method that will be developed in Chapter 6, which emphasizes a focus on performance through time, resource accumulation and interdependence, and heavy use of time charts!

Summary

Growth of any resource will ultimately be limited by the availability of other resources required, or by its own potential.

Attempts to push the business beyond that limit will commonly trigger feedback that drives increasingly powerful outflows that hold back the firm's growth. Eventually, these outflows match any gains that are achieved. Continued efforts to grow can push the business badly out of balance, with dire consequences for service quality, stress on staff, and other difficulties.

Delays arising from the time needed to notice or react to such imbalances can cause the business to overshoot a stable state or even swing repeatedly from overstretched to underloaded. This can make it extremely difficult to interpret the true state of the business, and cause management to make decisions that may be wildly inaccurate or even precisely the opposite of those required.

Spreadsheet thinking, and the ubiquitous tools used for this purpose, are inherently ill-suited to capturing or communicating the behavior of business (or other) systems through time. System dynamics provides the proper method for these tasks, and the software tools to implement the approach.

6

The Strategic Architecture—Designing the System to Perform

Key issues

❏ A process for developing a strategic architecture for any situation facing any single enterprise

❏ Illustrating the strategy dynamics analysis for a new-car launch

❏ Using the strategic architecture to seek means for substantially uprating business performance

It is now possible to combine the components from the first five chapters to assemble a picture of the firm's strategic architecture that can be used to seek performance-enhancing opportunities. This chapter will guide you through the process by following the example of new product development in the car industry:

- Chapter 1 explained and illustrated the meaning of "dynamics"—the time-path of performance.
- Chapter 2 explained the importance of strategic resources, specified how to identify them, and showed the importance of their special characteristic—accumulation and depletion over time.
- Chapter 3 showed the importance of quantifying change, and how the arithmetic works to produce an accurate time-path for all the key elements of the business and its performance.
- Chapter 4 explained how growth of a resource depends on the existing levels of resource already available, creating the possibility of self-reinforcing growth—or decline.
- Chapter 5 showed how resources can constrain each other's development through balancing feedback that limits growth.

Combining these structures for the firm's principal tangible resources creates an integrated, comprehensive map of the enterprise that can capture the dominant drivers of performance over time. *The firm (or other enterprise) is an intrinsically dynamic resource system, whose performance depends on the mutual reinforcement and balance between its component resources and asset stocks in its environment.*

The portrayal of the structure and relationships by which all these parts are connected generates the "strategic architecture" of the enterprise. Given this architecture, we can now examine carefully the role of the management team. This breaks down into two initial tasks:

- *diagnosing* the existing strategic architecture of the business, to understand how it *currently* operates and to explain its recent performance; and
- *designing* or redesigning the strategic architecture, to be *capable* of performing strongly (which may require either adapting a current architecture or designing something that is largely or totally new).

A further task—selecting goals, performance indicators, control mechanisms, and policies that most effectively *direct* how the business system performs—will depend on further concepts and structures to be developed in later chapters. However, diagnosis and design together offer powerful means to improve performance.

Industry example—new product development in car manufacture

Like many industries, car manufacture features a continuing imperative for producers to innovate. Simply introducing new models is not enough—to remain competitive, firms must incorporate new technologies and design philosophies in each new generation of vehicles. While many improvements are modest advances on what has gone before, substantial steps occasionally take place. Such discontinuities have included the VW Beetle, the Mini, MPVs (people carriers), off-road models, and the recent radical new approach to small-vehicle design in the Mercedes A-class, the 2-seat "Smart" and others.

A company attempting a radical shift in technology or design faces several challenges. R&D progress must be rapid to avoid being overtaken by rivals' innovations. Potential buyers and distributors must be made aware of, and receptive to, the new concept. Production capacity must be built, in anticipation of demand rates that will be difficult to forecast. These initiatives must be timed with care since they all consume cash at a rapid rate, and sales volume, revenue, and profitability must come in quickly before the cash drain becomes unacceptable.

Figure 6.1 shows the status of one such firm, 5 years after a particular research effort was started and 2 years after the product's market launch. Progress has been disappointing, with slow sales and poor cash flows—the business is still losing money at a rate of nearly $5m per month, though the deficit is reducing. Total sales to date mean that there are still fewer than 10,000 of the new vehicles in use. The early spending was devoted to R&D, but, 1 year into the project, investment was switched into building production capacity, for which there is a 2-year lead time. In Year 2, market development efforts started, preparing car

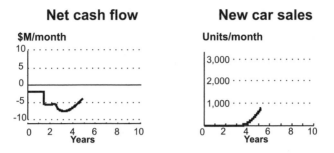

Figure 6.1 Early progress for the car development project.

owners and dealers for the launch. Although early sales have been slow, the resulting revenues have at least reduced the rate of cash outflow from Year 4.

Factors that could have gone wrong to cause the present situation include:

- failing to create a product that meets owners' unfulfilled needs, including the risk of launching before the new vehicle is ready;
- launching too late, when the new vehicle is no longer interesting, either because competitors have come up with something similar or because another fashion in car purchase has taken off;
- failing to build the market, by investing too little in marketing or setting prices that are too high.

This case will be developed, to illustrate each of the steps in the dynamic diagnosis.

A seven-step process for capturing the Strategic Architecture

The DRSV method requires a disciplined, analytical approach if it is to be used effectively to deliver improved business performance. Unlike traditional approaches to planning, which frequently fail due to weaknesses in their method and an inability to adapt, DRSV can be made into a living reference for the firm's evolving structure and behavior. Any inaccuracies, changes, or innovations can be readily identified and amended in the light of emerging information. Indeed, it may become necessary to redesign management information systems to clarify for everyone in the organization the reality of the architecture in which they operate.

The DRSV discipline extends to an organized, staged process for laying out the current architecture and seeking enhancements. For the explanation that follows, it is assumed that the purpose is to enhance the strategic performance of the entire enterprise. However, the same process is equally amenable to attacking more focused issues such as performance improvement in a single function or evaluating how best to undertake a particular initiative.

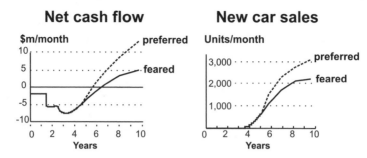

Figure 6.2 Alternative future sales and cash flow from launching a new vehicle type.

Step 1. Identify the time-path of performance

Chapter 1 explained the fundamental importance of taking a time-path perspective of performance, not just "roughly" but with the specifics of *scale* and *time-
path* accurately defined as well. It is worth investing some time in getting this step
right, since starting with a poorly defined issue or the wrong indicators will lead
the subsequent diagnosis badly astray.

Follow the process and advice offered in Chapter 1, taking particular care to:

- pick indicators that relate to something concrete about the business—
  customers, sales volume, etc.—rather than (or at least as well as) financial
  measures;
- avoid ratios, focusing instead on absolute measures for the state of the
  business;
- select a time horizon that is appropriate to the time-scale of the issue that
  concerns you.

For the car development case, the unit sales rate for new vehicles offers a top-
level performance indicator, with net cash flow as a measure of financial progress
for the project (Figure 6.2).

Step 2. Identify those few resources at the heart of the business

Chapter 2 specified how to obtain a robust list of resources for a business,
covering both tangible and intangible factors. It also offered tips to make sure
that the list was sufficiently comprehensive to cover the dominant elements of the
business, yet not so extensive as to confuse and duplicate. Follow the guidelines
in Chapter 2 to:

- build a list of the strategic resources in your business (whether the business
  you currently operate or one you intend to adapt toward or to create from
  new);

- specify sound measures, both for the resources themselves and for their rates of change (forcing oneself to put current *numbers* on each item, if only estimates, is a powerful encouragement to define resources properly);
- select the few core resources at the heart of the business.

The most common mistakes in this step are:

- including activities and other non-resource items such as marketing or product development;
- focusing on financial items rather than substantive business factors;
- selecting abstract items such as culture or innovation;
- failing to get a shared definition or measure for each item;
- picking too many resources from the list to start from—just three or four items, covering both the supply side and demand side of the issue, are generally adequate to define the heart of the business.

Table 6.1 offers tangible and intangible resources involved in the car development case. From this list, the key demand-side resource is vehicle *owners*. (Don't confuse this with purchase rate—since the product is a durable item, revenues arise from the initial sales, rather than from frequent repurchase of consumable items. The increasing pool of owners is the strategic resource, which is the cumulative result of unit sales.) The key supply-side resource is *production capacity*, which limits the rate at which potentially interested customers can be supplied. Between production and customers lie the *dealers* whose support in promoting the new vehicles is necessary for interested buyers to be able to have access to the cars, and therefore buy them.

Product functionality will limit the number of potential customers who can be persuaded to buy these new vehicles—many car buyers could be intrigued by the novel product, but, unless it fulfills perceived needs at an attractive price, sales will be slow. Functionality is also manifest in how well the cars perform in practice—do they fulfill well the functions they claim to offer and are they reliable? If not, owners will sell them quickly, damaging the model's reputation.

The resources left aside for now include *cash*, since this is a large manufacturer who can commit heavy expenditure to get this product launch right. This is not to say that cash is unlimited or doesn't matter, but the cash situation is an important outcome, rather than a fundamental constraint. The *fleet of vehicles* in the hands of owners is left aside because the initial issue concerns the purchase rate of new buyers. The fleet would become an important consideration at a time when second-hand vehicles are numerous, and the manufacturer would be concerned about the reliability, value, and reputation of this older population of cars.

Finally, the car's *reputation* is also left to one side at first, since the issue concerns how effectively the new market can be developed. This reputation will become important later in determining second-hand values and repurchase rates.

Table 6.1 brings together these resources and adds measurement units, defines flow rates, and offers likely drivers for those flows.

Table 6.1 Tangible and intangible resources in car development.

	Units of resource	Units of inflows and outflows	Drivers of gains and losses
Tangible resources			
Cash	$m	$/month	Sales revenue, R&D spend, marketing, capacity increases, operating costs, …
Dealers	Number	Dealers won or lost per month	Buyer demand, discounts
Customers	Owners	New buyers/month	Price, availability, reputation for functionality, and quality
		Owners selling cars/month	Vehicle functionality and quality
Vehicle fleet	Vehicles	Sales per month Cars scrapped per month	Purchases Ultimate breakdown
Production capacity	Units/year	"Units/year" per month	Investment, production engineering effort Plant closure
Intangible resources			
Product functionality	Features and performance (0–1)	Improvements per month vs. user requirements	R&D investment
Product reputation	User rating vs. expectations	Change in user ratings	Actual functionality and quality

Step 3. Get quantitative—identify the inflows and outflows causing the core resources to grow, develop, or decline

Working *just* with the core resources from Step 2, follow Chapter 3 to map out how each resource develops, both in moving from stocks of *potential* to *actual* resource and in evolving from stage to stage. Laying out the picture of how each resource develops clarifies the nature of the *flows* that are involved in this development process. These flows are crucial, since they are the *only* place in the system where management can have any impact on long-term performance.

Work out the arithmetic for each rate of gain, loss, or transition between stages (see Figure 3.1 for an example), and start to lay out the time charts for resource flows and for the level of each resource stock over time. Many of the remaining figures in Chapter 3 illustrate how this works. This stage can be carried out in isolation for each of the three to four core resources. There is no need as yet to worry about how resources affect each other, and discussing these links at this stage will only cause confusion.

Two tips may help at this point:

- Make sure that the time axis on these charts matches the timescale of the issue you are trying to understand and anticipate.
- Make sure that these time charts are consistent and accurate (it is most unfortunate if inflows and outflows seem to indicate growth, when the arithmetic actually implies decline!). If in any doubt, follow the process illustrated in Figure 3.9 or go back to the period-by-period arithmetic in Figure 3.1.

The result of carrying out this step for the car development case is shown in Figure 6.3. At top left is the progress the R&D team is making toward achieving a vehicle that fulfills the functional objectives that are required. This is an example of an intangible resource, a topic that will be dealt with in detail in Chapter 7. For now, note that early efforts make rapid progress toward achieving the sophisticated vehicle the firm is seeking, but that this progress slows as the easiest developments are accomplished.

At top right, production capacity reflects a decision after 1 year to start construction. The plant actually comes on-stream during the third year, but takes the rest of that year to build up to full capacity, as early teething problems are resolved. At bottom right is the growth in the number of dealers actively promoting the new vehicles.

The more complex part of this case concerns the development of customers. Marketing efforts start in Year 2, in anticipation of production starting shortly thereafter. At first, awareness rises sharply, as the novelty of the vehicles attracts attention, but it is hard to sustain this early excitement, and consumer interest grows less quickly. Nevertheless, by the end of Year 3, nearly one million people are intrigued enough to consider the vehicle for their next purchase.

It is the flow of *sales of new cars* that highlights the issue of concern. In spite of the vehicles' good features, buyers are just not choosing to buy it, so the population of people owning the new vehicles has barely moved by Year 4. Figure 6.3 raises some methodological issues.

First, although it is often an important discipline to trace out stocks and their related flows simultaneously, this is unnecessary for production capacity. Simply note how much capacity comes on-stream, and when. Second, note that *production capacity* is the special type of resource that itself includes a "per time period" unit of measure (see Chapter 2).

The customer flow illustrates the importance of being precise about what the "stuff" is that is flowing from stock to stock—this chain is tracking *people*, whether they are at any moment merely interested in this vehicle, are in the act of buying one, or are current owners. The chain is *not* tracking the fleet of vehicles themselves, though that may be a concern at a later phase of market development. Consequently, the outflow at the far right is the rate at which new vehicle owners are selling their cars into the second-hand market. It would be

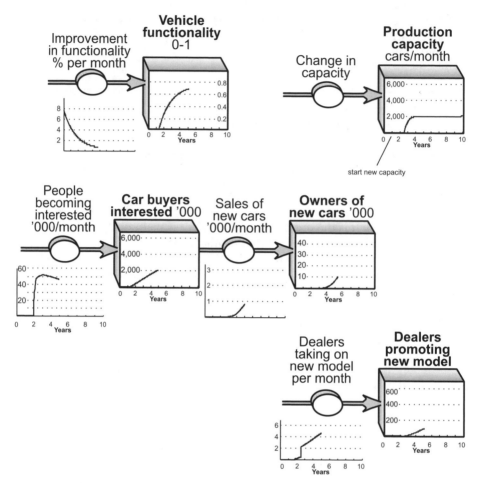

Figure 6.3 Core resource stocks and flows for a new vehicle launch.

hoped that their experience with the vehicle will encourage them to buy a replacement of the same type.

Step 4. Identify how *flows* of each resource depend upon existing *levels* of resources and other drivers

Chapters 4 and 5 explained how to capture the interdependence between resources—the inflows and outflows of each resource ultimately depend upon the current levels of others (and/or of the same resource itself). Taking each resource in turn, establish which other resources either help or constrain its growth, and add other factors both within and beyond the firm that affect its

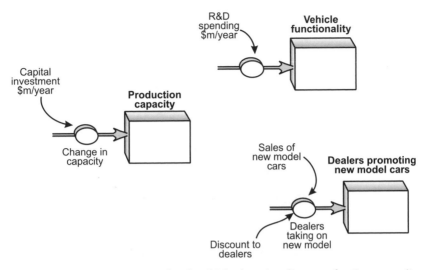

Figure 6.4 Factors driving growth of vehicle functionality, production capacity, and dealer support.

growth and decline. This step was illustrated with a simple example in Chapter 4, Figures 4.4 and 4.5.

For the car development example, the flow drivers for vehicle functionality could include other resources, especially the team of development engineers and the stock of available technologies. However, in this case, it is believed that both these resources are adequate and therefore not involved in the immediate challenge. Functionality therefore grows in response to the rate of R&D spending the firm chooses to commit. Production capacity, as has already been noted, simply reflects capital investment decisions (Figure 6.4). Dealers become committed to promoting the vehicles if they expect to make money from doing so. Consequently, they are interested both in the rate of sales and in the margin they will make, determined by the discount between the retail price and the price at which they are supplied by the manufacturer.

Tracing the forces determining the rate at which buyers purchase the new vehicles can be broken down into two parts. First, consider what is needed to make a buyer *want* to purchase a car at any moment (Figure 6.5). Price and functionality together determine whether the vehicles offer good value for money compared with competing models in the same class. In addition, car owners may be persuaded to consider this product for their next purchase by the firm's marketing efforts, and by recommendations from existing owners—a word-of-mouth effect. Finally, whether owners wish to buy the vehicle *now* will depend on whether they are currently planning to replace their existing car. So, the potential sales rate is limited by the number of consumers interested.

The second factor explaining the actual purchase rate is whether would-be buyers *are able* to buy the car. Two resources must be in place to ensure that

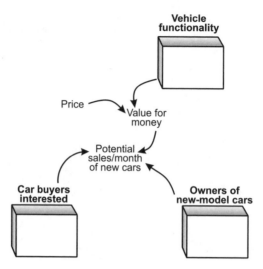

Figure 6.5 Factors determining *potential* sales of new cars.

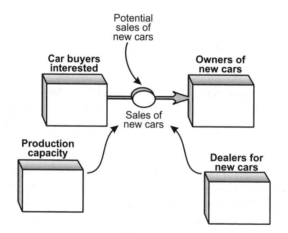

Figure 6.6 Factors determining *actual* sales of new cars.

vehicles are available: the firm must have enough production capacity and there must be enough dealers stocking the cars for buyers to find them (Figure 6.6).

To complete the chain of buyer flows, it is also necessary to add the original source of buyer interest and the loss of owners as they dispose of the new vehicles onto the second-hand market. Buyer interest is driven by the firm's marketing efforts, and how long owners will keep their vehicles reflects the functionality they experience while owning them. Adding these two factors to the consumer flow chain produces Figure 6.7.

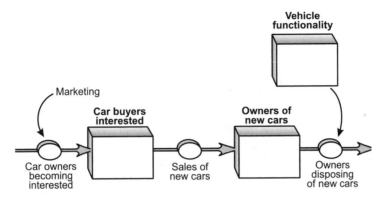

Figure 6.7 Marketing builds up interest in new vehicles, and functionality determines how quickly owners dispose of them.

Certain features commonly arise in Step 4:

- *Price, or some other financial benefit, often drives flows of firms or people.* Clearly, the relative price of a telecoms service, a consumer electronics product, or a service provided by a professional service firm will have some impact on the gain or loss of customers. *(In addition, of course, price may also determine customers' purchase frequency, though this is a separate mechanism from the actual gains and losses of customers.)* Similarly, the potential margin available on a product or service may motivate new dealers to stock a product, and salary or other rewards will affect the ability to hire, develop, and retain staff.
- *Some form of functionality will also drive flows* such as the services offered by the telecoms provider, the user features of the consumer electronics product, and the actual services offered by the professional service firm. An equivalent "functionality" may also drive other resource flows (e.g., the challenge and excitement of a job will affect hiring and attrition rates among staff).

In this case, the comparison between price and functionality of the new vehicles is a strong driver of the *potential* sales rate (Figure 6.5):

- *Rivalry is a common driver of flows.* Rivalry is largely captured by *relative* or *differential* comparisons of price and functionality between the firm and its competitors. For example, a telecoms firm's rate of subscriber losses will reflect the price differential between their service and that of rivals. The consumer electronics firm will win customers at a rate that reflects the relative functionality of their product compared with that offered by rivals. However, resource flows may also feature specific actions by rivals, like focused efforts to attract your staff or customers. (The dynamics of rivalry reflect certain further specific structures within DRSV, which will be developed in detail in Chapter 8.)

In the new vehicle case, rivalry is implicit. Price and functionality are both compared with what competing vehicles in the same class are offering, and the impact of marketing efforts depends upon whether rivals, too, are advertising.

Finally—*focus on how people* **actually** *make the decision to "flow"*—*do not assume that they behave as you think they should, or according to rational evaluations or standard models.* Do telecoms subscribers look at the monthly bill, calculate what they expect the bill to be with a rival supplier, then rationally compare the difference with what they think will be the costs of moving, or do they simply respond to rivals' claims to be cheaper? Are consumers motivated to buy an electronics product by a rational comparison of its product features, or are they swayed by what their friends have bought, or what stores are stocking? Do the staff in professional service firms leave because of work pressure, slow promotion rates, or poor expectations for future financial rewards?

In this case, car buyers' perceptions of value for money can only be confidently discovered from market research, not simply by assuming some ratio between price and functionality. This is likely to be especially true when the product is substantially novel, compared with anything that the industry has offered before. The strength of any word-of-mouth feedback from early buyers of the vehicles to persuade others to consider buying them must also be discovered, rather than assumed. The impact of vehicle availability on sales will need to be studied carefully: do keen buyers simply give up if they can't find the cars at their nearest dealer, or do they continue searching until they find one?

Step 5. Combine the resource dependencies from Step 4 into a strategic architecture of the business.

With only a few core resources, and with the drivers of growth and loss clearly defined in Steps 3–4, it is usually fairly clear how these elements combine to arrive at a core architecture. Check that this map is properly defined:

- make sure that the flow-drivers from Step 3 are properly represented;
- ensure that all links back to other resources are captured; and
- add the connection to financial and other performance measures.

The result of this step for the new vehicle case is shown in Figure 6.8. Note that dashed lines have been used to distinguish how the financial outcomes arise from the fundamental resources in the system.

Step 6. Get quantitative—again—to see how the strategic architecture explains performance to date and into the future

It is at this step that substantial debate and insight typically arise:

- *Add time charts for the key resources, the flow drivers, and performance outcomes.* Use debate and judgment to fill in unknowns. Where detailed information is not available, make estimates, check with people whose experience is likely to give them good insight into values and trends, and cross-check alternative views and sources.

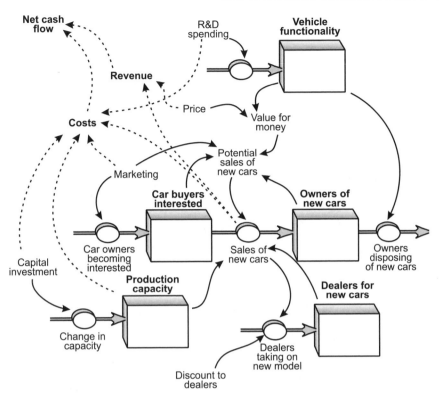

Figure 6.8 Building up the set of flow drivers for development and launch of a new technology vehicle.

- *Finally, assess and quantify the dependency of each resource flow on the combination of factors that are thought to drive it.* In many cases, research sources already exist to provide confident views on such questions. Customer research may offer some insight into the relative balance of factors that are in practice causing customers to be gained or lost, for example. Where research does not exist, though, it is often practical to collect good information. If you do not know why employees are leaving, it is relatively simple to put in place exit interviews to find out.

It is now possible to trace possible explanations for the new vehicle launch problem (Figure 6.9), and anticipate how the business might develop in the future.

Starting with the time chart for *sales of new cars*:

- Production capacity is entirely adequate for the modest sales rate. Dealer support, however, is poor and growing slowly. This could be due either to unattractive discounts or the vehicles' slow sales rate itself. If vehicle sales are slow, even deep discounts will not provide dealers with a substantial cash income, so the problem seems to lie with the sales rate—we have slow

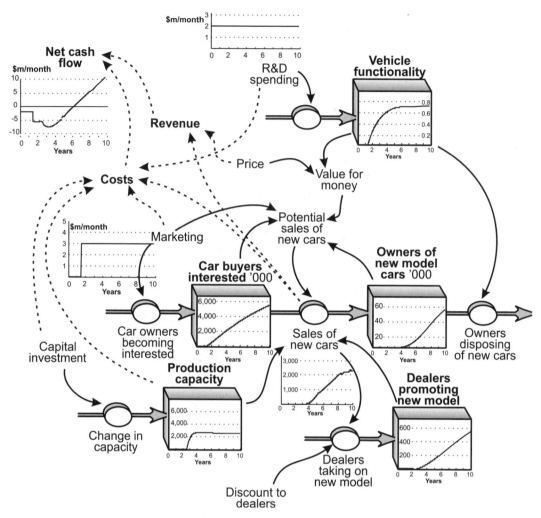

Figure 6.9 Anticipating prospects for development and launch of a new technology vehicle.

sales, so dealers don't want the cars, so we have slow sales. The company will have to look elsewhere for an escape from this self-perpetuating problem.

• The only remaining driver of *actual* sales is the *potential* sales rate. This depends on four items. The number of people interested in the vehicles appears to be healthy, at over two million. The stock of existing owners is too low to provide any significant word-of-mouth recommendation. The marketing efforts appear to have succeeded well in creating interest, so it seems that the problem lies with *value for money*.

The company embarked on the project on an assumption that its new vehicle would be so appealing that they could charge a substantial premium over rival products in the same class. However, it appears that they have overestimated consumers' admiration—a hypothesis that can be quickly confirmed by research.

Step 7. Revising policy to uprate performance

The six steps outlined above bring the management team to a point where they are able to evaluate alternative future strategies. The strategic architecture, as illustrated in Figure 6.9, highlights the points in the system where management can intervene. Such leverage points typically arise in two categories:

1 *Management **decisions** that directly impact on important flows in the system.* Examples include pricing, advertizing spend, pay rates, discounts, and so on.
2 *Management **commitment of effort** intended to grow or retain certain resources.* Examples include new product development efforts, hiring targets, and service-level commitments to improve customer retention rates.

Once again, an organized approach to this step is helpful:

- Start with the place (or places) in the architecture where Step 6 indicated the focus of the challenge to lie. This will usually be just one location (e.g., the *potential sales* item in our example), but may occasionally be more. For example, it may be found that the firm is both failing to provide capacity to service its current demand and failing to build that demand itself.
- Focus on the decisions or links into that part of the architecture that management can influence. Here, the options are to revise pricing (Type 1 intervention) or boost product functionality (Type 2 intervention).
- Estimate the *scale* of policy revision, and the *scale* and *timing* of any resulting effects. If this firm cuts its price by 10%, how much will the *potential purchase rate* change? If it doubles its R&D spending, how quickly will the vehicle's functionality be raised, and to what level?
- Trace through the *consequences* of these policy changes. If the *potential purchase* rate increases, how much will the *actual* purchase rate move, and over what timescale?
- Next, anticipate any further problems that may arise from altering the performance of the part of the system where the current challenge is focused. Will it be necessary for the car firm to change dealer discounts to ensure that would-be purchasers can find the vehicles that it now hopes they will perceive to offer good value? Will there be sufficient capacity to meet the likely increase in sales rate?
- Finally, work through how any performance outcomes may evolve over time, as a result of the proposed changes. How much will this firm's price cut reduce revenues and margins, and how will this, and the increase in R&D costs, hit cash flow? How quickly will the expected increase in sales rate raise revenues, and how much of that will be lost in higher dealer margins? What further capital will need to be invested in capacity?

It is entirely possible that this evaluation of the revised strategy will produce an answer that is unacceptable (e.g., the cumulative cash outflow would not be tolerated). If this is the case, then the process in this step will have to be repeated for a different set of alternative policies. However, an important implication of DRSV is unavoidable:

> *The firm's resources at any moment impose fundamental limits to the scope for performance enhancement and the speed with which this can be accomplished. Any attempt to push beyond this limit **will** have the result of creating stresses in the system that will ultimately prevent further improvement or trigger collapse.*

Investors, whether independent shareholders or the corporate center should be alert to overambitious profitability commitments made by (or imposed upon) management.

Figure 6.10 traces out two alternative futures for the new-car launch.

Case A

- In an attempt to boost consumers perception of value, R&D spending is raised considerably, from $2m/month to $5m/month.
- Recognizing that R&D improvements will take some time, the price of the cars is immediately reduced, from $40,000 to $32,000.
- In anticipation of increased demand, dealer margins are raised from 20 to 30%, and new capacity is ordered to bring the total up to 8,000 vehicles per month.

After thinking this through, the management team identify that to sustain this response will be extremely expensive. Not only will profitability be hit by the lower price, steeper dealer discounts and increased R&D, but the new capacity will also be costly. They feel they have no choice but to live with the pain for a while, and then look for the earliest opportunity to boost cash flows.

Case B (after following Case A for 1 year)

- The R&D improvements are expected to enable the cars to be relaunched a year later, at a higher price of $38,000.
- To sustain the sales rate at this time, marketing will be boosted to $5m/month, funded by reduced R&D.
- With the expected increase in sales volume, there should be no need to give dealers the deeper discounts they enjoyed during the 1-year recovery, so these are reduced once more to 20%.

Working through the expected sales volume, margins, and costs leads to the conclusion that the firm can be confident of breaking even early in Year 8, with sales and cash flows rising sharply to overtake what would otherwise have been likely.

Note that some of the variables do not appear to differ substantially between the three scenarios (continue as is, Case A, and Case B)—car buyers interested

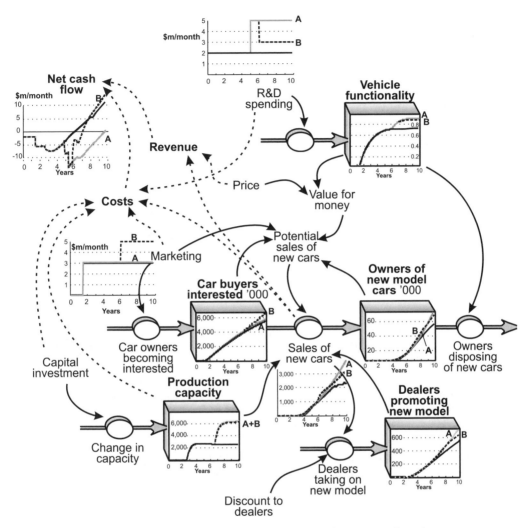

Figure 6.10 Alternative strategy responses for new-car launch.

and total owners of the new models, for example. The explanation is simply that these are *cumulative* stocks of resources, which already have a reasonable history. The important difference between the three scenarios, though, is that these resources are now on a different growth *trajectory*, which is manifest particularly in the rate of vehicle sales and the resulting cash flows.

Strategic Architecture: diagnosing performance challenges

The process described above should make it possible to arrive at a sound picture of the firm's strategic architecture. Step 7 summarizes what, in practice, may be a lengthy and complex evaluation. To assist in diagnosing performance problems, a search process can be followed to steer the team to a clear understanding of the causes of their current performance.

The logic of the improvement-seeking process is as follows:

- minimize any "leakage" of resources, since any efforts to raise growth will be disabled if important resource gains are simply lost again;
- identify whether the necessary drivers of resource inflow are all in place and operating effectively;
- identify any balancing mechanisms in the system, including those due to depleted potential resources, and seek policies to lift the constraints they may impose on growth;
- ensure reinforcing mechanisms that *should* be operating to drive growth are doing so, and seek to add new ones; look for reinforcing mechanisms that risk driving catastrophic collapse, and either implement breaks in the feedback or new balancing mechanisms to prevent such reversal;
- where the system is unbalanced, or risks becoming so, seek acquisitions, disposals, or other stepwise solutions to bring it into balance quickly.

Task 1. Minimize any "leaks" in the system—resource loss rates that are higher than they could be

There is little point in seeking to uprate gains in the system if the organization simply loses them again. This may apply to any of the core resources, but is most common among the simplest people resources—customers, intermediaries, and staff. Too often, customers are won, only to be lost again by poor products or service, staff are hired and trained, only to leave again for any of a host of reasons, and new distributor arrangements are set up, only to fall apart due to failures to sustain the relationship.

There may, of course, be cases where the organization has very good reason deliberately to implement loss of resources. Staff movement may be needed to make room for new talent, poor-quality customers may need to be discontinued, or a too-wide product range may be dissipating marketing and sales efforts. Nevertheless, even in such cases, it is vital that only the *right* resource items are lost, so attention to retaining valuable resources remains imperative.

Outflows inflict far greater damage on performance than is caused merely by the loss of the customers, staff, or dealers themselves—the effort that went into winning them in the first place will have been totally wasted, and could have been deployed on other tasks. Paradoxically, therefore, performance may even be enhanced by stopping certain efforts. Do any of the following apply to *your* situation?

- reduce sales efforts and focus instead on looking after existing customers;
- cut back the rate of hiring, and attend instead to keeping, developing, and valuing the staff you already have;

- slow down efforts to open up new channels to market, and make sure instead to sustain those you recently started; or
- reduce the rate of new product introductions, and focus instead on enhancing the functionality of those you have and squeezing a longer commercial life from them.

To ensure such dissipation of precious resources is reduced to a minimum, examine the time charts for all outflows in the system. Challenge whether each rate should be lower than it is, checking against at least four criteria:

- Has this leakage *previously* been lower than it is at present?
- Are there *parts of the business* (regions, departments, etc.) where loss rates are particularly low?
- Do rivals, or other *benchmark firms*, manage to sustain lower loss rates?
- How low a rate of loss *might be feasible*, at best?

Once the possible scope for loss reduction has been identified, the team can seek means for moving the organization toward that new, lower rate by referring to how the best standards are currently being achieved and identifying how to implement or move beyond them.

Continue this search for dissipation of resources by *looking for backflows* of resource along the chain of development, especially among customers. Is there any evidence that once-loyal customers are starting to source from rivals too, are they purchasing less frequently, is awareness among customers dropping, or are those who *are* aware becoming more likely to reject than admire our products or services?

Identify why the leaks in the system are occurring, whether due to inadequacies among other resources or inappropriate policies.

Where leaks or backflows involve *people*, exit interviews are a particularly powerful source of insight as to where attention should be concentrated. It is already common to conduct exit interviews among staff, but often these are not structured to spot the specific drivers of attrition in an organized manner. Nor is there usually any direct connection from the results of such interviews to redesigned processes or policies that might act to reduce attrition in the future.

Customers too can be "exit-interviewed". If customers tell you they are switching to a rival due to poor product performance, attention needs to focus on fixing that problem; if poor service support is to blame, then focus on identifying why that is the case.

Pay particular attention to resource losses that are due to inadequacies in other resources. Both the product performance and service support problems just mentioned may be directly attributable to inadequate resources (e.g., production engineers or service staff). These causes deserve particular attention since they will typically take time to resolve, as new resource is developed.

Task 2. Identify whether the necessary drivers of resource inflows are all in place and operating effectively

The team should examine each resource inflow, and ensure that all the necessary resources, mechanisms, and policies are in place to enable growth:

- Is the marketing budget sufficient to reach enough potential customers to make the desired win rate feasible? Is the number of sales staff sufficient to achieve the win rate of customers that is both required and possible? Is the product's functionality adequate for them to win customers, and are the production, delivery, and installation resources in place to turn orders into completed sales?
- Is the hiring and training capacity in place to capture staff at the rate required and make them productive quickly? Is there sufficient awareness among *potential* recruits of the employment opportunities and attractiveness in the firm?
- Are sufficient development efforts and facilities in place to allow product functionality or reliability to be raised at the necessary rate, and to the level required?

It is important to appreciate at this stage that the purpose is *not* to create a list of additional efforts or spending needs that the firm could not realistically afford— it is rather to *redirect* the efforts and spending that are made. Indeed, it is common for this task to identify savings of time and money.

As well as confirming the drivers for inflows of resource, similar thinking should be applied to each flow that *develops* resource forward through the system—winning increased awareness or loyalty among customers, developing products quickly from prototype or niche status to extensive market take-up, and developing staff to levels where they can make a stronger contribution to the enterprise.

Even where other resources and expenditures should be adequate to build a certain resource at the required rate, it is still possible for inflows to fall short, due to lack of clarity among staff about what they are expected to achieve. It may therefore be necessary to clarify to the staff groups involved the priorities that exist and why:

- Should sales staff be focusing attention on retaining existing customers, on developing more trade with those customers, or seeking new customers?
- Should product development efforts be focused on improving functionality or reliability of existing products, or on extending the product range?
- Should line managers be concerned to consolidate employees' satisfaction with their current roles, accelerating skills development, or bringing on new talent?

These first two tasks have largely focused on optimizing the *flow rates* of resource acquisition, development, and retention. The next two tasks are concerned with ensuring that *feedback* mechanisms enable the business to develop.

Task 3. Identify and eliminate any balancing mechanisms that may be preventing progress at present, or may do so in future

Chapter 5 explained how the development of one resource may be hampered by inadequacies in other resources through balancing feedback mechanisms. The team should examine the strategic architecture they have developed for the business, focus on each resource in turn, and identify whether its own growth may cause imbalances that hamper its further progress:

- If customer or distributor acquisition is successful, will the increased requirement for service, support, or supply run up against limited resources in other functions?
- If plant expansion efforts succeed in boosting output, are *all* the additional resources in place to enable that extra capacity to contribute—supply sources, warehousing, outbound distribution capacity, installation manpower?
- If staff hiring or development efforts are successful, is the training capacity in place to cope, and does the organization have the capacity to absorb the new people?
- When new promising products are launched, is the supply chain, installation capacity, and service support adequate to support them?

In each such case, a useful question to trigger insight is, *"If we are successful in winning these customers (or finding these staff, or launching these products), what are all the things that could go wrong or get in the way?"* Management then needs to focus, not so much on the primary resource itself, but on developing the plans needed to bring on the range of *other* resources without which the primary growth objective will be frustrated.

In extreme cases, it may even be necessary to develop contingency plans. These take two principal forms:

- If there is a risk of resources being won far more quickly than we can cope with, could we bring in temporary sources of support from elsewhere? The Egg low-cost savings bank, described in Chapter 5, was quickly overwhelmed within 3 weeks by new-customer demand some 20 times higher than its most optimistic expectations. Fortunately, it was able to draw on call-center support from a competent third party to relieve a large part of the pressure.
- If we can neither cope with the growth ourselves, nor find alternative sources of support, should we deliberately slow down or stop the growth until we can catch up with the pressure? In parallel with the outsourced call-center support, Egg briefly cut back its marketing efforts and warned would-be customers of possible delays.

(While these two policy responses in this case may seem somewhat self-evident, it is far from obvious *how much'* to respond, for *how long*, or with what likely impact.)

*Task 4. Ensure reinforcing processes that **should** be driving growth are doing so, and seek to add new mechanisms*

Only after the previous three steps have been completed should management turn to the tempting task of finding reinforcing mechanisms to drive growth. There is no point implementing such devices, simply to see the large numbers of new customers lost again or poorly served by inadequate support. Nor is it much help to bring in large numbers of new hires, only to have them leave again due to inadequate training or career opportunities.

Every business has the potential for resources to reinforce their own and each other's growth mutually, as described in Chapter 4. Examine the time charts to see whether rates of resource gain confirm that these processes are actually operating. Start by examining each isolated resource:

- At what rate are existing customers contributing to the winning of further customers (likewise for dealers and other channel partners)? At what rate *might* this reinforcement occur if we implemented policies to encourage such feedback?
- To what extent are existing staff contributing to the recruitment and retention of new staff, and to developing these new hires once they have been attracted to us? Again, at what rate *might* this reinforcement occur if we designed policies to stimulate it?
- How effectively are we capturing the technological or service lessons from recently developed products to further enhance both those products themselves and subsequent products in development?
- Are we effectively capturing lessons from plant operating changes to further enhance production efficiencies?

As described above for minimizing resource outflows, look for parallels or exemplars from strongly performing parts of the business, from previous time periods, or from other companies in your own or other industries.

A particularly common failure arises when excellent learning about such feedback mechanisms is not captured and spread from one part of the organization to another. It is remarkably common to discover that one region's sales manager has created powerful reinforcing mechanisms to build customer growth that others are not aware of, let alone implementing. Similar observations arise between different departments' staff-development policies, different product groups' market-development successes, and different production facilities' efficiency improvements. There are few quicker gains to be had in many firms than simply providing the feedback from outstanding successes in one part of the organization to others. A most regrettable consequence of the drive, in recent years, to slim down management has been the often extreme levels of pressure executives experience. The price has been an often absurd inability to learn from important experiences of others.

Having reviewed and confirmed that *existing* reinforcement is operating as it should, the team can next *seek additional reinforcing mechanisms* that may be brought into action. A simple and relatively common example arises when firms fail to make full use of staff groups for more than their restricted, functional task. Sales staff can bring back opportunities for new products, administrative staff can contribute to customer development, and firms undertaking organizational change can use "early adopters" among their staff to inspire and reassure others, accelerating the progress of change.

The team should examine the overall resource map, then:

- focus on those resources (from previous steps) that appear likely to be the most difficult to grow or develop;
- seek opportunities to add further growth-reinforcing mechanisms;
- confirm with knowledgable staff that the proposal is feasible;
- ensure that any new mechanisms will not conflict with other growth drivers;
- ensure that any resulting success will not lead to other imbalances or, if it does, that plans are in place to build the complementary resources needed.

It may also be possible to add reinforcing growth mechanisms by seeking new strategic resources to add or create:

- consumer goods suppliers use wholesalers to extend their reach into more retail outlets;
- manufacturers seek outsource suppliers to leverage their production capacity;
- pharmaceuticals firms link with university research departments to leverage their rate of new product introductions;
- professional service firms codify their knowledge base to raise the productivity of their staff.

Such routes to further growth are clearly already common, but DRSV makes it possible to evaluate, in detail and in scale, the organization-wide repercussions, over time, of such initiatives.

Finally, one vital precaution should be taken—*examine the new resource-system structure and look for any possibility that* **negative** *reinforcement could arise.* Ensure that balancing mechanisms are in place to act against such collapse quickly enough to protect against disaster. Common examples arise among customers and channels, and also between these market-based resources and critical staff groups. It is essential to ensure that any loss of customers or dealers does *not* risk stimulating further such losses. So severe can this danger be that, in some cases, it may be necessary rapidly to redeploy sales, marketing, and support efforts away from developing new business so as to catch the decline before it gets out of hand. Where loss of key staff may trigger customer or dealer losses, or vice versa, urgent action may again be needed to reassure and retain those who remain.

Task 5. If necessary, use stepwise solutions to remove resource limits and imbalances

In cases where resource limits and imbalances are serious, it may be impractical or take too long to grow, develop, or reduce the necessary resources. In such cases, step changes may be appropriate. These arise at two levels:

- focused actions may be taken to bring a single resource into line with the rest of the system, either as it is or as it is planned to become;
- larger actions may be appropriate to bring the business to a totally new level, with a better balance and stronger growth potential.

Dealership agreements, licensing of products or process, and outsourcing are common examples of actions focused on moving a single resource up to a new level. Redundancy, customer-base rationalization, and product-range reductions are examples of actions needed to bring excess resources back to affordable levels and reignite higher growth.

While such stepwise responses are hardly a novel approach to relieving resource constraints, DRSV raises certain important issues regarding their implementation:

- It is important to ensure that the *rest* of the system, into which a new tranche of resource is added, is capable of absorbing it. It may be necessary to build up complementary resources in advance, or at least start them on an increasing trajectory so that they become able quickly to cope with the influx.
- If this is not achieved (or even if it is), some post-acquisition losses of the new resource may be triggered, either among the acquired population itself or among the resources previously thought to be reliable. It is common, for example, for staff to resign following the taking on of new people. Losses may also arise among other resource categories—inward licensing of new products may cause product-development staff to become disillusioned and resign, and the opening up of new direct customer relationships may cause dealers to desert to rivals.
- Where substantial *reductions* of a resource are instigated, similar continuing consequences may arise—redundancy programs trigger increased attrition among other staff, customer-base rationalization may worry important customers, reducing loyalty and increasing loss rates, and product-range rationalization may cause outflows of customers, distributors, or staff.

Whatever the specifics of the situation, the management team must think through the probable secondary effects, not just in outline, but in scale, and over time. Policy responses can then be put in place to minimize any adverse, secondary consequences or, if satisfactory precautions cannot be found, then the major event can be postponed or cancelled.

Where a full-scale acquisition, alliance, or disposal is considered, all the issues just raised for stepwise change to a single resource are repeated, but across the entire organization. Full discussion of the issues that such events may raise is beyond the scope of this chapter. However, the imperatives indicated by DRSV can be developed to provide guidance for any large-scale change:

- seek to minimize unwanted losses of resource triggered by the event;
- ensure drivers of resource growth and development are in place to take the business forward subsequently;
- ensure that each resource will not be prevented from growth by inadequacies in others that may arise from the event;

- finally, be particularly alert for any risk of catastrophic collapse arising from interdependencies between critical resources.

Summary

A disciplined, organized process is essential for building up a picture of the strategic architecture for the firm (or a part of it), focused on the issue of concern. Identify the time-path of the particular performance item in question, identify the relevant resources, and select the few core items only. Put time charts on these resources and on the inflows and outflows for each, then identify the other items on which these flows depend. Take care to capture how these dependencies *actually* operate, rather than how you may wish them to or how standard assumptions or models dictate that they should. Combine these interdependencies into a single map of the firm's architecture. Finally, get quantitative again, by completing the time charts for any new items and performance outcomes that have arisen as the complete picture is put together.

There are common structures that recur in many sectors of business, but it is *always* necessary to build up the structure that applies to *your* situation. Similarities also arise between the issues that arise in such cases, but the actual behavior of each case can *never* be inferred by reference to other cases, only by close attention to what is happening here and now.

In new ventures, or extreme cases requiring transformation, it may be necessary to lay out a business architecture that is not currently in existence. However, for most continuing businesses, the current architecture provides a foundation for seeking performance improvements.

Such improvement opportunities can be discovered by following a process of investigation (in the correct order). First, seek to minimize losses of key resources, then make sure that any inward flows or development flows of resource are responding properly to the forces that should be driving them. Look to identify and remove any imbalances that may be holding back growth, and free up or initiate new reinforcing feedback mechanisms. *Look most carefully for any structures that could trigger catastrophic collapse* and identify means to cut critical connections in such cases.

If the changes required to the level of a single resource cannot be practically accomplished sufficiently quickly through normal gain and loss processes, seek means to acquire or lose tranches of resource through one-off events or programs. Make sure, though, that the rest of the system remains in balance, and that any adverse secondary consequences are protected against. Major, organization-wide acquisitions, disposals, or rationalizations should be scrutinized to ensure they comply with the same criteria for performance and robustness.

Part II

Further Concepts

7

The Hard Face of Soft Factors—the Power of Intangible Resources

---

Key issues

❏ The characteristics, measurement, and importance of intangible resources

❏ "Indirect" resources—reflecting how people feel about important issues, and the resulting impact on resource flows

❏ Direct drivers of change affecting intangible resources

❏ Resource "attributes"—qualities that change as resources are won or lost

❏ The impact of time delays and changes in perceptions over time

❏ Dealing with "negative" perceptions

❏ Coping with changing expectations

❏ Integrating intangibles into the strategic architecture

❏ An example of intangibles in a professional service firm

The early chapters have focused on the most direct drivers of business performance, especially those that account for revenues, costs, and profits. These factors have consisted almost entirely of tangible resources—items that are easily seen, counted, touched, hired, bought, and sold.

Traditional methods for assembling a fact-based strategy deal with similar factors, though without the integrated, time-based structures described in the chapters so far. When it comes to softer issues, though, such as staff morale, product functionality, or investor support, managers are left with little guidance—everyone knows they matter, but *how* do they affect an organization's performance?

Soft factors play a crucial role in competitive performance. Highly motivated staff are more productive than those with poor morale—a strong reputation in the market helps customer acquisition, a firm with strong backing from investors will have more freedom to take investment opportunities, and a production-cost advantage results in more margin, which can fund the development of other resources.

If we are to tackle the time-path of strategy comprehensively, then, we have no choice but to deal with such intangible factors rigorously. The rationale for dealing with intangibles is as follows:

• strategic performance at any moment depends on the current level of tangible resources to which the business has access;
• the only means of changing performance into the future is by building and sustaining levels of these tangible resources;
• so, the influence of intangible resources *must* be felt through some impact on the firm's ability to capture and hold on to those same tangible factors.

Unfortunately, while intangible items clearly make a large impact on management's ability to build the business, they can be the most intractable factors to manage. While firms may easily borrow cash, buy or build production facilities, or hire staff, it is difficult and time-consuming to build the morale of a workforce, grow a reputation in the marketplace, sustain support from investors or achieve a cost-efficiency advantage over rivals.

Applying just one of these advantages to a firm's strategic architecture will increase the "gain" (i.e., rate of growth) of the business engine. Even small differences can accumulate substantial performance changes if they persist over time. Now, consider the likely competitive performance of a firm with an advantage in *all* these intangible resources compared with one that doesn't. Given the power of a well-designed strategic architecture of related resources to drive growth, there is clearly considerable scope for a firm with strong intangibles to outperform rivals by a substantial margin. Furthermore, since it is both hard to identify exactly what these intangible factors are, and time-consuming to do so, they provide the basis of that holy grail—*sustainable* advantage.

Before describing and illustrating intangible resources, it is important to note that, for developing strategy, the word "tangible" is not used in the narrow sense to refer purely to inanimate, physical assets. It also includes people-based resources (e.g., staff), related enterprises (e.g., customers, suppliers, and intermediaries), and tradable assets such as patents and brand names—literally anything you can touch, including cash. Tangible items also include other useful and identifiable factors available to the business such as its range of products and services.

Intangible resources come in two forms:

A   *"indirect" resources, reflecting people's feelings or expectations regarding issues that concern them;*
B   *characteristics or "attributes" associated with tangible resources.*

A few resources that may be thought of as intangible do not fit neatly into the two categories above, though it may not be clear whether they are in fact intangible in the strategic sense. A firm's knowledge base may be tangible if it is manifest in the firm's library of patents, since these can be sold or licensed. In other circumstances, the knowledge base may be intangible, and may only be evident in, for example, the range of products or services offered to customers. However, there is little to be gained from semantic debate about how to put such examples into tidy categories. It is enough to recognize that resources exhibit different degrees of tangibility, ranging from the extremely tangible (e.g., cash or physical plant) through to the clearly intangible (e.g., reputation or staff morale). The important issue is to be clear what is meant by each item, and look for measures that provide reliable information on its health.

We will examine the particular features and behaviour of indirect and attribute resources later, but, for now, we will start with a discussion about some general characteristics of intangible resources.

Features and impact of intangible resources

Certain features of intangible resources have important consequences for their dynamic behavior and hence their role in the firm's resource system:

- *Intangible resources take time to accumulate.* In the early 1970s, European and US car industries' product quality lagged far behind that of Japanese manufacturers. It took nearly two decades for most to catch up. The challenge here was not limited merely to raising the measurable quality of the vehicles themselves—faults on leaving the production line, breakdowns, and warranty claims—a further substantial effort was needed to change the *perception* of quality among car-users.
- *Intangibles can be destroyed rapidly.* Important resources, carefully nurtured over many years, can be damaged through accident or carelessness. Oil companies are rarely popular, but Shell International has paid close attention to its public image for many decades. Its reputation for environmental responsibility, then, suffered badly from a decision to sink the obsolete Brent Spar oil rig in the Atlantic. This example also illustrates that such damage may not accurately reflect the objective merits of the case—it was subsequently established by Greenpeace itself that Shell's proposal was far less damaging than the initial publicity suggested. (Interestingly, this episode itself damaged the credibility of environmentalists with the media, making it more difficult to gain their interest on subsequent campaigns.)
- *Special cases arise with "hygiene" factors*—issues that are usually disregarded until something goes wrong. We take for granted that an airline has acceptable safety standards, so a reputation as a "safe" airline is not usually a source of advantage. But, a disaster or scandal about safety procedures can cause a sharp drop in that reputation, creating a serious competitive disadvantage that lasts many years.

- *Damage to intangible resources has powerful effects on tangible factors.* Shell's loss of reputation did immediate, measurable damage to the company's customer base at the petrol pumps, particularly in Germany, with equally measurable impact on its revenues. In a different context, the tidal wave of investor support for new ventures in 1999/2000 led to a flood of managerial talent away from traditional careers. As the fragility of earnings from these ventures became apparent, a sharp reversal in support caused many dot.coms to find the stream of keen new talent was suddenly less easy to entice. Moreover, the limited pool of experienced e-business talent exposed many of these firms to disastrous losses of key individuals.

Measuring intangible resources

Since we are seeking to build a fact-based, quantitative approach to evaluating strategic performance, some means is needed to measure these important intangible factors. Certain intangibles, especially the more direct ones, come with a ready-made measure, as illustrated in Table 7.1. Where such measures are available, they should be used, avoiding the temptation to talk in abstract terms. The quantitative performance of the business over time cannot be understood by relying on statements such as "we have an experienced workforce" or "our delivery performance is excellent".

Other intangibles do not offer such convenient units, but reliable measures are still required. Many can be measured on a 0–1 scale, where 0 represents a complete absence of the resource and 1.0 is the maximum level that can be achieved. Employee morale, for example, may be gleaned from internal surveys, and measured on such a scale. Customers' perceptions of service levels may be measured in the same way.

Beware, though!—the reference level for measures of intangible resources may alter over time. Examples of this problem are numerous. Consumer-service standards that are at first thought to be exemplary, driving strong growth in customer numbers, may come to be the expected norm. Excellent employment and career conditions that attract the best recruits at one point in time can be quickly matched by rivals. The cost performance of products and services changes rapidly with improvements in the underlying technology, so that a cost-effective solution today loses its competitive lead, often quite fast. This is

Table 7.1 Measures of illustrative intangible resources.

Intangible resource	Common measure	Units
Product quality	Reject rate	*Fraction*
Delivery performance	Delivery lead time	*Days*
Cost-efficiency of production	Unit cost	*$ per unit*
Staff experience	Average service	*Years*

a further reason to use hard measures, rather than qualitative judgments—if our unit cost for a product remains at $90 per ton, while our rivals improve their costs from $100 to $80, our cost-efficiency "resource" changes from strong to weak. It is far preferable to treat the unit cost itself as the resource and compare it with the equivalent for rivals. (Note that "cost efficiency" is in fact a result of a complex system of more detailed asset-stocks, but can often be treated, as here, as an attribute in its own right).

"Indirect" resources, reflecting people's feelings or expectations regarding issues that concern them

Table 7.2 offers some examples of indirect resources, and specifies how they might be measured. Indirect resources rarely have an objective measure, but can usually be identified by survey. Such indirect resources, while difficult for management to reach and influence, have a powerful effect on the behavior of important groups of people (e.g., whether staff stay or resign, whether customers remain loyal or leave, and whether investors continue to back management and provide funding). So, Table 7.2 also shows resource flows that may be affected by levels of these indirect factors.

Indirect resources have certain characteristics that give them a strong influence over the rest of the firm's system. Changes in the indirect resource may be quite different in magnitude from changes in the reality they reflect—in the Shell example above, the indirect resource (reputation) moved much more severely than Shell's actual efforts on environmental protection. Indirect resources may also lag behind the intangible resource they reflect, as is illustrated by the distinction between car-makers' build quality and their reputation for quality.

Having discussed the nature and measurement of intangible resources, we can now move on to consider the mechanisms that cause them to change.

Table 7.2 Examples of indirect resources.

Tangible resource	Indirect resources	Possible measures	Resource flows that may be affected
Customers	Annoyance level	*Research rating: 0–1*	Customer loss rates Recommendations to new customers
Potential customers	Reputation for quality (service or product) or reliable delivery	*Research rating: 0–1*	Customer acquisition rates
Staff	Morale	*Research rating: 0–1*	Attrition rates Hiring success
Investors	Investor confidence	*Research rating: 0–1*	Additional finance raised

Direct drivers of change to intangible resources

This first type of resource change simply replicates the process described in Chapter 3 for tangible resources—from a certain starting level, management action or other factors lead to a gain or loss of the resource stock. A firm may increase the average skill level of staff by providing training, raise the average size of its customers by helping them build their business, or increase support from investors by telling them about exciting investment opportunities. On the downside, the average level of staff skill can deteriorate without practise, average customer size can fall if their business declines, and investor support can wane if their interest switches to other investment opportunities. Figure 7.1 illustrates the dynamics of such a resource in the case of employee skill levels.

This picture and its illustrative numbers raise some important points:

- The framework distinguishes between the management action (amount of training given) and the impact it has on the resource that concerns us (effect on current skill level). This distinction is important, since a given input may generate a range of outcomes, depending on the effectiveness of our efforts and the influence of other factors. For example, work pressure may make our training efforts relatively ineffective.
- It shows the use of an index measure for the intangible item, with 0 meaning complete absence of skills and 1.0 being the greatest level of skill we can imagine for the tasks that concern us.

But, there is something unrealistic about this picture. It implies that a constant rate of training raises skill levels in a persistent, linear manner by a fraction of 0.05 per month. This is clearly unlikely, as the defined limit will soon be reached—the maximum level of skill we can imagine for the task. It is more realistic to suppose that the closer current skill comes to the maximum level the weaker will be the incremental benefit of further training. This is a

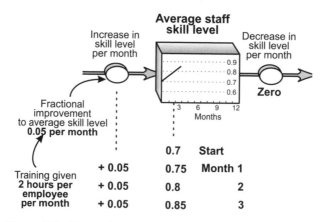

Figure 7.1   Direct changes in average employee skill level.

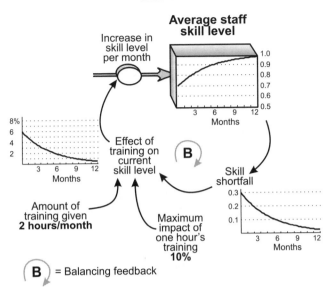

Figure 7.2 Limits to growth of an intangible resource—the case of staff skills.

balancing mechanism, like those discussed in Chapter 5, and a further reason to distinguish the amount of training input from its effect on skill levels.

Figure 7.2 shows how this declining impact of training on an increasingly skilled workforce may be captured. Initially, 2 hours per month of training per person has a strong effect, causing a steep increase from an initially low average staff skill level. As the average skill level rises, however, the potential for *further* benefits from training is progressively reduced.

While this framework may seem a somewhat mechanistic approach to measuring and evaluating real skill levels and training impacts, it does provide a structured means of understanding the current situation and making well-informed judgments as to the impact of management policy. In practical situations, skills' audits can provide useful starting information, and the firm's actual experience of training efforts offers good estimates of training impacts. While the actual *impact* of training in any particular situation may be somewhat different than is shown in Figure 7.2, the key *relationships* will be similar.

There are similarities, too, between the *deterioration* of tangible resources from Chapter 3 and the decline of this intangible skill resource. Skill levels may erode without constant practise and reinforcement—even without staff attrition (which will be dealt with later in this chapter). It is also feasible, though not inevitable, that the rate of decline will be faster the higher is the current skill level. Figure 7.3 shows how average staff skills might decline if this forgetting mechanism is at work. Note that "decrease in skill level" is identical to "skill forgotten", but is kept separate to allow other drivers of decline like staff attrition to be added later. Again, this is an idealized framework, which management will need to reflect on and adjust before applying it to any practical case.

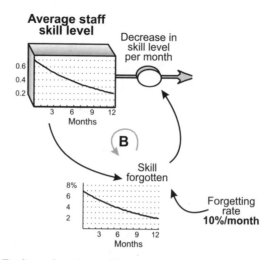

Figure 7.3 Decline of an intangible resource that is not being refreshed.

Table 7.3 Examples of intangible resources and drivers of growth and decline.

Growth drivers	Intangible resource	Decline drivers
Advertizing	*Perceived product quality*	Loss of interest Rivals' advertizing
Bonuses, encouragement Business performance	*Staff morale* *Investor support*	Overwork Alternative investment opportunities
Satisfied clients	*Service reputation*	Service quality below expectations

Similar structures to Figures 7.2 and 7.3 arise in many situations, some of which are listed in Table 7.3.

Combined impact of growth and decline drivers on intangible resources

A case concerning staff morale illustrates the behavior of an intangible resource exhibiting both growth and decline drivers. Many restaurant businesses benefit strongly from marginal increases in utilization, since gross margins are often healthy and site-dependent fixed costs like rent are high. It therefore makes sense to adopt a pay policy designed to reward staff for any sales they generate beyond a certain threshold level. This may be particularly important where there is no opportunity for staff to receive tips from customers. Under these circumstances, high customer traffic generates good bonuses, leading to strong staff morale and productivity. On the other hand, the same high

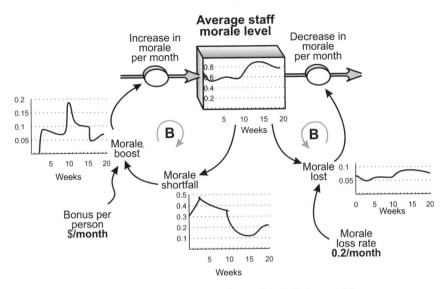

Figure 7.4   Combined impact of morale depletion and bonuses.

customer traffic will overload staff and, since their capacity to serve people even at peak productivity is limited, bonus opportunities are limited too.

The illustration in Figure 7.4 follows the fortunes of one such restaurant, where the excitement of opening caused staff morale to start strongly at 0.7. (*Again, this simple measure may seem crude, but is sufficient for many situations. One software company had a delightfully elegant way of tracking staff feelings—before starting work for the day, employees' screens offered a simple message "How are you feeling today?" with a pointer that could be moved from 0 to 1! Naturally, such devices must be treated carefully to avoid cynicism and annoyance.*)

The manager thought that this enthusiasm would continue, but the hard work wore people down, and morale dropped quickly (Weeks 1–3). She decided to do something about this, and offered her staff bonuses that gave each person about $20/week additional pay. Morale climbed back to over 0.6 during the following 3 weeks, but this was still not sufficient to keep staff enthusiastic, so in Week 10 bonuses were increased to $50/week. Motivation rose to a new high of 0.85.

Unfortunately, the generous bonus payouts were too costly—even at high rates of customer traffic, much of the margin was being given out to staff, which risked putting the restaurant out of business. The manager did not, though, want to risk the loss of customers that may have resulted if bonuses were cut right back again. At a meeting with staff, she agreed with them new bonuses worth about $40 per week, if strong customer demand continued—down on what they enjoyed before, but at least enough to keep them committed to the business. Morale was no longer so good, dropping back to below 0.8, but was sustainable at this new level.

While this story is clearly a stylized depiction of the true subtleties of staff morale, it at least offers some means of grappling with the issue. One executive offered a metaphor he found helpful in thinking about the same issue in his own business. He imagined each member of staff with a "fuel tank" of morale on their back. He thought of the fuel level dropping as hard work got people down, but refilling again as achievements and rewards made people feel better about their work.

The key messages from this example to transfer to other cases are:

- the importance of asking *what is happening* in the particular situation;
- estimating *the scale and rate of change* in the realities of the case (if you have not been collecting information on such soft issues up to now, make your best estimate, ask others for their views, and start collecting that information for the future);
- identifying *why* those changes are taking place; then
- asking *what you can do* to influence those changes.

Finally, remember why achieving this understanding is important—the level of each intangible resource has a direct and powerful influence on your ability to win and hold on to other resources. In the restaurant case, the critical revenue generator is the population of regular customers. Low morale affects service quality, which immediately drives regular customers away. In this particular case, the catchment market was highly localized, and the outlet's reputation spread quickly, leading to an almost immediate fall in new customers when service deteriorated (Figure 7.5).

Time delays and changing perceptions

It is actually rather rare for people's feelings to adjust so immediately to changing circumstances, as the restaurant case suggests. More commonly, such indirect resources move up or down over time, due to one or both of two mechanisms:

- *Repeated or continuous experience of the same condition over time.* Staff morale may be unaffected by occasional peaks in workload, but will deteriorate if work pressure continues at a high level. Customers' perception of service quality may tolerate occasional errors, but will be badly damaged if mistakes are frequent.
- *The time taken for word to spread among a population.* Improved product quality must be reflected in a stronger reputation among potential customers if the improvement is to cause an increase in sales. Similarly, organizations' successful adoption of new methods depends upon the whole staff population coming to understand and have confidence in the changes being made.

Both mechanisms may be either useful or damaging, depending upon circumstances. It is useful, for example, that staff and customers tolerate occasional difficulties without immediately becoming dissatisfied. On the other hand, it is tough to provide those same groups constantly with enough good experience to

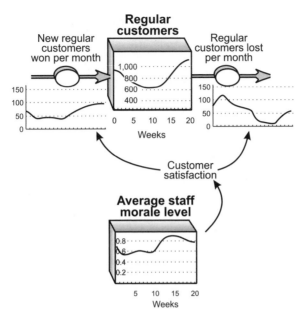

Figure 7.5 The impact of morale on restaurant customer numbers.

raise their perception to a new, higher level. Investors too often tolerate occasional lapses in performance, but are unimpressed by any improvement unless it is sustained.

The structure that captures how perceptions change in response to repeated experience of a new reality is similar to the skills and training example developed in Figure 7.2. People are surprised when experiences differ from their current perceptions, but then adjust their expectations.

Figure 7.6 shows how this adjustment process has worked in the case of passenger rail services. In many countries, rail travel has long been viewed as too unreliable for important journeys. As a result of privatization, reinvestment, and other publicly sponsored efforts to get travelers off the roads, many rail services have received investments and new management designed to improve reliability. These efforts have mostly been successful, but the perceptions of the traveling public have not been so easily altered. Passengers have continued to complain of poor services long after reliability improved.

In Figure 7.6, the rail operators manage to improve service reliability over a 12-month period from a situation where only 50% of journeys arrive on time to a new performance where 90% are punctual. Regular travelers, who provide the majority of rail business and are the key population among whom reputation is formed, have long memories for service failures. Although reliability rises, travelers' perceptions are initially little different than their recent experience, so a gap opens up between perception and the new reality.

In case A, it takes about 12 months for travelers to accept that things really have changed. Gradually, there is a positive change in perception. Some react

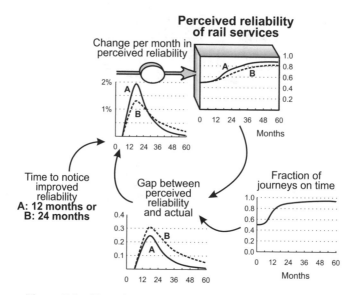

Figure 7.6 Changing perceptions of rail service reliability.

sooner and some later, so perceptions do not change in a straight line, and even some 24 months after service improved there remains a residual shortfall in perceived reliability.

Case B shows the result of still longer memories and greater skepticism among travellers. If they take an average of 24 months to accept the new reality, the gap between perceived and actual performance remains larger, for longer. It now takes many years for overall reputation to creep toward accepting that the improvements are real.

This illustration raises important issues:

- Perception may be a soft factor, but clearly matters, since it directly affects success in winning new business. (In this case, perception also has an important indirect influence on political support for public investment.)
- While this situation may be deeply frustrating for the managers and staff involved, it is an inevitable consequence of the importance that the service plays in the lives of their customers.
- The firm is not powerless in this situation. Management can act to accelerate closure of the gap between perception and reality, through publicizing the real improvements. They might also invite comparison with less attractive alternatives like long delays in road traffic. It may also be useful to over-correct for those few failures that do occur, through high-value refunds or free travel for any travelers still suffering delays. Such responses cause a corrective shock to customer perceptions, precisely because they are unexpected.

- To accomplish a real shift, and to manage the improvement, we need information. Researching customer perception and its causes can be costly, but the potential returns are high. If the perception gap in this situation can be closed along Path A rather than Path B, it requires only a very small increase in the rate of new traveler acquisition to make a considerable difference to revenues within the firm's planning horizon.

Figure 7.6 explains in detail how the perception adjustment process commonly operates, and it may sometimes be necessary to examine exactly how the details of this mechanism are developing. In many cases, though, a shorthand notation may be sufficient. Simply note that there *is* a gap between perception and current reality, estimate what the current, historic, and expected future of these two values might be, and show them on a single chart. Figure 7.7 shows how this is done for actual and perceived reliability of rail services, and how it connects to the growth of customer volumes.

Similar shorthand methods may be used for other perception resources (e.g., workload vs. staff morale), but should be applied with caution. Management should seek a clear understanding of the relationship between actual conditions and people's feelings about those conditions. This debate should be extended to cover plausible, but unexpected events (e.g., in the railways case, the likely impact of an extended period of disruption caused by major construction work).

Finally, note that groups other than customers may adjust their perceptions. Few people are so adept at changing their expectations than investors! No sooner do companies report record results than investment analysts rush to upgrade forecasts and shareholders look forward to ever-higher returns. The same mechanism, of course, applies within corporations, with headquarters' staff taking the role of "investors" and adjusting their expectations of the performance to be achieved by subsidiary business units.

Intangibles hit national strategic performance too

Intangible factors can cause trouble at the country level, as well as for individual firms. In 1990, Venezuela formed the National Council for Investment Promotion, CONAPRI, a nonprofit organization with the mandate of promoting Venezuela as a location for foreign direct investment (FDI). Key tasks included enhancing the business environment, building the country's image, and facilitating the investment process.

CONAPRI's early success in image building resulted in the rate of FDI enquiries growing from a trickle to over 100/month in less than 2 years. One critical resource was key to this success—a 30-year record of democracy, stability, and political maturity. However, in February 1992, an attempted coup disrupted this strong foundation. Critical resources were immediately thrown to new levels—potential investors, both interested and already committed, were lost, and the vital image asset was severely damaged.

CONAPRI was left with an enviable promotion platform and a positive reputation for its own performance, but high awareness for a badly tarnished product. The organization's policies had to shift, from investor acquisition to brand repair. Under these new circumstances, continued effort to "win customers" was not just unachievable but positively damaging as well. Such efforts would merely have brought to the attention of potential investors the alarming features in a situation of which they might otherwise have been only distantly aware.

I am grateful to Adolfo Taylhardat, former head of CONAPRI, for permission to report this case.

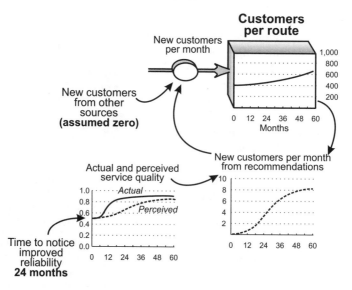

Figure 7.7 Shorthand for service quality perception in rail travel.

Trust—a fragile resource

Until recently, Sotheby's and Christies' auction houses dominated the market in fine arts, thriving on the confidence and trust among would-be sellers of valuables that each built up over decades, even centuries. Both houses, then, suffered badly from investigations into anticompetitive practises between 1990 and 2000. The multimillion dollar financial penalties on the two organizations were bad enough, but collateral damage has proved even more severe, including the departure of their talented salesforces, who fostered close relationships with potential sellers of artwork.

Chief beneficiary of the discomfiture shared by this leading pair was Phillip de Pury & Luxembourg. Being only 200 years old, Phillips is a relative newcomer to the art market, but the impact of its arrival, especially on Christies, has been intensified by rivalry between the bosses of the two groups. Unfortunately for Christies, the damage to its reputation drove sellers and salesforce together into the arms of the new upstart. While it may be possible to replace this salesforce over the coming few years, the accumulated experience will be harder to replace, as will the trust that the group formerly possessed in the market it serves.

I am grateful to Edward M. Blair III for bringing this case to my attention.

Negative perceptions

A challenging feature of modern business life is the tendency for customers, staff, and others to assume that everything will be perfect— products will work reliably, service will be provided in an instant, deliveries will be immediate, complete, and exactly convenient to each individual's needs. This has arisen not simply because people are increasingly demanding but also because so many firms *have* raised standards to very high levels.

Often, then, the best a company can hope for is to avoid causing annoyance. The CEO of Otis Elevators once remarked that the best his company could achieve was, "*to go unnoticed— the elevator arrives immediately, and moves people rapidly and quietly to the required floor.*" Utilities firms face the same problem—consumers simply assume that electricity, gas, and water arrive with no problem, and only notice these services at all when something goes wrong. In spite of heroic efforts by firms to drive positive motivation among their people, staff too may simply expect that their working lives will be smooth and trouble-free, and react only when this expectation is disappointed.

The most realistic means to portray people's feelings under such circumstances may not be to assess their positive attitudes, but rather their level of annoyance or irritation. Then, capture the process by which disappointing quality, service, or working conditions combine to raise the level of these "negative" resources. At the same time, people may be forgetting or forgiving past failures, so, if the firm stops disappointing them, their annoyance level will fall.

Consider the experiences of the many Internet retailers who were welcomed by consumers for the convenience of purchasing products at attractive prices, without the need to visit stores. These purchases were made in the full expectation (not unreasonable) that the ordered products would be available, and would be delivered reliably and quickly. In the excitement of early growth, many firms failed to appreciate how demanding it would be in practice to achieve this high-reliability order fulfillment. Even outsourcing the task to logistics specialists failed in many cases to eliminate the problem, as the chosen contractor too struggled to cope with unfamiliar and unexpected challenges.

Even when the crisis was resolved, these Internet retailers continued to face a tricky judgment. Providing a totally reliable and instantaneous service will always be unrealistically costly. Consequently, firms will need to understand the impact of service disappointments on customer-perceived quality, as well as the wider reputation among the public that results.

"Annoyance" levels and the unfortunate episodes that drive them are readily captured. Assuming first that nothing ever goes wrong, the stock of annoyance for the average customer (a negative resource) should be empty. Each problem that occurs, however, adds some annoyance and the stock starts to fill. Provided that these problems are not *too* frequent, customers will begin to forgive past failures, and the stock of annoyance will drain away at a rate that is characteristic of the particular service and customers involved. The rate of new annoyance comes into balance with the rate at which old irritations are forgotten.

An important reason for viewing customer perceptions in this way is that it can have highly nonlinear consequences. Customers put up with a background level of failure because their annoyance is not raised sufficiently for them to act. If problem frequency rises, however, their irritation may rise beyond a level that triggers action—they cease to do business with you. For example, many consumers put up with minor and occasional irritations from their banks, but if a particularly serious error or insensitive treatment arises, their patience snaps and they move their account elsewhere.

Figure 7.8 illustrates this mechanism for a new Internet retailer. The business usually manages to meet 90% of deliveries successfully (Line A—bottom chart), and the service is highly popular, so grows by word of mouth, with low customer churn (Line A—top charts). Customers are irritated by their memory of past

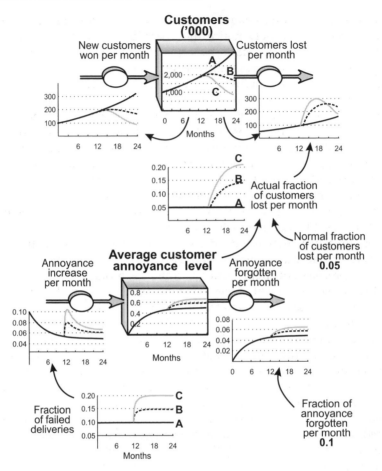

Figure 7.8 Annoyance levels for a new Internet retailer—and its consequences.

failures, but experience them sufficiently seldom that they continue to trade with the firm and recommend it to friends.

Many kinds of people jump when their annoyance has built too far!

In May 2001, Senator Jim Jeffords deserted the Republicans and gave Democrats control of the US Senate. Newspaper reports of the time explain that Jeffords was not infuriated by a single major conflict, but rather was progressively irritated by a succession of minor incidents and repeated indifference to his concerns by the White House.

If delivery failures become more common (Lines B and C), the average level of annoyance rises marginally, but just sufficiently to push customers "over the edge"—churn rates escalate, and recommendations collapse, with dire consequences for the firm's customer base and revenues.

The media and other commentators find it easy to criticize firms who encounter such difficulties, and protest that it was just "common sense" to make sure the supply system is in place and working. While it may seem careless, even incompetent, for firms to get into such difficulties, those not involved can rarely have much appreciation of the challenges involved. The UK direct savings bank, Egg (referred to in Chapter 5), carried out extensive market analysis of its potential, only to discover on opening for business that new customer acquisition rates were many times greater than its most optimistic expectation. Even when business has apparently settled down, very small changes in customer acquisition rates, or responses to marketing efforts, may be sufficient for service demand to move rapidly outside the expected range.

In some cases, it may be hopelessly impractical to provide sufficient resources to guarantee a totally reliable service at all times. Phone service and Internet service providers, restaurants, airlines, holiday companies, and many others face extraordinarily high peaks of demand, on top of a normal background rate with which they can easily cope. Such firms have no choice but to evaluate an acceptable balance point between having sufficient capacity to cope with most of the peaks, while not incurring uncompetitive costs from having vastly excessive capacity for normal trading conditions.

Note some further important points that build on the issue of customer annoyance:

- A more complete map of the Internet retailer would highlight a second highly nonlinear balance point. The delivery failure rate itself will increase sharply when business volumes move from being just within, to just beyond, the firm's logistics capacity. This will exacerbate the risk that the firm can move extremely fast from just coping to hopeless failure.

Similarly sensitive balance points arise in many contexts. In the years up to 1997, exceptionally strong economic growth in Indonesia had pushed consumer incomes of a sizable minority of people up to levels where they could afford a new family car for the first time. Market growth rates of up to 100% p.a. continued for several years. Unfortunately, the Asian economic crisis of 1997/1998 caused the country to share with others in the region a reversal in GDP and consumer spending. Although the fractional drop in incomes was actually quite modest, sales of new vehicles collapsed to a far greater degree than expected, with unit sales at the worst point running at just 20% of the previous peak monthly rate. This extreme nonlinearity reflects the sensitivity of car sales to the stock of consumers just above, vs. just below, the level of wealth where a car is affordable.

- Although customer annoyance is shown in Figure 7.8 as a simple, fixed number at any moment, there is in practice a "distribution" of annoyance among the firm's customer base—some will have been unlucky enough, or purchased often enough, to suffer more than the average number of problems, and individuals exhibit varying levels of patience with problems. This can make it difficult to detect just where the sensitive point lies, due to a continuing background rate of annoyance.

- Where possible, the solution is to track carefully the number of first-time complainers, since this indicates when the business is beginning to move into the danger zone of escalating annoyance.
- Very similar structures can capture important annoyance mechanisms among staff. Employees may tolerate occasional peaks in workload, non-routine demands, or disappointing bonuses. However, increasingly large or frequent irritations may raise overall dissatisfaction and trigger dissent, quality problems, or attrition.
- Similarly, investors (whether independent shareholders or corporate staff in multi-business firms) may tolerate small, infrequent shortfalls in business performance, but will exhibit escalating annoyance with continually disappointing results. The event triggered by this accumulation of annoyance is often the removal of the management team!

Chapter 5 described a common feature of balancing feedback structures—the potential they offer to cause "overshoot" behavior. (Service quality is initially excellent, causing new customers to be won, a process that continues beyond the point where the system is overloaded. The resulting poor service drives customers away, again beyond the point where service capacity is adequate once more.)

What that discussion did not explain, however, was how to quantify the perception-adjustment mechanism that might cause such overshoot conditions to occur. The process outlined in Figure 7.8 provides that explanation. The Internet supplier problems offer the potential for exactly such an overshoot to occur—if we were to continue the story of Cases B and C a little further, delivery performance would recover as customer numbers fall, irritation levels would drop, and growth might resume.

Resource attributes

Many tangible resources have corresponding intangible characteristics that affect their impact on the rest of the firm—staff possess experience, products possess functionality, customers bring with them the profitability they contribute to our business, and so on. To make use of these attributes, it is just as important to measure them as it is to measure the tangible items themselves. Table 7.4 offers some measures that are useful in different cases. Choice of measures will be case-specific, depending upon the influence that the attribute in question has upon *other* tangible resources. Note that a single tangible resource may have more than one important attribute, as the examples of bank loans and retail branches in Table 7.4 demonstrate.

We have already seen in Part I that managing resources is tricky, due to their accumulating behavior and interdependence. To this challenge, we must now add the problem that a change in the level of a tangible resource brings with it a change to its associated attributes—we may run out of good-quality customers, or may have to accept a drop in experience when we try to build our staff

Table 7.4 Examples of intangible attributes of tangible resources.

Sector	Tangible resource	Intangible attribute resources	Possible attribute measures
Many	Customers	Spending power	$'000/year
Many	Staff	Experience	Years
		Skill level	Fraction of tasks that can be done
Many	Products (physical or service)	Functionality	Fraction of user needs fulfilled
Many	Distributors	Market reach	Potential sales/year
Manufacturing	Production facilities	Capacity	Units/year
		Cost-efficiency	$/unit at full capacity
E-commerce	Web-site pages	Appeal to visitors	Site rating
Banking	Loans	Value	$'000
		Interest margin	Percent
		Risk	Probability of default
Retailing, hotels ...	Branches	State of repair	Index 0–1
		Catchment population	'000 people

numbers. Note too that intangible attributes may be "potential" rather than actual, and still require efforts on our part if they are to be developed. Examples in Table 7.4 include the catchment population around retail sites, who will only be won if our stores offer an attractive product range and good service.

Changes in intangible attributes can be captured by looking at how they are made up. Take for example a firm concerned that it has too many unprofitable products in its range. *(Product range proliferation is a problem in many industries, commonly resulting from a determination to reach all conceivable customer segments and hence keep increasing sales, combined with enthusiasm on the part of product develop-ment and marketing teams.)* To picture the extent of the problem, take the annual profit contributed by the most popular product alone, and add to it the contribu-tion from the second most profitable, then the third, and so on. Continuing this until the entire product range is accounted for produces a curve of cumulative revenue vs. cumulative products (Figure 7.9). Note, this is one of only *very* few graphs in this book that are not time-charts!

This picture is not just a record of the present situation, it should be used actively as a tool for management to debate and agree policy. The extent of the poor-performing product problem is visually clear, together with the average product revenue (A divided by B). Management can discuss the relative merits of pruning the product range by various degrees:

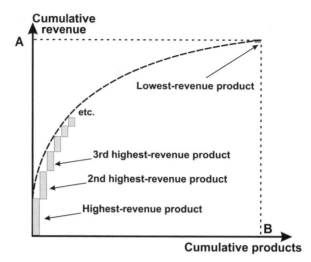

Figure 7.9   Revenue-generating profile of a product range.

- If the product range is rationalized, what reduction in support costs should be possible?
- What is the risk that removing products may cause customers to leave?
- Could we inadvertently strengthen rivals by giving them a more viable business in product types we are abandoning?
- What is the scope for replacing poorer products with better ones (i.e., more like those towards the left)?

Figure 7.9 is a powerful starting point for understanding attribute resources—it makes explicit the quality profile of a tangible resource, in this case "products". Similar attribute curves are particularly useful when they concern sources of revenue, profitability, or cost. Table 7.5, though, includes some examples of more subtle resource attributes.

Table 7.5   Intangible attributes that may exhibit a quality profile.

Tangible resource	Intangible attributes	Additional important attributes
Customers	Customer revenue	Customer profitability
Salesforce	Sales success	Customer retention performance
Production plants	Unit cost	Product quality
Staff	Experience	Productivity
Bank savers	Size of deposit	Wealth
Media audience	Viewing hours	Attractiveness to advertizers
Charity donors	Annual donations	Opinion leadership

Getting the resource-quality curve wrong can be costly

The demand for mobile telephony—anywhere, any time—can seem almost unlimited. It certainly seemed large enough to the backers of Iridium to justify investing $5bn to deploy a large fleet of low-orbit satellites. These would enable Iridium, from 1998, to offer a telephony service for travelers visiting regions beyond the reach of terrestrial cellphones. The call charges would be very high—over $5/minute—so only the most premium segment of potential users were ever likely to be won.

Rather than the half-million users expected in the first half-year, Iridium folded after just 9 months, with only 15,000 subscribers. Had the uptake been more modestly short of expectation, the growth trajectory might just have enabled Iridium to drop call charges enough to accelerate adoption and hit a point where the business architecture could be self-sustaining. But a 30-fold shortfall was never likely to be closed.

The situation is very different, though, for the newly-risen Iridium, whose assets were bought by a group of private investors for a knock-down price. The new firm needs only a tenth of the subscriber base of its predecessor, even at one-fifth of the cost per minute, to survive, pushing way to the right on the customer-quality curve.

Whilst simple attributes, like revenue by product in Figure 7.9, may be easily identified, measured, and debated, it is important to focus on the *correct* attribute for the intended purpose. Product revenue is one useful measure, but does not necessarily correlate with product *profitability*. Figure 7.10 shows this distinction, and illustrates further common features of attribute analysis:

- In many cases, the product range includes negative profit contributors—the right-hand end of the curve slopes downwards again, showing that the positive profitability of the profitable products is partly negated by the unprofitable products to the right.
- The "best" product (or customer, or salesman . . .) on one measure is often not the best on another. The largest customers, for example, often drive the hardest bargain on price, to the extent that they may even be unprofitable to serve. In the insurance and personal loans industries, the most productive salesman (in terms of new policies sold per month) often exhibits a high rate of early redemptions.
- Conversely, the "best" resources on an important measure (e.g., profitability) may not apparently be the best on a simple, gross measure. Most banks are engaged in a competitive pursuit of "high net worth individuals", because these customers have the largest potential deposits and borrowing needs on which margin can be made. But, they are also the best-informed and the most promiscuous in their use of banking, simply following the best deals from bank to bank. This can make them, far from the most valuable customers, the most costly to serve.

The shape of the curves in Figure 7.10 should not be simply accepted as given, but can often be challenged. The banking industry in most countries features a particularly unpleasant version of Figure 7.10, in that the majority of customers have long been unprofitable to serve. The Portuguese bank BCP made a dramatic assault on its local industry by transforming the shape of this curve. Having established a low-cost operation through innovation in service to higher-income customers, BCP created an ultra-low-cost banking operation

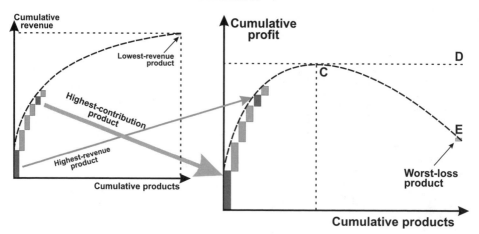

Figure 7.10 Profitability profile of a product range.

targeted specifically at lower-income people. The result was that most of the customers who were unprofitable to competitors were profitable to BCP, in effect lifting a large portion of the curve segment C–E in Figure 7.10 from downward to upward sloping.

In extreme cases, the "tail" of problem products (or customers, etc.) can completely wipe out the contribution from the profitable products, and Point E in Figure 7.10 drops below zero. Such cases are especially punishing, not simply because the business is unprofitable overall. The tail absorbs management attention, and imposes heavy and unproductive resource demands on the rest of the system. Unprofitable branches in retailing are often disproportionately costly for delivery, are often left with the least able management, and exhibit high staff turnover.

Figure 7.10 is an improvement on 7.9, but must still be handled with care. There are several reasons why it may be unwise to rationalize the business by eliminating all products to the right of Point C.

It may not be possible to cut overhead costs in line with the number of products. Eliminating all products between C and E would merely raise the overhead burden on the profitable products to the left of point C, turning some of them into losers. The curve is simply "squashed" to the left, but with the profit peak at a lower level than D.

Poor resources may be linked to good ones. Retailers may not want to give space to a product range that does not comprehensively serve their customers' needs, so suppliers have to include unprofitable products, simply to have their range accepted.

Dependencies between resource items may not be positive, however. Hiring "star" employees into an established team may demotivate existing staff and damage overall performance. Existing clients for professional service firms may switch business away if the firm takes on the clients' key rivals. New product introductions steal sales from established products, often turning a profitable item into a loss maker. Great care is needed in setting policies for new product introductions that do not inadvertently undermine an otherwise healthy business.

> Remarkably, certain firms pursue policies that appear purposely designed to bring about this damage. A famously innovative global manufacturing firm controls salesforce costs via strict head-count limits, while at the same time driving the organization to introduce new products. Whenever a new product arrives, therefore, the salesforce has no choice but to give up promoting established, profitable products to free up time for the new item. The result is a constant churn of perfectly successful products and very short product lives, sacrificing market after market to competitors who gratefully accept the gift!

*Individual resource items often **move** their position on the quality-profile curve.* Newly introduced products are commonly unprofitable, but, if well positioned against customer needs, will move to the left. Poor-performing staff may grow in stature and performance (and vice versa!), talented managers can transform low-productivity production plants into highly efficient units, and so on. Ideally, each individual resource item (each product in this case) should be tracked over its life cycle as it moves its position on the quality-profile curves in Figures 7.9 and 7.10. For a product range with any more than a handful of products, this will be a substantial task. However, so long as any manager has responsibility for a reasonable portfolio of products, it should be possible for this analysis to be carried out and constantly updated.

These cautionary points should not be overdone. It is commonly argued that customers or products are interdependent, and have great "potential", whereas in reality no such link exists and the promising potential never seems to be fulfilled. Management needs an objective assessment of the quality profile of their product range, their customer-base, their staff skills, and any other resource item important to the performance of their business system.

Since intangible factors have such an important effect on competitive advantage, evaluating the attributes of key resources as described above is vital to any assessment of changing strategic performance. This has an important implication for the *robustness* of the firm's resource system, in that loss of just a few tangible resources from the left of the curve (e.g., key customers or staff) can have devastating effects on the rest of the system. Many professional service and corporate financial service firms fear the defection of top-performing staff to rival firms. Such individuals may take high-value clients with them, along with other vital staff. In such situations, the firm's architecture needs to be designed to be robust to such losses, rather than being destroyed by them.

A framework for managing resource attributes—the "co-flow" structure

The resource system now needs a means to capture the dynamics of attribute resources, reflecting both possible *improvements* and *deterioration* in quality. Three distinct mechanisms cause attribute levels to change:

1   Direct actions and effects cause attributes to increase or decrease, without any change to the tangible resource itself. The earlier discussion of staff skills illustrates this (Figures 7.1 and 7.2)—training raises skills, while forgetting depletes skills, even if there is no change at all in personnel.

2   In addition, though, bringing in new tangibles with more of the desired attribute raises the average quality of those in the firm's available pool, while bringing in poorer-quality resources dilutes the average quality held. So, hiring unskilled people reduces average skill levels.

3   Conversely, losing tangibles that have more of the desired attribute than the average of all those currently held diminishes the average quality of those that remain, while losing poorer-quality resources leaves us with a pool that is now somewhat better. So, losing unskilled people leaves a smaller, but more skilled team.

A framework known as a "co-flow" captures this process, so-called because the inflow of the tangible resource (e.g., staff) brings with it a *connected flow* of the intangible resource (e.g., their skill). Similar effects occur in many other contexts such as the improvement in average customer size from winning big new customers or a retailer's improvement in average site quality from buying better sites than those in its current portfolio.

> A helpful way to think of an attribute builds on the idea of the tangible resource as the water in a bathtub. The intangible resource can be thought of as the temperature of that water. If your bath is half full, but too cold, it can be warmed up by adding hot water. The hotter the new water is, the less must be added to raise the average temperature. It will heat up quicker if you let out some of the cold water at the same time. Business resources have a neat characteristic that bath water does not share—you can selectively remove the coldest water (the least skilled staff, the worst accounts, the least successful products) and so leave hotter water behind!
>
> Taking this analogy further, product obsolescence, decline in customers' businesses, and staff forgetting their skills can be thought of as your bath cooling down. Management efforts, on the other hand, work like a heater directly in the bath—training to raise skill levels, product development to improve the product range, and business development to improve the profitability of an account base.

To illustrate the adjustment in attribute levels caused by the arrival of new tangible resources with a different quality from those already held, Figure 7.11 portrays a company providing computer maintenance services to businesses. The company has started successfully, winning 100 clients, each of whom has on average 80 items of equipment to maintain. However, these large clients are now all used up, so only smaller potential clients are now available, each with an average of 30 units to maintain.

The *loss* of important attributes when losing tangible resources is captured in a similar way (Figure 7.12). This time, instead of winning clients, the computer service firm is losing them. What is worse, it is the *largest* clients who are leaving—each lost client is 50% bigger (in terms of units to service) than the

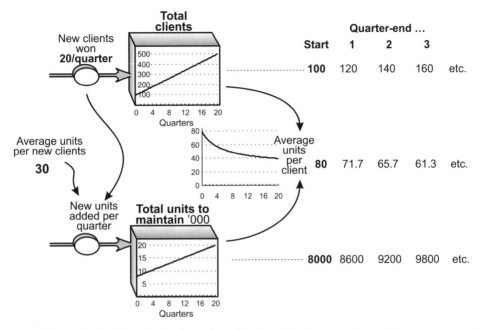

Figure 7.11 "Dilution" of average client quality in computer maintenance.

average, as can be seen by comparing the two right-hand charts. Over just 3 years, while 60% of clients are lost, *80% of business volume goes.*

The examples of attribute co-flows in this section of the chapter use average values as an approximation for the quality profile of each tangible resource. In many cases, it will be necessary to lay out the *actual* quality profile, as in Figures 7.9 and 7.10. In this way, the exact implications of alternative policy options can be worked through. A retail bank used this method in detail to trace through the revenue, margin, and cost implications of a branch rationalization program, including two key knock-on effects: (a) the likely retention rate of customers from closed branches into remaining branches, and (b) the reinforcement of customer-loss rates caused by the closure program itself.

Having set out the basic principle of attribute flows, it is now possible to work through a more complete illustration of the computer service company's strategy. This needs some additional information.

The potential market is heavily skewed, with just a few extremely large clients, a good number of substantial users, and a very large "tail" of small businesses.

The size of the largest clients, and the heavy cost of their computer maintenance, gives them considerable negotiating power, and the price/unit that the supplier can obtain is low. Medium-sized and small users are willing to pay better prices, not only because they have less bargaining power but also because they have little capability of their own.

There is a variable cost of supporting clients' installed equipment, as well as a somewhat fixed cost per client of sales and administrative effort.

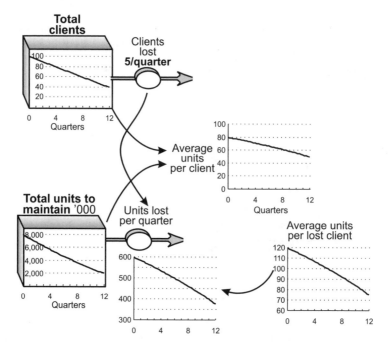

Figure 7.12 Losing clients and the quality of the client base.

To deal with the change in client quality, it is necessary to capture the revenue contribution of each client (i.e., the number of units to be maintained, multiplied by the unit price of each contract). The result is a "resource" of "total revenue $'000/year". This seems to break a basic rule of the resource-system view, that resources cannot include items from the profit and loss account. However, revenue is being used here as an indicator of client quality, so can best be thought of as "revenue-generating capacity".

The resulting resource levels and interactions are shown in Figure 7.13, with the key tangible resource—clients—in the middle stock, and the two attributes—total units to maintain and total revenue—in the stocks at bottom and top. The key policy choice that concerns us is where to focus the firm's sales effort. These policies are shown in the gray ovals—how many clients, and of what size, to add or lose. The firm's history is as follows.

The business starts out with just 50 small clients. For the first year and a half, the firm continues to pick up more small clients (bottom left chart), at good prices (mid-left chart). Profitability (not shown as yet) is poor and getting worse, since the fixed cost of client support is not covered by the low revenues and margin from the small amounts of business per client.

From Quarter 6, a new chief executive takes over, committed to taking a major piece of the market. All selling effort is switched to winning major new clients, averaging 500 units each. The effort needed is so large, and the number of potential clients of this size so few, that success is initially very limited.

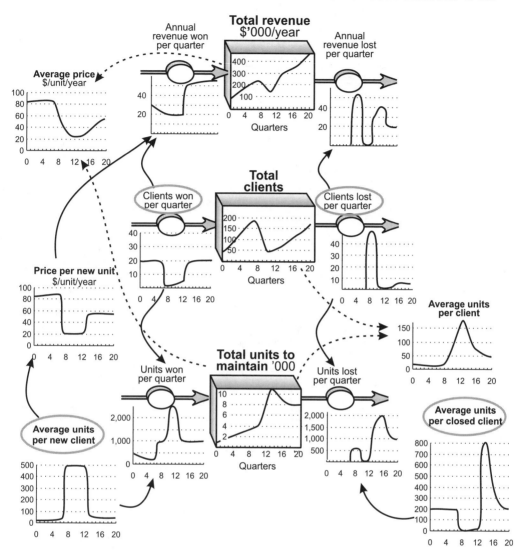

Figure 7.13 Managing client quality and profitability in computer maintenance.

However, with experience in the big league of the market, clients are soon being won more quickly—5 per quarter from Quarters 10 to 12. Note that 500 units is the *average* size, and some will be larger still.

At the same time, the smallest clients are dropped. From Quarter 7 to 10, some 50 clients per quarter are shed, averaging 10 units each.

The result is that average client size grows sharply, reaching nearly 200 units/ client by Quarter 12 (chart at middle-right).

Unfortunately, the financial consequences of this bold strategy are unattractive (Figure 7.14).

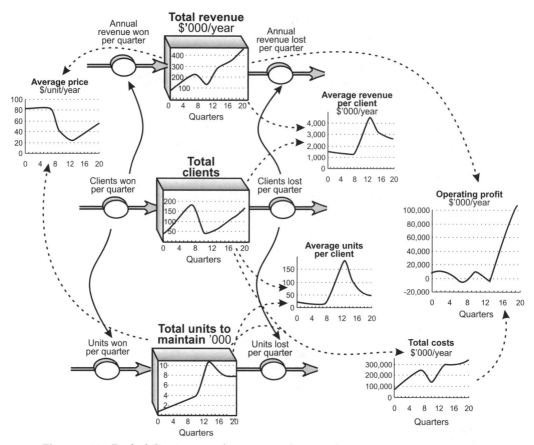

Figure 7.14 Profitability impact of managing client quality in computer maintenance.

Profitability improves from Quarters 7 to 10 as the smallest clients are dropped, leaving some mid-sized and profitable clients. From Quarters 10 to 12, however, the very low price negotiated by the largest clients now being won depresses operating margins—it is simply not possible to fulfill these contracts at a profit, in spite of the scale economies that arise.

From Quarter 12, a more balanced strategy is adopted—see Figure 7.13 again.

Sales effort is switched to mid-sized clients (average 50 units each). The firm's recent success in taking the largest clients gives it credibility with mid-sized firms, and sales success is strong, bringing in 20 clients each quarter.

At the same time, the very largest clients are "lost" to competitors. This is a progressive process, with just 2 very large clients being sacrificed first, then followed by further clients who are not quite so large.

The financial outcome (Figure 7.14) is that average contract prices recover (leftmost chart), average client size and revenue both dissipate, but total revenues continue to grow ahead of costs. The result is rapidly improving operating profits.

Changing expectations

Executives face a further challenge in trying to manage intangible factors—the target moves! The functionality offered by a product or service is a common illustration of this effect. When introducing new products and services, firms struggle to provide sufficient functionality to make them useful enough for customers to buy. As usage rises, suppliers compete by "improving" their offering—increasing its functionality by adding to the sheer number of features included in the product or service (Table 7.6).

If a supplier chooses *not* to take part in this improvement process, their once-exemplary product becomes merely average, and then obsolete. They would be left behind, not because their offering has actually become worse, but because customers' expectations have risen. This happens for two related reasons:

- users become accustomed to what is currently offered; and
- suppliers seek constantly to rise above their rivals by offering more benefits in their product or service.

This process eventually runs out of momentum. There is a limit to how many features customers can benefit from in any product or service, and there comes a point where adding a new feature does nothing useful for the majority of users. Nevertheless, in the battle to be seen to offer an advantage, firms continue to add features, often well beyond the limit of what is useful to customers. Consumer electronics devices and office software both illustrate how far this process can be pushed—both product categories now offering functionality that is far in excess of the ability of most customers to use, or even understand.

This development of product functionality, the raising of customer expectations, and the inevitable limits that the process faces need to be understood if the evolution of sales and profitability over product life cycles are to be managed. The steps in the process are as follows:

1 *Identify the list of features, elements, or functions that combine to make the product or service useful*, in order of importance (i.e., starting with those that are

Table 7.6 Basic and extended benefits for selected products and services.

Product/service	Basic benefits	Extended benefits
Video recorders	*Record and playback*	Timer recording, program indexing
Mobile phones	*Reliable calling, number store*	Voicemail, three-way calls, games
Word-processing software	*Text editing, spell checking, autosave*	Mail merge, outlining, revision tracking
IT services	*Data-processing outsourcing, application development*	Business process redesign, strategy development

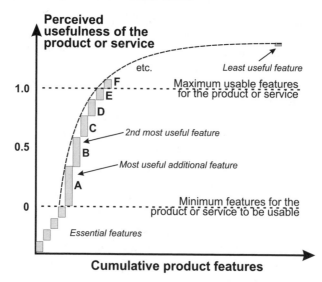

Figure 7.15 Limited usefulness of product features.

crucial to retaining the users' interest, and ending with those that are merely "nice to have" or superfluous to many potential users).

2   *Assess the overall usefulness that customers would perceive from a product or service possessing a smaller or larger set of these features* (Figure 7.15). This perceived usefulness will vary between different individual customers. It may be necessary to repeat the exercise across several contrasting customer segments, each with their own characteristic mix of needs (e.g. business users vs. young consumers, in the case of mobile phones). If this segmentation is necessary in your case, focus first on completing the exercise for a dominant segment, and only later move on to adapt the findings for other segments.

3   *Identify the features of your own product and service,* and so place yourself on the customers' scale of usefulness *relative to competing suppliers.* Competing products may not offer the same range of incremental features (i.e., you may offer features A, B, D, and E, while a competing product offers A, B, C, and F. Figure 7.15 can still be used to evaluate the comparative usefulness of rival products).

4   *Estimate the rate at which rivals, and you, are advancing the features offered,* and assess how customers are changing their view of the usefulness of the product or service:

- note that the "required minimum" might be moving (e.g., a mobile phone with no voicemail was once acceptable, but is no longer);
- the maximum features with which customers can cope may also be advancing (e.g., web-browser functionality today offers features that

early users would not have found useful, due to the lack of related services);

- consequently, customers' perceptions of the relative attractiveness of your product or service will be changing (typically declining), even though its actual features remain the same.

5   *Use this picture of comparative features and perceived usefulness to evaluate the pace of product development that you should be adopting.* Customers typically do not view features and usefulness in isolation from price. Their view of product usefulness should therefore be compared with pricing to assess the value for money that rival products are felt to offer.

In the following example of a consumer electronics product (Figure 7.16), we are engaged in a race to win the potential customers we expect will find the new product useful (bottom chart). Market research has told us that, without a minimum of four specific features, no one will find the product useful. Our product-development efforts make progress in raising the product's features, so we come to market with a usable product in Quarter 12.

We continue to add features to the product, so, from Quarter 13, we offer more than customers expect (leftmost chart). This excess of features vs. expectations means that they perceive the available product to be more useful than they thought. The more features we add, ahead of customers' expectations, the more useful the product is felt to be and more of the potential user base buy our newer products. (The perceived usefulness shown at upper right is, strictly, an accumulating stock, but it responds sufficiently fast to rising features that this representation is safe.)

We continue to push more features into the product, but, by Quarter 32, users see little extra benefit in the additional functionality. Since the market offers products with just about everything customers could want, the undeveloped pool of potential customers is empty.

Adding other practical considerations to the dynamic played out in Figure 7.16 raises important issues for strategy:

- The timing of product development efforts is critical—if there were rivals in this scenario, and they had come to market earlier or raised product functionality faster than us, the potential customer pool would be empty before we could get started.
- Note the importance here of upgrade sales. Long after the potential market has been developed, we continue to enjoy sales to users who are upgrading.
- This illustration has shown the consequence of user expectations lagging behind what is actually available. In some cases (e.g., PC operating systems), customers expect *more* than is offered, and don't bother to upgrade until they hear that the product offers still more features. In extreme cases, like motorcycle marketing, buyers are so motivated by new features that they hold off buying in the expectation of still-better products to be released in the future. This has led to customers ignoring whole generations of machines.

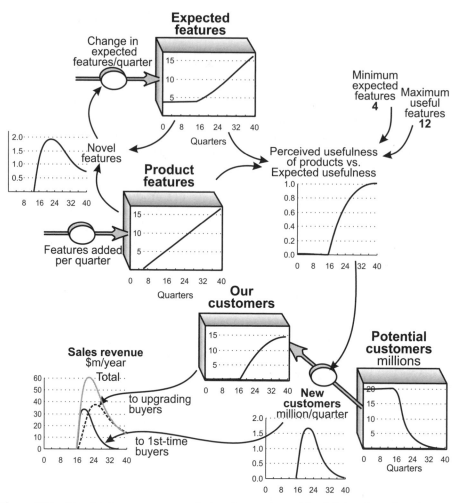

Figure 7.16 Developing a consumer electronics market with additional product features.

- To reflect the different expectations of different user segments, Figure 7.16 can be repeated. For example, the air travel industry sought for decades to serve a perceived increase in customer needs by adding service features. However, for certain large segments, nothing more than the most basic service elements were wanted (and at an appropriate price point!). It is not sufficient, though, even in this apparently simple case, to assert "low-cost, no-frills". Airport convenience, flight times and frequencies, and range of destinations remain important features of the service.
- The cost and risk of product development imposes an imperative to extract high sales volumes from each product generation, before it becomes obsolete and is discontinued. In the halcyon days before PCs, when mainframe computers ruled, IBM were masters of this process, announcing new

product families, but continually supporting major customers. Since the new products promised radical increases in data-processing potential, users purchased substantial new capacity of the *old* product generation in anticipation of the new needs they would soon be able to satisfy.

Finally, note that similar "feature-development" mechanisms may affect any group whose feelings impinge upon the performance of the firm's strategic architecture. Employees have constantly-changing expectations of rewards and working conditions, and management can either exceed or fall short of those expectations. These expectations too evolve over time, in response to what is commonly available, either from the firm itself or from other employers. It is also possible to offer benefits that staff do not value, including many that become fashionable from time to time. For example, while many employees like to be "empowered" to take responsibility for important decisions, others do not, preferring to be told what is expected. Firms that add this "feature" to employment conditions can find staff satisfaction falling, while they thought they were changing employees' lives for the better.

Integrating intangible resources into the strategic architecture

Chapter 6 described a systematic process for identifying resources, capturing their behavior, creating an integrated picture of the core business architecture, and explaining the resulting business performance. Without intangible resources, however, that process could not achieve more than a rough first cut at explaining business performance. The process for generating the strategic architecture therefore needs to be extended to encompass the vital intangibles.

It is not generally practical or helpful, however, to attempt to add every intangible item to the architecture and produce a "monster" map of the entire system. It is more helpful to start by isolating and operationalizing the small pieces of important structure. Some of the examples in this chapter have already indicated how this is done (e.g., Figures 7.8 and 7.14), but the following steps should ensure that the most important elements are properly dealt with:

1 *Identify indirect resources.* Review the original resource list (Chapter 2), and check that relevant indirect resources have been included. Remember that any group of people may hold feelings, attitudes, or perceptions that influence gains or losses of other resources, so check the *tangible* items on the list and question whether any indirect resource may be driving those flows. Customers and staff are the groups most commonly found to possess attitudes involved in driving strategic performance, but investors, suppliers, dealers, co-suppliers, and other business partners also feature in certain cases.

2 *Map the structure and time-path information that captures how these indirect resources are behaving.* Figures 7.2 and 7.3 show how change drivers for an

indirect resource are captured, and the lower part of Figure 7.8 provides an example where negative perceptions are important.

3 *Make the connections that show how these indirect factors drive gains and losses of other resources* (Figure 7.8, upper section).

4 *Identify resource attributes.* Reviewing the original resource list (Chapter 2) and core architecture, question whether each tangible item possesses any important attributes (Table 7.4). "Important" implies that an attribute makes a significant difference, either to the strength of influence on other resource flows or else to the financial performance. Define a clear measurement for the attribute.

5 *Map the structure and time-path information that captures how each resource attribute is behaving.* Figures 7.11 and 7.12 show how this is done. Take care to ensure that all important influences on the attribute are included—gaining or losing resources with a different quality from the current stock, as well as direct changes to the attribute itself. Also make sure to include both the effects of deliberate managerial actions and the impact of forces over which management has little or no control.

6 *Make the connections that show how these resource attributes affect the rest of the system.* Figures 7.13 and 7.14 give an example of this step.

7 *Adjust the core architecture (Chapter 6) to reflect both indirect and attribute resources.* In cases that are not too complex, it may be possible to redraw the core architecture to include the new structures explicitly. In more complex cases, it may be necessary to keep separate the small pieces of structure produced in Steps 2, 3, 5, and 6, and include in the core architecture only the time-path changes that these substructures generate.

An example structure—professional services

The performance of professional service firms is strongly affected by intangible factors—staff experience, reputation, and so on. Figure 7.17 illustrates the core architecture of tangible resources for such a firm. (Similar structures apply to many support functions within larger firms like IT services, especially where such departments have to "win" business from operating divisions.)

The basic relationship between staff capacity and the organization's client base arises through workload and staff pressure. If there are too few staff to cope with the workload from clients, work quality suffers and clients are lost. The key management policies (shown as gray and italics) concern hiring, firing, and promotion of staff, together with efforts to win and lose clients. (This is only the heart of the system, remember. Many additional concerns such as target client groups, sale of follow-on work, range of services, and knowledge building can be added.)

The firm makes money from fee income minus costs, of which salary-related staff costs are the dominant item. Appropriate measures for the other items in the architecture might include:

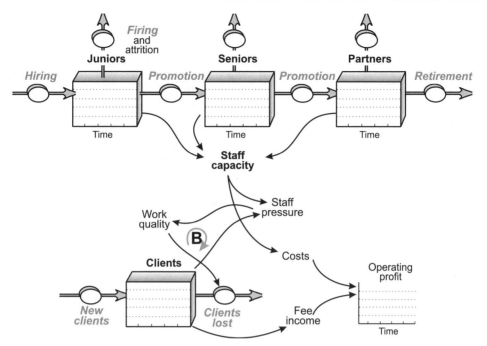

Figure 7.17 Core architecture for a professional service organization.

- "staff capacity"—maximum number of client projects that can be handled simultaneously;
- "staff pressure"—working hours per week vs. accepted ideal;
- "work quality"—typically, this is assessed by an internal post-completion review, but ideally this should be backed up by client assessment.

A more thorough version of this structure would examine the capacity of each staff group separately. This becomes necessary because juniors, seniors, and partners fulfill different roles in professional firms. The workload from the client base would also need to be split among these groups to arrive at a view of the specific "staff pressure" affecting each seniority level.

An important link not shown in Figure 7.17, which may arise in certain cases, concerns the close relationship between clients and individual professionals within the firm. Especially where the advice is qualitative, rather than analytical, clients can become devoted to their one trusted advisor. Consequently, in sectors such as public relations and advertizing, firms are vulnerable to loss of clients when key professionals leave (a causal link would be added, between partner attrition and client loss).

The first intangible we can add is a common example of an attribute "co-flow"—the experience that the professionals themselves carry with them. This is most simply measured in years. (Years of experience clearly do not equate directly with skill. Technical expertise and process skills such as management of

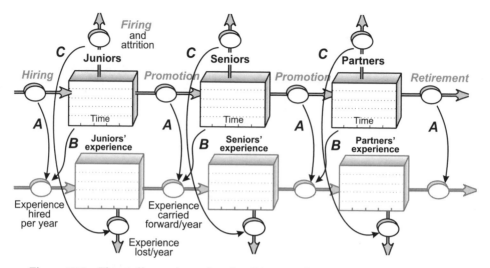

Figure 7.18   The staff experience "co-flow" in a professional service organization.

projects, clients or colleagues may change as experience grows, but ideally these should be defined and evaluated explicitly.)

The experience of each staff group is affected by four factors (Figure 7.18):

- individual professionals bring their experience with them when they are hired, or join a new grade (Link A);
- experience is lost from a grade when staff are promoted, but is added to the next grade up (Link A);
- experience builds simply as a result of time passing (i.e., the resource accumulates), even with no inflows or outflows of people (Link B);
- finally, experience is lost when individuals leave, or are fired (Link C).

For the simple case of tracking average years' experience (or "tenure"), most firms should have good data. However, it is not so common for such firms to track the average *total* experience (i.e., including time before they were hired).

Figure 7.19 shows the firm's architecture with the staff experience chain added. The impact of this change on the rest of the system is to revise the assessment of the work capacity of the total staff population—capacity is reduced if professionals in any group have less experience than is normal for their grade. This might arise, for example, from too rapid hiring or promotion, or from unexpectedly high attrition.

Finally, two indirect resources may be important—the morale of the staff and the firm's reputation in the market in which it operates.

Typically, professional staff tolerate quite high levels of pressure, provided these do not continue for too long. However, extended periods of overwork gradually "grind people down". This may most immediately affect staff

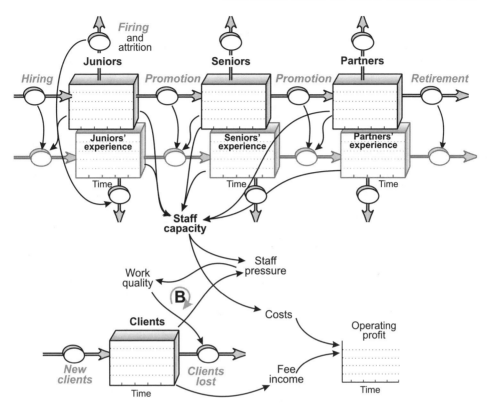

Figure 7.19 Adding staff experience to the architecture of a professional service firm.

capacity, but has the more insidious effect of raising attrition rates as staff leave for positions with more reasonable workloads.

Note that the impact of work pressure on morale is not exclusively negative—highly-motivated staff expect a degree of pressure, and become bored and frustrated if they do not feel their career offers a challenge. Consequently, care is necessary to ensure that changes in morale are properly reflecting what is going on, rather than simply assuming that "more pressure leads to falling morale".

Reputation rises or falls as word gets around in the market about the quality of work the firm carries out. The speed with which this takes place depends on the industry and the particular work, projects, or clients involved—a high-profile success for a well-known client can boost the reputation of its advisor substantially. Equally, a substantial and public failure can quickly damage a firm's reputation. Reputation then affects the firm's ability both to win new clients and to hire good staff. Newly-qualified MBAs, lawyers, accountants, etc. all know which firms have the strongest reputation for their chosen career path.

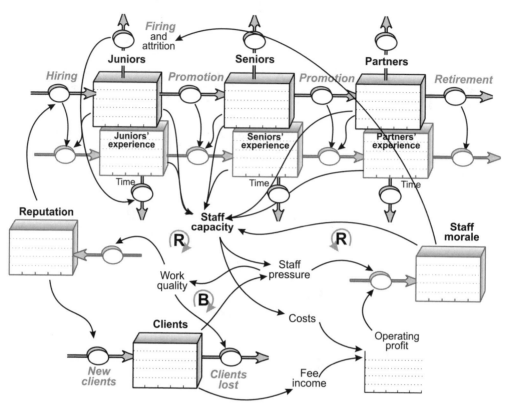

Figure 7.20 Adding indirect resources to the architecture of a professional service organization.

Note, by the way, that the small structure at bottom left of Figure 7.20 concerning work quality, reputation, and the client base is extremely common. Similar structures arise in many cases, not just professional service firms:

- imbalances in the business create pressure on staff, infrastructure, or other resources crucial to delivering products or services, which damages the immediate quality of work or service;
- this has a relatively rapid effect of making customer losses happen more quickly;
- the indirect consequence is to damage reputation, which makes customer acquisition more difficult or slower.

The key observation here is that only *current* customers can have any experience of the current quality of work. *Prospective* customers have no first-hand experience of this quality, so can only be influenced by what they hear through the firm's reputation.

Summary

Intangible factors have a powerful impact on business performance over time, by affecting strongly the rates at which tangible resources are won or lost.

Since intangible factors have such a strong impact on performance, it is essential to define and measure them clearly, and to track how their values change over time.

Indirect resources reflect the perceptions and attitudes of key participants in the business system—the feelings of staff and customers are most common, but investors, suppliers, dealers, and business partners may also be important.

Attribute resources are the second intangible category, reflecting important qualities of tangible items. Gains and losses of tangible resources always carry with them gains and losses of these attributes, just as water entering or leaving a bathtub carries its temperature with it. Attributes may also change directly, with no change to the quantity of tangible resource.

Time delays arise where indirect resources or other perceptions by key people adjust in response to changing realities. These time delays may obstruct managerial efforts to make improvements (e.g., when service quality increases go unrecognized) and may also store up trouble for the future. It is therefore important to track such perceptions, and act to influence them.

Certain intangibles may be "negative" resources (e.g., reflecting some irritation or annoyance among customers, investors, staff, or others). These negative resources hold down the rate at which the organization can build other resources or cause other damage. More seriously, they can reach tolerance levels where substantial behavior changes are triggered by what seem quite small events.

The core strategic architecture for the business, built up as described in Chapter 6, can be adjusted by adding the structures and time-path behavior caused by key intangible factors.

8

Into Battle—the Dynamics of Rivalry

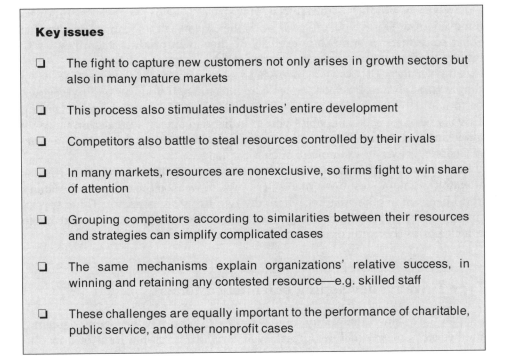

Key issues

❏ The fight to capture new customers not only arises in growth sectors but also in many mature markets

❏ This process also stimulates industries' entire development

❏ Competitors also battle to steal resources controlled by their rivals

❏ In many markets, resources are nonexclusive, so firms fight to win share of attention

❏ Grouping competitors according to similarities between their resources and strategies can simplify complicated cases

❏ The same mechanisms explain organizations' relative success, in winning and retaining any contested resource—e.g. skilled staff

❏ These challenges are equally important to the performance of charitable, public service, and other nonprofit cases

Chapters 1–7 have shown how executives face a constant challenge to build and retain resources over time, if they are to deliver continually improving earnings or other performance objectives. They are generally not alone in this effort, though, and struggle to accomplish these aims against others who are just as determined. From this point of view, competition is as relevant to nonprofit organizations as to commercial firms—charities must win donors, just as airlines must win passengers.

All rivalry processes can be captured by just three dynamic structures, each applying not only to customers but also to other resources that may be scarce and fought over such as staff and sources of supply. The three forms of rivalry are:

1   the race to develop potential resources (e.g., winning first-time buyers);

2   the tug of war to switch resources away from competitors and to prevent the reverse; and

3   the struggle to win a share of attention from customers and other resources that may be shared with competitors.

These mechanisms imply a specific development of the underlying theory, which is discussed briefly in the Appendix.

These three mechanisms frequently operate simultaneously. For example, in fast-moving consumer goods, competitors rush to win new consumers whenever a new type of product is introduced, and strive to have competitors' products removed from stores and replaced with their own. If they cannot ensure that either consumers or stores buy exclusively their own product, then they try to capture more share of purchase than their rivals.

A further form of rivalry also arises in certain special situations—namely, a simple effort to wreck rivals' strategic architectures. If you can build your own performance by assembling a strongly integrated set of resources, understanding a rival's resource system enables you to inflict damage on *their* performance by unpicking that system. The pharmaceuticals rivalry case, introduced at the start of Chapter 1, was an example of such a challenge.

In extreme cases, firms may launch such wrecking attacks with no particular attention to gaining resources themselves (e.g., to weaken the competitor's ability to do battle in another market where the two firms *do* compete). These special circumstances are quite rare, though—organizations nearly always have scope to benefit positively from competitors' failures, and strive to do so.

Type 1 rivalry: developing potential customers

Chapter 3 explained that many finite resources can only be grown by depleting another stock of *potential* resources. Type 1 rivalry takes the form of a race to drain this stock of potential customers faster than rivals. Potential customers flow into a developed customer base for each rival.

The Chinese mobile telecommunications market has been the fastest growing and potentially largest market in the world. With a population of 1,300 million, it is not surprising that mobile subscribers had by late 2000, already reached 60 million, growing at 2 million per month. China Mobile and China Unicom were the dominant providers at that time, though China Telecom (the dominant fixed-line operator) planned to enter the market, with many other potential rivals eagerly seeking entry. With just two players in place, rivalry was a relatively simple, if desperate race to win new subscribers first, in the hope that, once captured, these customers could be persuaded to stick with their first provider.

Consider the challenge facing either of the two service providers early in this process of market development. On the one hand, there is a huge potential demand, so capturing any substantial share should be extremely lucrative. On the other hand, your competitor will be chasing the same opportunity and, if you fall behind, they may gain such an advantage that your longer-term position will

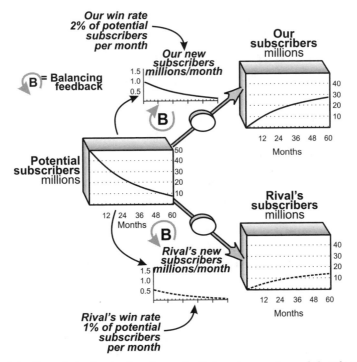

Figure 8.1 Type 1 rivalry to develop potential customers in mobile telecoms.

be untenable. (The limited granting of operating licenses clearly constrains the number of directions from which a challenge will arise, but a smaller number of rivals may just mean that each will be stronger.)

Assume, for now, that there exists an initial fixed number of only 50 million consumers who would find a mobile phone service attractive and realistically accessible. These potential subscribers will sign up to a provider if:

- the expected price is attractive;
- the supplier has a reasonable reputation;
- they are made interested by the supplier's marketing; and
- they have the opportunity to join the service, through retail stores, call centers, or other channels.

Figure 8.1 shows this process playing out over time, with our firm being better, overall, on these measures—we win 2% of the potential customer base each month, while our rival wins only 1%. Chapter 3 explained in detail the process of depleting a stock of potential resource, and Figure 8.1 now shows how this process operates when rivals are "fishing in the same pond". Depleting the potential pool creates balancing feedback, imposing limits to growth on both firms and ultimately stopping progress altogether.

This first scenario reflects some strong simplifying assumptions—for example, that network capacity and coverage can be provided quickly enough to serve this burgeoning demand, and that retail distribution of handsets and service sales is in place. However, it already raises important observations:

- Since the stock of resource (customers) determines performance, and this stock can only be influenced via the rate of flow from the potential pool, *competitive outcomes depend upon the relative win rates*—the fraction of the potential customer pool each rival wins in each time period.
- The initial rate at which the customer base is developed can be rapid, but slows as the potential pool is depleted. This unavoidable effect is often ignored in strategic plans—firms commonly assume they can win customers at a constant rate until the market is used up. In practice, development rates often slow down still more quickly, since the most amenable customers are taken up first. Suppliers of WAP phone handsets such as Nokia and Ericsson suffered this fate during 2000/2001, when an initial flurry of interest from keen gadget buyers gave way to much slower sales among consumers who found the functionality disappointing.
- Growth of the rival's customer base depends not only on its own success but also upon *our* win rate. Capturing customers quickly not only builds our own resources but also denies them to rivals.

The Type 1 rivalry structure provides some dynamic precision for the much misunderstood concept of *first-mover advantage*. Our accumulating customer base by, say, Month 24 already gives us 16 million subscribers "in the bank". If our rival at that point makes strenuous efforts and raises their win rate, not just to match our own, but to *double* that rate (i.e., 4% per month), they still barely catch us, in spite of a short-term outstanding jump in the rate of customer acquisitions (Figure 8.2). The loser in this early race then faces further disadvantages, notably from the switching costs that will obstruct the efforts of later rivals to steal customers from their first choice of supplier.

The scale of this single-resource first-mover advantage substantially understates the full impact of the benefit. The additional subscriber base acquired during the first 2 years will, through contributing to cash flow, channel growth, and other resource developments, further enhance the overall strength of our resource system. Conversely, the practical constraints noted earlier, concerning provision of retail distribution and network capacity, will work to slow the rate at which either rival can develop.

Developing potential customers

A large assumption behind this first example of Type 1 rivalry was the fixed number of 50 million potential subscribers. This is not, of course, realistic. The potential pool itself will grow to some extent, driven by operators' collective marketing efforts, external factors like economic development, and a variety of feedback mechanisms (e.g., word of mouth).

It is important to clarify exactly what is meant by "potential" resources. Consumers or other customers typically move through a chain of development

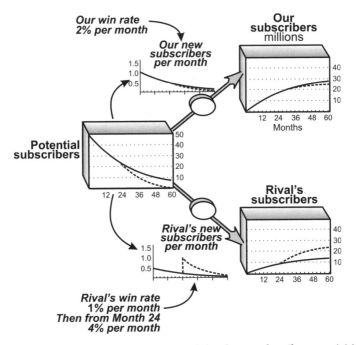

Figure 8.2 First-mover advantage in mobile phone subscriber acquisition.

(e.g., from unaware to aware, to understanding, to actively seeking to buy, to active, to loyal). The precise character of customers in each of these stages, and how they are detected, will vary from case to case. So, for example, the behavior of people actively considering a new car purchase will be very different from the shopper thinking whether to buy a can of beans. Rigorous market analysis methods should, therefore, be applied to determine these customer characteristics accurately. (*Customers do not actually "move" at all, of course, but change from one behavior pattern to another. Nevertheless, it is helpful to think in these terms to focus on the key flow rates [i.e., the number of people per time period who are changing their behavior from one mode to another]*).

For the case of Chinese mobile telecoms, the 50 million "potential" customers can be defined as the number of people who are actively considering purchase at this moment, as evidenced by them reading advertizements for phones, or talking about mobile phones with friends.

Where does *this* stock of potential customers come from? The source can best be conceived of as "those people who might ever, feasibly, become customers", given current demographic, economic, and other conditions. This suggests we take the entire population, minus small children, minus many of the elderly, and minus the fraction who would never be likely to afford a phone. Interestingly, this stock too is changing. Demographic changes such as lower birth rates and longer life expectancy will bring new people into the stock and remove them at a

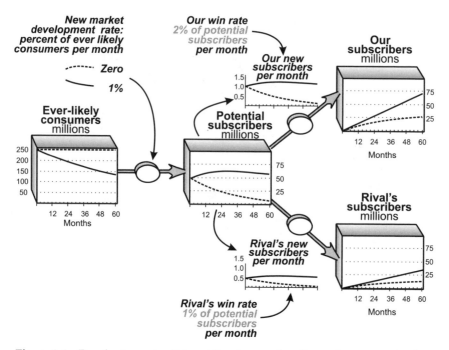

Figure 8.3 Developing potential mobile phone subscribers—impact on rivalry.

changing rate, increasing consumer wealth will bring down the fraction of people who could not conceivably afford a mobile phone, and reducing prices for phones and calls will also lower the threshold. For simplicity, though, assume for now a fixed pool of consumers "ever likely" to buy a phone—say, 250 million.

Figure 8.3 shows the consequences for rivalry in market development if just 1% of this "ever likely" pool turns into active "potential subscribers" and our two firms compete as before. A number of points emerge from this scenario:

- gradual conversion of the "ever likely" pool of subscribers sustains the potential subscriber base (over this timescale), even though both rivals are constantly capturing them;
- our competitor may think they are doing fine, with a constant win rate, but in fact are falling further and further behind.

To this core structure can be added the impact of marketing, price, and exogenous factors affecting the emerging rivalry in Chinese telecoms. However, before expanding this example, a generic framework for Type 1 rivalry can be developed.

Generic framework for Type 1 rivalry

First, the exploitation of a potential resource by each competitor is driven principally by marketing and the relative value offered. To this must be added the self-limiting constraint posed by the finite scale of the potential pool itself, which creates a balancing limit to the exploitation rates of all competitors (Figure 8.4). Note that this figure shows the development of customers for several rivals, in the form of multiple flows for *"rivals' new customer rates"* and multiple stocks for *"rivals' customers"*.

In addition, there is the possibility of reinforcing growth, driven by word-of-mouth mechanisms. Finally, customers' costs of taking up the product or service may constitute a barrier, slowing the rate of uptake. Many Chinese consumers may be able to afford some rate of monthly expenditure on mobile phone calls, but they will not become active subscribers unless they can afford the handset and connection charges.

Note that the same principles in Figure 8.4 will apply to any contested resource, notably staff, but also, for example, to advertizers, dealers, or partners. For each such group, marketing may be carried out, a trade-off will be made between the cost and value of dealing with each rival, those involved will consider the costs and risks of joining one of the rivals seeking their attention, and word-of-mouth mechanisms will arise.

"Relative value" in customer development is a balance between price and functionality (see Chapter 7 for discussion of functionality). It may be tempting

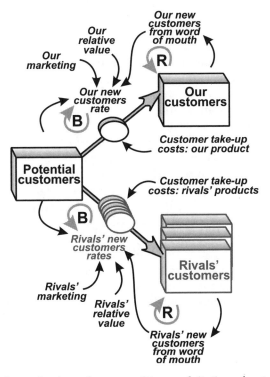

Figure 8.4 Generic mechanisms for competitive exploitation of potential resources.

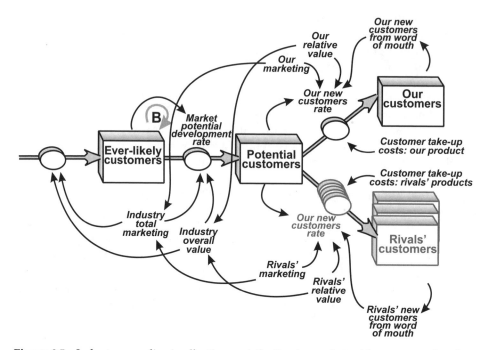

Figure 8.5 Industry suppliers' collective contribution to market-wide customer development.

to use a simple ratio between functionality and price as the driver of customer-acquisition rates. However, this is rarely realistic. Customers take up products because the *scale* of benefit is attractive, given the price. It is therefore more reliable to evaluate how much the product or service is worth to them, then look at the difference between this amount and the price. *(For a full treatment of this issue, see established marketing texts on value-based pricing.)*

The concept of "relative value" has parallels in developing other potential resources. Potential new hires are attracted to an industry by a trade-off between expected career prospects, job interest, salaries, other benefits, the effort to gain entry, and so on. Potential advertizers are won to new channels by a trade-off between the cost of advertizing in that channel and expected reach and impact on the target market.

Competitors' collective efforts to build their own resource base will have the side-effect, whether deliberate or accidental, of developing potential resources (Figure 8.5). The most immediate effect will be to turn ever-likely resources (customers, staff, etc.) into available potential resources. Note that another self-limiting mechanism will constrain this growth, as the ever-likely pool itself is drained.

It is generally feasible to assess the reach and impact of rivals' collective marketing efforts on the rate at which new customers are developed. *"Industry overall value"*, though, needs careful treatment—it is almost certainly *not* an average of the value offered by all competing suppliers. Customer-development rates are more commonly driven by the *most attractive* product or service on offer—or something close to the most attractive, allowing for the possibility that not all customers will be aware of the best that is available. This gap may be particularly wide when functionality and price are changing quickly— potential customers may constantly hold an outdated view of what is available. To understand accurately the impact of industry overall value on the development of potential customers, then, needs careful use of market research.

Again, there are parallels for development of resources other than customers— awareness of career opportunities and potential reward will swing new trainees toward choosing the educational path that will take them toward a newly attractive sector. Potential business partners, too, may be fought over. Such partners will awaken to the possibility of new revenue streams they might gain by joining forces with competing service providers—a powerful example in recent years being the development of extensive business partnerships forged by enterprise resource planning (ERP) software providers like SAP.

Figure 8.5 shows the further possibility, as discussed for the Chinese mobile phone market, of an industry's collective efforts causing the growth of new customers ever likely to be available. A simple example of this effect arises in the PC market where, until recent years, large fractions of the population would not have classed themselves as "ever likely" to find such products useful. But, the combination of growing online services, improved usability, and tumbling prices have switched on the possibility that whole segments of consumers might one day be persuaded to consider purchasing a PC.

Finally, there is the possibility of industry-wide word-of-mouth and other growth effects (Figure 8.6). Simply put, the more customers already exist for a general category of product or service, the more new customers become aware and actively consider taking it on. Similarly, increasing awareness converts people or businesses who had never before been likely users into at least considering themselves as not being excluded.

To this internal industry growth mechanism must be added the influence of exogenous forces. These are conventionally divided into four—political, economic, social, and technological (so-called PEST analysis). While these factors are often considered by firms in evaluating industry opportunities, the framework being developed here makes possible a rigorous, fact-based evaluation of the scale and pace at which they may drive change:

- Political changes can open up entire industries—clear examples in the last couple of decades being privatization and deregulation. A particular case concerns the increasing approval of drugs for over-the-counter (OTC) sale, rather than prescription only, a change that is gradually altering consumers' perceptions that they might one day purchase OTC rather than visiting their doctor.
- Economic changes constantly bring new customer groups into existence. The entire infocoms sector (telecoms, information services, and media) is developing worldwide at a rate determined by economic development. Poor

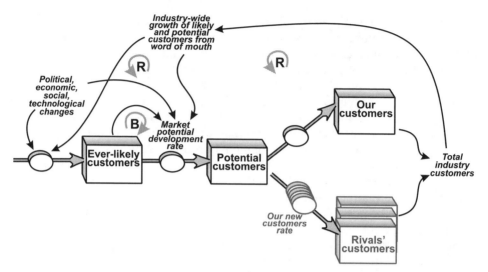

Figure 8.6 Adding reinforcing growth mechanisms to market-wide resource development.

consumers in many countries, who were previously unlikely ever to take up such products and services, find themselves able to do so as GDP and consumer incomes rise. Again, it is quite possible to measure these effects and track their progress through time.

- Social changes too drive the migration of consumers, employees, and others into and out of the likely, potential, and actual resource base of different industries. Rising education standards create an increasing pool of potential trainees for many new industries, ageing populations create new markets for services to the elderly, and so on. For example, the Brazilian aircraft maker Embraer enjoys a dominant position as a career-path for skilled young engineers—a stream of talent stimulated by high and rising education levels.

- Technological progress is largely manifest in two dynamics—the changing feasible functionality of products and services offered, and the reducing unit cost of offering them. Consumer electronic products are perhaps the most obvious case, where industry-wide progress makes products possible that most consumers would never have considered just a few years earlier, and at increasingly affordable prices.

Figure 8.7 brings together the structures discussed thus far into a single, generic architecture for industry-wide customer development.

Illustration of industry-wide development

We are now in a position to consider the effect of actions and decisions taken by the rival suppliers on how the Chinese mobile telecoms market develops. Each

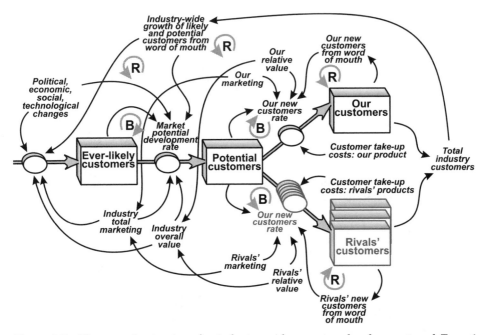

Figure 8.7 The generic structure for industry-wide resource-development and Type 1 rivalry.

competitor seeks to win potential subscribers into their currently active subscriber base, using marketing and price as the principal weapons. Retail distribution through stores will also be important, but is ignored for now—we assume that all suppliers have sufficient retail presence to enable the consumers they attract actually to subscribe to their service.

If a given rate of marketing spend reaches a certain fraction of potential customers, then the *number* of potential customers considering each rival's service is constrained by the size of the potential pool. The perceived value of each alternative then determines the proportion of those people deciding to take up the service. If both operators are believed to offer essentially similar levels and standards of service, this perceived value is largely a comparison between the price charged and the expected price. Detailed analysis of information emerging from the evolving market provides reasonably confident relationships like those illustrated in Figure 8.8.

Figures 8.9 and 8.10 show how the evolution of pricing alone operates through the generic mechanisms described above:

- take-up costs for the service are assumed to be insignificant, so that subscriber acquisition is sensitive only to usage price and marketing;
- marketing spend by rivals is taken to be constant, and modest, so that the dynamics are driven exclusively by changes in usage tariffs;
- as the rival services are launched, some 50 million consumers are expected to find the service affordable (250 million additional consumers might one day

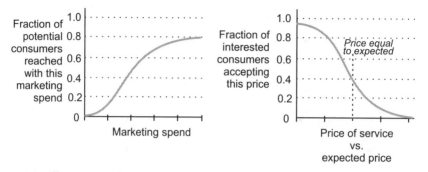

Figure 8.8 Illustrative relationships between price, marketing, and consumer take-up in emerging mobile telecoms markets.

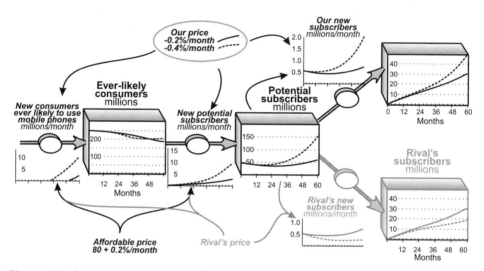

Figure 8.9 Impact on market development and Type 1 rivalry of competitive price reductions.

find a mobile phone service accessible, and industry price reductions progressively bring the service within their reach);

- both rivals offer an initial tariff that costs subscribers Yuan100/month (approx. $12) at typical usage rates, but each pursues price reductions in an effort to both develop and exploit the potential subscriber base;

- as operators cut prices, subscribers adjust their expectation of monthly usage costs, so that if either supplier lags too far behind in price reductions, their acquisition of new subscribers slows down or stops. *(The details of this adjustment in expectations follows principles described in Chapter 7.)*

In the first scenario (solid lines), both service providers cut prices at an average

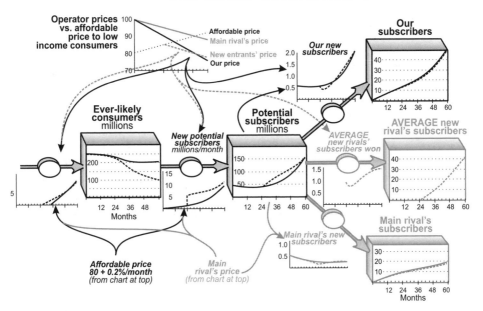

Figure 8.10 Impact on market development and Type 1 rivalry of aggressively price competitive new rivals.

rate of 0.2% per month. The potential market is progressively used up by both suppliers, but the service remains beyond the reach of the remaining population. The two suppliers achieve equal progress, winning some 30 million subscribers each over 5 years.

In the second scenario (dashed lines), our firm reduces prices at 0.4% per month, so that, by Year 5, we are offering a service costing under Yuan65 per month for a typical user. This aggressive price reduction has several veffects:

- As described earlier, we rapidly draw ahead of our rival in attracting the potential consumers.
- Our price reductions drive down consumers' *expected* price, so that our competitor, although reducing prices as before, no longer manages to win consumers so quickly.
- Our price reductions also open up the market to a rapidly emerging new group of potential subscribers. The discontinuity is so great that new consumers begin to consider buying a mobile phone much more quickly than the two operators actually win them.
- Furthermore, by Year 5, the price reductions, together with increasing wealth as the economy develops, bring the service within reach of some of the poorer population who would not previously have been thought of as a feasible market.

Finally, the example can be extended to show multi-firm rivalry. The Chinese regulatory authorities were considering the issue of licenses to additional operators in 2001. As is common in many markets, this event would trigger entry by several new rivals, at least one of whom could be expected to use aggressive price reductions to drive subscriber acquisition.

Figure 8.10 shows how this scenario might play out if three new operators were to enter in Month 24 with tariffs that imply an average monthly cost of 85 Yuan to the average subscriber. Our own firm has, as in the latest scenario, been reducing prices faster than the main rival, but this new entrant price is a further 5 Yuan per month below our own current charges, and within reach of many new potential subscribers. The new scenario (dashed lines) also assumes that this low-priced entry is so costly that the new entrants cannot maintain such a deep discount, and fail to match our reducing price trend. *(Note that the subscriber acquisition rate and subscriber stock in Figure 8.10 are shown for the average rival—these items should be multiplied by the number of new entrants to arrive at reconciled totals.)*

Compared with the previous case (solid lines), key features of the new scenario are as follows:

- The new rivals immediately start attracting a flood of new subscribers from the existing potential pool.
- This rapid acquisition rate would fall sharply as the potential pool is depleted, but their bold pricing also triggers a rapid inflow of new potential subscribers.
- They also initiate an earlier growth of new likely consumers during the period when their pricing first brings the cost of mobile phone use within reach of poorer people. The faster development rate of potential consumers causes, paradoxically, the ever-likely pool to be drained to a lower level than in the previous cases. However, this reflects the plausible possibility that the attractive prices now on offer cause consumers to actively seek a phone as soon as they can afford one. *(Similar effects have been observed in developed markets as mobile phone prices have come within reach of younger consumers—as soon as they could afford one, they actively sought to subscribe, usually by exerting pressure on parents!)*

Neither of the two former operators suffers unduly from this new entry, as compared with their previous performance. The new entrants stimulate roughly as many new subscribers as they capture. However, note that this is not much of an achievement for the main rival, who was already losing out to our own firm with its more aggressive pricing schedule, and now falls behind the new entrants too.

Extending the telecoms industry dynamics

This exploration of an evolving telecoms market describes a clean illustration of Type 1 rivalry dynamics, driven by changes in a single factor—price. Naturally, a complete analysis of industry evolution in this case would require important additional mechanisms to be added. For example:

- *Increasing usage*. As prices fall, not only will customer acquisition accelerate but usage by *existing* subscribers will also grow (call-minutes per person per month). As in other mobile phone markets, this will be a major effect.

- *Tariff structure*. Complex issues arise in the choices that rivals must make about monthly charges, usage tariffs, initial contract charges, and handset subsidies. There is no "right" answer to these dilemmas, only better or worse responses to specific situations—a market's development will emerge as consumers respond to the relative appeal of the options offered. The Italian market, for example, led the way in growth of prepaid services. However, this arose, not so much because Italian consumers were vastly more interested in this payment method than consumers in any other country, but because one supplier decided to launch and promote the scheme. The strong appeal of this option to key consumer groups then left rivals with little choice but to join in, creating strong reinforcing growth for prepayment at the expense of alternatives.

- *Revenue opportunity*. Total usage (billion call-minutes per month) is, with price, the critical revenue driver. Together with the economies of scale available as the networks and their usage develop, this will strongly affect the price reduction policies of competing suppliers. It is only to be expected, then, that the imperative to build a customer base and revenue stream in such situations has frequently driven industry prices down so strongly that positive returns are difficult or impossible to achieve.

- *Marketing*. The discussion of generic Type 1 rivalry mechanisms highlighted the powerful role that competitors' marketing expenditures can play, not only to capture customers themselves but also to drive potential demand. The analysis of pricing effects demonstrated in Figure 8.9 can be repeated to assess the likely scale and timing of marketing effects.

- *Retail availability*. Where independent retail stores exist for sale of handsets and service contracts, a Type 1 rivalry dynamic will occur for acquiring retail distribution. A service provider will win independent retailers to its service if it offers an attractive "price" (i.e., the margin to stores on each contract it sells), if its marketing promises to grow end-user demand and if its successful sales rate confirms to retailers that they would do well to offer the provider's service. Three additional factors arise, however. First, retailers may offer the services of several providers—in this case, Type 3 rivalry will arise, as rival operators fight to have these shared retailers push one service at the expense of others. Second, even where independent retailers promote only one service, they may be persuaded to switch from one provider to another, if, for example, their early choice happens to be to go with a service provider who fails to build a strong market share. This is an example of Type 2 rivalry. Finally, depending on regulatory conditions, service providers may be free to build their own retail network—in which case, Type 1 rivalry arises once more, but now as a race to acquire the most attractive store locations.

- *Capacity*. While all these mechanisms are complicating the demand-side goals and policy choices of rival service providers, they must also pay attention to correct scale and pacing of investment on the supply side. This concerns not just the rate at which they build the network to extend geographic coverage and capacity but also the provision of customer support, billing systems, and other infrastructure.
- *Subscriber churn*. Following on from the previous point, rivals will have to pay close attention to subscriber churn, caused either because their own service provision is inadequate or because rivals offer better alternatives and change consumers' expectations. (See Chapter 5 for advice on how to evaluate the risk of self-inflicted customer churn and on developing sound responses.)
- *Rivals' policies*. Finally, it will be necessary to complete the analysis with understanding of the policy structure being followed by rivals. Each firm will be taking a view on its own probable success in building a customer base, demand, and revenues, comparing this against the costs of supporting this level of provision, and deciding on its best policy for investment rates, pricing, and marketing efforts.

Limits to rational analysis

We have built up a nicely logical, analytical "method" for plotting out what happens over time as markets develop. But, this impression of certainty is misleading. Particularly in novel markets, the development rate will be highly uncertain, possibly ranging across several orders of magnitude. Who would have expected, for example, on the day the first Pokémon cards were distributed that the market would build to the extent it did.

Nevertheless, the structural understanding described above remains invaluable, as shown by the launch of Swap-it-Shop, a second-hand market for children's unwanted games. At the same time as Swap-it-Shop was launching, several competing online services for children were in the early stages of development, so the business faced the likelihood of intensive rivalry to win and retain a user base among a notoriously fickle consumer group.

The business concept for Swap-it-Shop is simple—children become bored or grow out of games, toys, music, books, and other items, often quite quickly. At the same time, they crave new items that they either cannot afford to buy or cannot find. Swap-it-Shop was an online, virtual market with its own currency ("Swap-its") that children could use to bid for items they want. They acquired Swap-its from snack packets, as well as from auctioning their own items.

Prior to launch, this opportunity faced considerable uncertainty. How many children would find the service appealing, how frequently would they trade, would they lapse from the service quickly or slowly, and so on? Answers to these questions were critical, for a host of reasons, including how much "currency" of Swap-its to put into the market, how much warehousing capacity to construct and how much marketing to do. Pre-launch research and analysis gave only a limited indication of possible scale and timing (e.g., only children with Web access were likely to take part, and the number, and rate of change in this number, were reasonably well understood).

The crucial role of the frameworks, however, was to provide a focus for the information gathering that followed launch of the service. As soon as trading started, flow rates of children through the system commenced, the impact of the various drivers affecting those flow rates could be assessed, and appropriate marketing and operational policy changes implemented. All this happened extremely fast, over a period of just a few weeks, but the clarity of the structure enabled strategy to be adjusted with equal speed. Unfortunately, the emerging information showed both that the win-rate of children was modest and that churn-rates would be high. This at least alerted the firm to the dangers of gros over-investment that destroyed other e-business start-ups.

Type 1 rivalry in mature markets

Before moving on to discuss other rivalry mechanisms, it is important to note that Type 1 rivalry is not only of critical concern when new markets are emerging. Wherever new customers are coming into existence, the same battle will arise to capture their attention for the first time. This clearly arises in all consumer markets as each year's age cohort comes onto the marketing radar screen for rival suppliers of goods and services. Each year brings a new tranche of babies wanting their first shoes, teenagers opening their first bank account, young adults buying their first electrical durables, middle-aged people wanting new types of holiday, and elderly people needing care services for the first time.

A further cause for Type 1 rivalry to recur is the possibility that competitors may not succeed in holding on to those customers they initially win. Although direct switching of customers between rivals is properly captured by the Type 2 mechanism described below, customers can instead re-enter the "potential" category—disillusioned phone users, for example, have commonly given up a disappointing service, and thought about which alternative to take up instead. During this reflection period, they are just as amenable to being fought over by rivals as first-time subscribers.

Customer recycling rates, or churn, differs markedly between sectors. For example, while mobile phone subscriber churn rates of 20–40% per year are common, many online clothing suppliers have had to grapple with churn rates of 80–90% per year! Clearly, such differences have important implications for marketing strategies, since the firm that first manages to hold the churn rate down to 60% will enjoy a substantial advantage.

Only where no new customers are likely to emerge will Type 1 rivalry be absent. This may apply to many business-to-business markets, where well-known products and services are supplied to large, long-established buyers.

Examples include the sale of components to car manufacturers, the supply of paint pigments, the provision of tankers to oil producers, and so on. Even in such cases, however, the possibility of Type 1 rivalry may *still* arise whenever a new type of product or service is developed. This has occurred, for example, when anti-lock braking, safety air bags, and other innovations have been introduced to the car industry, then again as satellite navigation systems were introduced, and so on. In all such cases, the generic structures for Type 1 rivalry should be applied if the scale and pace of market development and competitive outcomes are to be understood.

One-time purchases

For durable goods such as fridges and TVs, as well as for certain other purchases, like major holidays, the idea of a "customer base" may not seem relevant. In business-to-business markets too, certain purchases may be so infrequent as to be essentially one-off in character. Examples include the purchase of major construction projects (like petrochemical plants) or office-relocation services.

In such cases, as explained in Chapter 3, revenues arise predominantly from the *flow* of new customers per period, rather than from purchasing frequency by the *stock* of established customers. It may still be important, nevertheless, to construct the framework for Type 1 rivalry, treating the customer base instead as an "installed base" of customers whose one-off purchase decision was in favor of your product, rather than rivals':

- First, you may continue to enjoy revenues from sale of related goods and services. So, anticipating the development rate of your own and rivals' installed base is vital to any understanding of these revenue streams.
- Second, replacement and upgrade opportunities arise from the installed base previously created. Customers effectively re-enter the "potential" pool, but with ready-made perceptions regarding the original supplier. Once again, then, future purchase rates can only be understood if the scale and character of our own and rivals' installed customer base is known.
- Finally, an installed based contributes to powerful word-of-mouth, reputation, and other system effects. For example, in petrochemical plants, power plants, and other construction projects, contractors who win early sales gain reference sites that demonstrate their ability to deliver high-performing facilities quickly and cost-effectively. In addition, they obtain learning benefits that enable them to perform still better on subsequent projects.

A further example of reinforcing growth mechanisms arising from an installed base concerns consumer durables. One-off sales of fridges, TVs, and so on create an installed base who may recommend the product to others. Perhaps more importantly, however, these sales motivate dealers to allocate more space to the supplier of the more popular models (Type 3 rivalry). The greater sales revenue may also provide additional marketing resources, leading to greater success in capturing later customers. Lastly, a good experience with a certain product may last long enough that consumers choose the same supplier's model when they come to replace the item.

Type 2 rivalry: capturing rivals' customers

As markets develop, a second rivalry mechanism comes into play—the *switching* of established customers between rivals. This struggle is a tug of war, in which each firm tries to pull customers out of their rivals' system and into their own. This mechanism can be illustrated by the intensely competitive market for the supply of vehicle fleets to large customers (e.g., distribution firms purchasing trucks, rental firms purchasing cars, and large companies acquiring vehicles for employees' business use).

There are often strong reasons to concentrate the purchasing of such fleets with a single supplier, including better prices and efficiencies in maintenance. Initially, therefore, we can consider the battle between rival vehicle producers as a simple effort to make customers switch—fleet buyers either purchase our vehicles or someone else's. (*The example could be extended to cover nonexclusive purchase by adding the Type 3 rivalry structures described later in this chapter.*) Consider a simple case:

- Just two vehicle suppliers are engaged in this rivalry (e.g., because they are the only firms offering the particular class of vehicles required).
- There are 200 equally-sized companies using fleets of 1,000 vehicles, which they keep for 2 years. Each therefore buys 500 vehicles per year at an average price of $15,000. No new customers are entering the market and none are leaving.
- A key factor in purchasers' decision-making is the cost per mile that they will incur in using the vehicles (fuel usage, maintenance costs, insurance, resale value, and so on). This class of vehicles costs in the region of $0.80/mile to operate, and they cover about 40,000 miles per year, so annual fleet operating costs are approximately $32m.
- In their efforts to win contracts, each rival tries to show that their vehicles are the most economical to operate, by improving reliability, fuel consumption, resale values, and so on. Contracts typically last for at least a year. Customers incur switching costs of $0.2m when they change suppliers (e.g., setting up new maintenance arrangements). However, even when savings exceed these switching costs, only a fraction of customers can be persuaded to switch each month (Figure 8.11), due to the efforts of the existing supplier's salesforce, and the time it takes for the salesforce with the advantage to get in touch with customers.

Figure 8.12 shows the dynamics of this Type 2 rivalry between two vehicle suppliers. We start with 80 of the market's 200 customers, but, in a recent innovation, the competitor has cut its vehicle's costs per mile to $0.80/mile (dashed line on bottom-left chart), vs. our vehicle's $0.83/mile. This gives

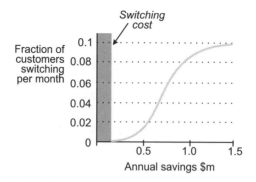

Figure 8.11 Vehicle-fleet customer-switching rate vs. annual cost savings.

customers a potential cost saving of $1.2m/year, so we are losing a large fraction (10%) of our current customers each month.

However, our production engineering efforts are reducing the customers' operating costs by 0.3 cents/mile per month for our vehicle, vs. 0.1 cents for the competitor. Although it takes a full year for us to eliminate the cost disadvantage of our vehicle completely, our customer loss rate nevertheless falls sharply, for two reasons. First, as the potential saving to customers reduces, our salesforce finds it easier to dissuade customers from switching. Second,

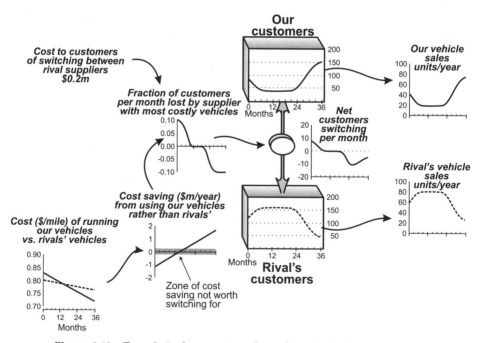

Figure 8.12 Type 2 rivalry as a tug of war for vehicle-fleet customers.

there are simply fewer customers left for our competitor to capture, making it increasingly likely that only the least easily persuaded customers remain.

For the next year, there is so little to choose between the two suppliers' vehicles that no customers can be persuaded to switch. *(It is more likely, in practise, that there will continue to be a small rate of switching in both directions.)* Thereafter, as our vehicle's cost advantage starts to widen, we manage to capture customers back from the competitor at an increasingly rapid rate.

This example illustrates certain common features of Type 2 rivalry:

- the progressive nature of customer switching is very common, with switching rates accelerating as the customer benefits move further and further ahead of switching costs;
- the "residue" of hard-to-persuade customers, too, is a common feature in many markets;
- There is a "path dependency" in the outcome of this case and comparable situations. Had we been just 6 months later in improving our vehicles' operating costs, the competitor would have captured so much of the market, and had time to continue improving its vehicle, that we would never have caught them.

Industry-level switching

Equivalent mechanisms arise at the level of entire industries, and become most evident when shocks occur. For example, car-buyers have been subjected to the shock of sharp increases in gasoline prices on several occasions (e.g., 1973, 1979, and 2000). Such shocks cause short-term changes in behavior, like reduced travel. Switching to alternative means of transport may also arise, when the framework illustrated in Figure 8.12 can again be applied. However, these effects are rather modest.

Certain longer-term effects are more significant, though difficult to unravel. Substantial changes in price, cost of usage, or functionality not only cause short-term responses but trigger switching behavior that may continue for some time. The gasoline price increases just mentioned caused car owners to change to more fuel-efficient models. But, this is not an instant change, occurring over several years as car owners come to replace their vehicles. This process is properly captured by a structure similar to Figure 8.12, with a stock of *"owners of less fuel-efficient vehicles"* migrating to a stock of *"owners of more fuel-efficient vehicles"*. The flow rate is driven by the relative usage costs of the two classes of vehicle, and constrained by switching costs and time of ownership.

Since fuel consumption is not only a function of current travel habits but also depends on the profile of the whole industry's fleet of active vehicles, this is the only means of accurately accounting for changes in gasoline sales over time.

The emergence of new resources and obsolescence of others can overcome even large obstacles to switching

The market for hand-held games consoles has for many years provided a fascinating arena for watching competitive dynamics play out—and promises to continue doing so! Early pioneers like Atari have faded into legend, and even recent winners such as Sega and Nintendo have fallen from leadership.

At first sight, it looks like network effects should make it easy for leaders to stay ahead. An established base of users has built up, at considerable cost, a stock of popular games that they can exchange and discuss with friends. Retailers are highly motivated to stock and promote the most popular platform and its games. Developers have strong incentives to commit to further game development for the largest potential market. However, powerful obsolescence effects make this system more fragile than it looks.

First, technological advance imposes obsolescence on the simple functionality of both the consoles and the games. On top of this comes the psychological process of obsolescence in the appeal of both individual games and the suite available for the platform. (Long-lived popular titles are rare.) Next comes the games developers' incentive to seek new opportunities to leverage their expertise. Retailers too are eager to find incremental revenues from new offerings, so store-distribution and shelf-space resources cannot be relied on to be sustained.

Finally, it is easy to mistake the rather distinctive user group of games players as an established market, in which Type 2 rivalry will dominate. Getting players to switch platforms seems to be the key. However, this ignores the powerful effect of demographics. Each year a new generation of gamers emerges. If the average player stays an active user of hand-held games for 10 years, then 10% of the new market emerges each year. At the same time, 10% of tired older players retire themselves, and mostly retire their equipment to the loft as they leave. A newcomer like Xbox, then, has the chance to win a place among a very large uncommitted market each year.

One-time competitive opportunities

A common consequence of such industry-wide switching behavior is the phenomenon of one-time opportunity. Deregulating markets in utilities such as water and electricity have provided many such cases. Incumbent firms often inherit inefficient assets, while new entrants are free to start up new, low-cost facilities. This enables newcomers to achieve a quick switch of price-sensitive customers. However, later entrants are unable to repeat this achievement—even if they can offer further price reductions, the remaining scope for saving has narrowed to be less than customers' switching cost, and much of the market remains in the hands of the early entrants, even though they are no longer the lowest-cost providers.

Figure 8.13 illustrates this phenomenon for an electricity market, where an incumbent supplier starts with 1 million consumers, paying a price that produces an average bill of \$400/year at typical consumption rates. Although this supplier is racing to reduce prices—by \$20/year for the average consumer—a new entrant in Year 2 starts offering prices of only \$320/year, and continues to reduce charges by \$15/year. This first entrant captures some 300,000 consumers during Years 2 to 4, but further progress stalls, as the average consumer's saving approaches their switching cost.

In Year 4, a second entrant starts offering prices equivalent to \$280/year (and falling). This is sufficient to capture a few more of the original supplier's consumers, but note that Rival 2 wins no business from Rival 1—the saving is too small vs. consumers' switching costs.

The second, third, and subsequent entrants inevitably face increasing diffi-

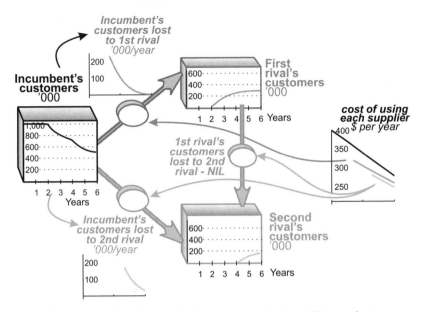

Figure 8.13 One-time switching opportunity in utility markets.

culty in finding ever-greater cost savings. In addition, they face substantial entry costs, not only in establishing the capacity to supply but also in marketing their proposition. It is therefore unsurprising that many new entrants have found the opening up of previously regulated markets to offer only a brief glimmer of commercial opportunity, while others who tried to enter have failed and withdrawn. The 2001 power crisis in California, when large parts of the state experienced frequent power outages, shows serious consequences of regulatory regimes that misunderstand this structure and its consequences for firm behavior.

Regulatory and technological changes are opening up competition in many markets (e.g., airlines, telecoms, and energy). When such changes occur, new entrants can start to take customers by offering significant price or functionality advantages vs. incumbents. However, it is much harder for other entrants or retaliating incumbents to offer sufficient *further* benefits to incentivize more switching, and the window of opportunity closes.

The framework in Figure 8.13 thus offers insight into the scale and timing of the one-time opportunity offered by sudden shifts. It also enables established firms to explore the nature, scale, and duration of countermoves that might keep the window closed. Many executives imagine that aggressive pre-emption is appropriate like cutting prices to below the expected entry price of new rivals. However, not only is this highly costly it is often unnecessary as well.

Game theory is commonly used to evaluate the retaliatory moves of rivals, a technique that requires estimation of the future cash flows each competitor can expect from a given strategy. These future cash flows, though, depend on the likely customer switching, which, as we have seen, will be a dynamic process

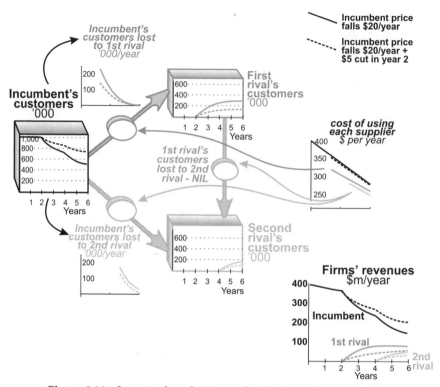

Figure 8.14 Impact of modest incumbent price cut on new entry.

rather than a one-off event. Consequently, it may not be necessary for an incumbent firm to pre-empt fully an attacker's expected price move, merely to narrow the gap sufficiently to deter a proportion of potential switching.

Figure 8.14 illustrates this point by repeating the electricity example, but (dashed lines) with the incumbent reducing price by just 1.3% in Year 2, cutting customers' average bills by $5/year at that point. This small cut brings the average customer's savings from switching closer to their switching costs. Consequently, customer loss rates are markedly reduced, with the first rival accumulating barely half the customer base of its original achievement.

The financial implications are also substantial (bottom chart). The incumbent's retention of customers is so great that it more than makes up for the cost of the price cut. Year 6 revenues are improved by some $60m/year.

Multiple competitors in Type 2 rivalry

As for Type 1 rivalry, it will often be necessary to understand customer switching among more than two or three competitors. Figure 8.15 shows a generic framework to deal with this more common challenge.

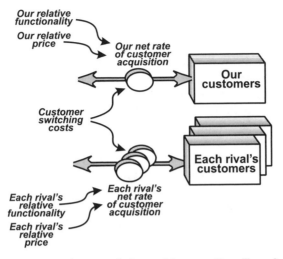

Figure 8.15   Generic framework for multi-competitor, Type 2 rivalry.

As in the case of Type 1 rivalry, net gains and losses of customers among the various rivals must be conserved. Where there are many rivals, a large number of inter-firm pairings occur. However, this need not cause severe difficulties. First, the principal rates of customer switching that are of concern generally arise in respect of one or two particularly powerful or aggressive rivals. Second, rivals can often be treated safely as a group. For example, established firms in certain retail sectors have suffered attacks from "category-busters"—new entrants with a particularly strong consumer proposition and powerful expansion plans such as Toys-R-Us, Staples, and so on. Any existing rival store chain will be predominantly affected by customer switching to that new rival, and may safely treat customer switching to and from local independent stores as a group. The use of firm groups to simplify rivalry will be discussed later in this chapter.

Type 3 rivalry: competing for sales to shared customers

Type 1 and Type 2 rivalry capture competitive dynamics adequately in cases where customers commit exclusively to one supplier at a time (e.g., consumers rarely buy utilities from several firms at once). Even where conditions exist that may make it possible for them to share their trade among suppliers, few tend to do so. Regulatory changes have offered telecoms users in some markets the opportunity to choose between alternative carriers for each call that they make. However, the clear advantage of using one particular service, plus the inconvenience of repeated choice for trivial savings, have combined to leave most consumers committed to a single supplier. Where consumers do use more than one fixed-line service, many still tend to commit totally to a single supplier for local calls, and a second supplier for long distance.

In business-to-business markets too, it makes sense for firms to acquire some categories of product or service from a single supplier. The high cost of taking on enterprise-resource-planning (ERP) software solutions, combined with the need for integrated information management, makes it most unusual for firms to adopt more than a single solution. Volume-discount considerations also motivate single-source buying for many more services such as logistics, cleaning and security services, even stationery supplies. In all such cases, the structures for Type 1 rivalry and/or Type 2 will capture adequately the competitive dynamics.

In many markets, though, consumers and businesses alike allocate their buying among two or more suppliers. In these cases, rivals are fighting for a larger *share* of sales to customers who purchase from several suppliers:

- producers of fast-moving consumer goods (FMCG) such as food, drink, and cleaning materials frequently compete for sales to consumers who sustain a portfolio of brands from which they choose;
- business purchases of raw materials are frequently sourced from multiple suppliers in order to sustain competition between rival providers, to ensure security of supply, or for geographic and other practical considerations;
- newspapers compete for share of expenditures from advertizers, who allocate their spend among several papers and among several alternative channels. For TV broadcasters, Type 3 rivalry arises for share of viewer time. A channel's success in winning share of viewing hours determines how attractive the channel is considered by advertizers. Conversely, advertizing revenues fund the quality of programming, which drives the share of viewing hours. We therefore have mutual interdependence between Type 3 rivalry for two distinct resources.

Type 3 rivalry often occurs in combination with Types 1 and 2, but its structure is most clearly illustrated with a customer base that is both static and completely shared. The appeal of rival products does not now cause customers to switch, but instead determines the rate of sales each rival enjoys (Figure 8.16).

Since *"our sales"* in Figure 8.16 result directly from the number of shared customers, their normal purchase rate, and the price, marketing, and attractiveness of our product, there does not seem to be much scope for dynamic complexity to arise. (*Remember that the curved arrows mean that items are simply and instantly calculated from others—so a change in price, for example, would instantly result in a change in our sales to the shared customers.*) However, several mechanisms commonly occur to make even this simple structure exhibit complex behavior over time:

- First, the stock of shared customers, itself, accumulates and depletes.
- Second, since this customer group is already shared, there is little friction to slow the switching of purchases among the active suppliers. While one might

Figure 8.16 Winning sales to a shared customer base.

hope that this would make it easy to persuade customers to favor one supplier over another, the very ease of this switching causes suppliers to expend considerable efforts to hold on to their share of customer purchases.

- Third, the sales that arise for any supplier to this shared customer base create cash-flow and other resource-building effects that can change their ability to compete for a still-larger share of business.

The supply of fast-moving consumer goods (FMCGs) is a particularly familiar process that features Type 3 rivalry. The development of consumer interest in products is a somewhat more complex process than the structure described in Chapter 4, where we assumed consumers were either simply "interested" in the product or not. In reality, consumers' interest and active purchase of products develops through a series of stages (Figure 8.17). Though these stages vary in detail between different cases, they are broadly as follows:

- The first challenge is to move people from being *unaware* to being *aware* that the product exists. Classically, this is the role of simple, relatively low-cost, mass advertizing.
- The next problem is to move consumers to the third stage, where they *understand* what is being offered—not just the product's functional purpose but also its connection to their lifestyles and values. This requires more sophisticated, costly advertizing, designed to communicate particular messages about the product to particular groups of people with particular needs.
- Consumers must then be tempted to try the product. Promotional trial offers fulfill this purpose. If this effort succeeds, and consumers continue to buy, they have been moved into the fourth stage on Figure 8.17—disloyals. Their first time of purchase is the event that moves them through the flow from

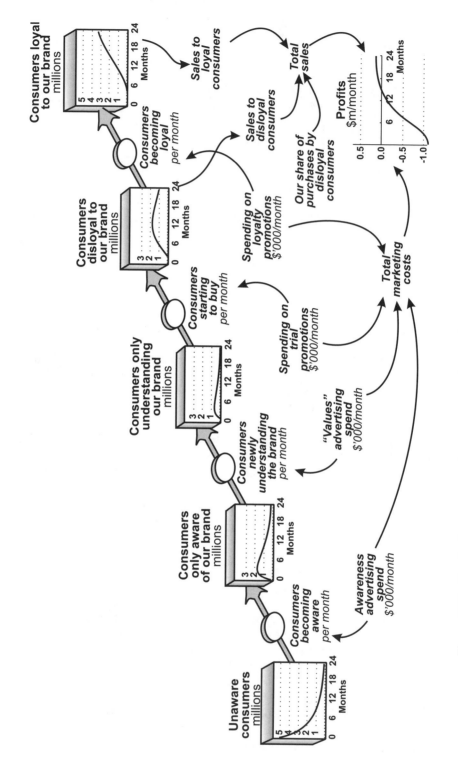

Figure 8.17 Developing consumers' awareness, understanding, purchase, and loyalty for products.

Stage 3 (understanding) to 4. So, if the trial fails, a consumer falls back immediately into Stage 3.

● Finally, consumers are encouraged to move on to the highest stage, becoming loyal to the brand, by which is meant that they will always seek the brand in preference to its rivals. Here, continued values advertising and loyalty promotions are key weapons, not only for moving consumers into the final, loyal stage but also keeping them there once they have been won.

In tackling the challenge described in Figure 8.17, the supplier is fighting against forces that are constantly pushing consumers back down the chain. Not only might a loyal consumer become disloyal, and start using rival products again, but disloyals may stop buying altogether as well—perhaps becoming loyal to a rival, or removing our brand from their portfolio of choices. Consumers may cease to understand the brand, slipping back from Stage 3 to 2, either because their needs or values change, or because the brand itself alters in the values it is seen to offer. *(This may be unintentional on the part of the brand-owner, as, for example, when BMW cars came to be popular with drug-dealers in certain cities.)*

The marketing chain in employment

It is becoming increasingly clear that the development chain for individuals' interest and choice of action, depicted in Figure 8.17, arises in more widespread situations than first thought. Work by McKinsey & Co. on the "war for talent" to capture and retain skilled staff, for example, recognizes that firms must effectively "market" their job opportunities to potential employees. Furthermore, these marketing efforts must also be directed toward *existing* staff in order constantly to reinforce the benefits of staying with the firm. (Doman *et al.*, 2000 and other articles on "talent" at www.mckinseyquarterly.com)

In most cases, the "disloyal" employment category does not apply, in the sense that skilled staff are working simultaneously for more than one firm. However, the disloyal category still exists, though in a different form. In this case, disloyals are those employees who are not totally committed to their current situation, and could readily be tempted to move (e.g., they typically browse job ads). Loyal staff are committed to staying where they are. Note that such loyalty may not always be for positive reasons (e.g., staff who fear they have little alternative but to stay where they are, due to high unemployment levels).

Finally, consumers may lose their awareness of the brand, not in the sense that they forget having heard of it, but simply that it does not occur to them to mention it in their set of known products (so-called unprompted awareness). There is only so much attention that anyone can give to named products and services, and it is hardly surprising that new names can only push their way into consumers' heads at the expense of others that are forgotten.

Many new e-business services fell into the trap of assuming simply that, by committing huge quantities of advertising spend, their audience would remember them, know what they offered, understand what they stood for, and become loyal customers. In the event, consumers only had mind space for one or two new providers in any sector, and, once these places were taken, later providers had little chance to attract attention. It is all the more remarkable then that many incumbent firms too decided to adopt names for their e-services that were completely disconnected from the long-established understanding that they had built among consumers. Presumably, many feared that the stock of negative emotions around their brands risked putting off the more with-it new consumers they hoped to attract. However, as is apparent from Figure 8.17, it is impossible to move people on to the "understanding" stock unless they are first "aware", so it is astonishing to observe that so many firms, and their highly-paid professional advisors, decided to ignore this hurdle and attempt the monumental task of creating a whole new mind space for their e-services.

It is mostly around the fourth stock that Type 3 rivalry plays out. These disloyal consumers are, by definition, sharing their purchases among several alternative products, and, with low costs of switching, can be moved frequently between them. Unless the brand-owner is highly successful in moving people on to become "loyals", the brand's total sales will be largely accounted for by purchases from this disloyal group, so capturing a large *share* of their buying is imperative.

Illustrating Type 3 rivalry for a consumer product

Having set up the brand-development transition, we can now focus more closely on the rivalry dynamic around shared customers for an example—a low-value consumer product category such as canned food or cleaning products. The following simplifying assumptions will be made:

- There are just two branded rivals, equally established in consumers' purchasing habits. There are 5 million fully-developed consumers, so no possibility of either we or our rival building additional demand.
- Consumers do not include in their portfolio of choices any unbranded or retailers own-brand products, so these further rivals can be ignored.
- Current advertizing spend for this category is in the range $0–1.0m/month, with diminishing returns setting in around $1.0m. Normal prices are $0.40/unit, from which product cost, retailer margin, salesforce costs, and advertizing spend are deducted to compute the brand's cash contribution.
- A single style of advertizing by both suppliers serves to build both awareness and understanding of brand values.
- The nature and effect of alternative promotional devices is ignored, leaving price as the only mechanism, besides advertizing, to win share of purchases from disloyal consumers.

The marketing chain in organizational change

A further case where individuals are encouraged to move through a chain of stages is where a substantial organizational change is being made. Such changes can be worrying to people when they must alter significant elements of their behavior (e.g., taking on new responsibilities). Here is how the chain works (Figure 8.18).

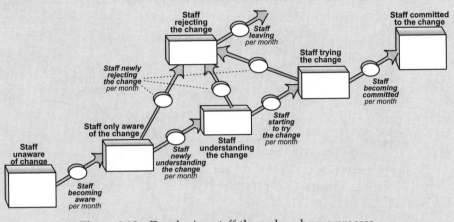

Figure 8.18 Developing staff through a change process.

People begin at the far left, unaware that any change is happening. The first shift required is to make them aware of the change. This can be a dangerous transition unless the organization immediately moves them on to the third stage—understanding the change. In the absence of other information, people will try to make their own sense of what is happening, and may easily misinterpret events. In contrast to the brand case, the possibility of some threat to the status quo gives people a strong incentive to move to Stage 3. People in the fourth stage not only understand the change that is occurring but are also trying out the new behaviors that are expected of them, personally. Finally, people reach the last stage when they become comfortable and confident in the new organization.

The challenge of organizational change becomes apparent when one considers how easily people can fall into the sixth stage—active rejectors. They may arrive there from Stage 2 (I hear there's change happening, I don't care what it's about, I don't want it), from Stage 3 (I understand the change that's happening, I don't like it, and I'm not having any of it), or from Stage 4 (I understand the change, I've given it a go, and I definitely don't like it).

Equivalent "marketing" mechanisms also apply to such organizational changes—awareness advertizing moves people to Stage 2, and values advertising (explaining the change and its implications) takes them on to Stage 3. As in the brands case, delivering the specific messages needed for this transition is harder than simple awareness building.

Incentives such as remuneration or other rewards may be necessary to move people on to Stage 4—trying the new way of doing things. An additional consideration arises, however, namely the need to remove or reduce perceived "switching costs". These consist not simply of concrete costs and inconveniences like relocation but also include anxieties about the personal risks involved. Reassurances about retraining and tolerance of failure are examples of policies that can reduce these switching costs.

There are, of course, examples of organizations that have transformed without any concern for the niceties of these transitions—simply announcing and implementing the new order and imposing it on their people. Their ability to succeed in this, however, still depends on the relative transition rates of their people between the stages in Figure 8.18. A firm may get away with such tactics if enough people are able to resolve in their own minds that moving to top right will be OK—at least relative to the risks involved in rejecting the change or leaving. In the extreme, though, if too many people become "rejectors", the draconian approach risks destroying the firm's staff base, and ultimately the business itself.

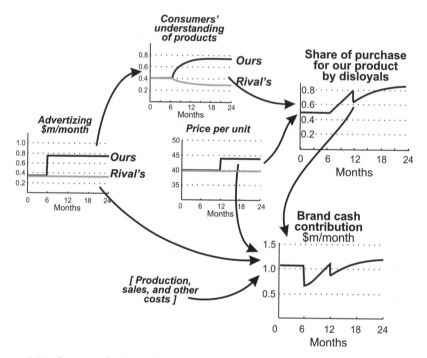

Figure 8.19 Impact of advertizing and price on share of disloyals' purchases for a low-value fast-moving consumer product.

In Figure 8.19, we and our rival start with advertising rates of $0.35m/month and retail prices of $0.40. We then try to break the competitive deadlock, and, in an effort to sustain its profitability, the competitor does not react:

- In Month 6, we raise our advertizing to $0.75m/month. The increased spend builds consumer understanding of our brand, and also distracts consumers somewhat from our rival's product. Consequently, our share of disloyals' purchases starts to climb. The initial cost of a higher advertizing rate hits the brand's cash contribution, but increased sales to disloyal consumers causes the contribution to recover over Months 6–12.
- In an effort to profit further from our now-increased share of purchases by disloyal consumers, we raise the price in Month 12 from 0.40 to 0.44. This unfortunately hits our share of sales volume, doing more damage to

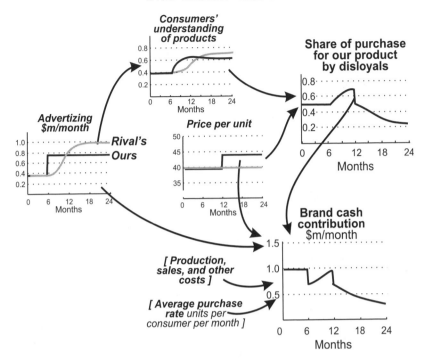

Figure 8.20 Competitor advertizing response to loss of share of disloyals' purchases.

contribution than we gain from the higher margin. However, our higher advertizing rate increasingly widens the gap in consumers' understanding of the two products, and the brand's contribution rises once again over the remaining 12 months.

It is unlikely that a serious player in a highly competitive market would tolerate such a serious loss of market share, so Figure 8.20 plays out a competitive response. In the first month after our advertizing increase, the rival ignores our increased advertizing, since its share of sales changes little and any increase will be costly. However, as its sales share continues to drop, it increases advertizing expenditure to try to recapture its former equal position. The mind share we have built up among consumers is substantial, though, so our competitor has to continue increasing its expenditure to make any progress.

By Month 12, the competitor's response is holding down our gain in share, and, in an attempt to sustain profitability, we once again raise prices from $0.40 to $0.44. This severely damages our share of consumer purchases, and consequently our cash contribution also suffers. *(Note that our share would have dropped from Month 12, even without our price increase, since consumers' mind share for the competitor's product would have been rebuilt to exceed our own.)*

Combining Type 3 rivalry with Types 1 and 2

It is unusual for Type 3 rivalry to exist alone. In mature markets, there is often a battle to create and sustain loyal customers (Type 2 rivalry), and, where new customers are emerging through time, Type 1 rivalry will be occurring too. To illustrate how Type 3 rivalry combines with the other mechanisms, the FMCG example just discussed can be adapted to reflect the challenge facing a new entrant challenging a dominant supplier. In this case, the new entrant has to develop consumers through the first three stages of Figure 8.17—from unaware to aware, and then to understanding the brand, before any chance of gaining even disloyal purchases can arise.

As this situation starts (Figure 8.21), the established rival has all 5 million consumers as loyal buyers of its brand (bottom-right chart). Their advertizing spend is modest, at $0.35m/month (dashed line, top-left chart), but is still in the process of communicating the brand's values to their consumers.

Since the incumbent has already developed the market, these three populations are already entirely loyal to their brand. In Figure 8.21, therefore, the stock of "rival's loyals" is always identical to the sum of the first three stocks of our own consumer-development chain. (Note—it is essential that these consumer stocks, like any resource, do not double-count the same people! Hence, the dashed line round the stock of rival's loyals, to indicate that this is not, in fact, a distinct resource.) Initially, all consumers are in the "unaware of our brand" stage.

We launch our product in Month 6, with an aggressive rate of advertizing ($0.8m/month). With such a large pool of unaware consumers, we are able to drive a rapid rate of new awareness. It may appear that we succeed in giving to only a small number of consumers either awareness or understanding of our brand, but remember that all consumers above Stock 1 in our chain are aware. The stocks of "only aware" and "only understand" are relatively empty, only because our strong advertizing and equally competitive price have conspired to drive them on to become purchasers.

The sales and cash-flow consequences of our successful launch are shown in Figure 8.22. The detail of our own building of awareness and understanding, prior to capturing active purchases by consumers, has been simplified into the single stock of the "rival's loyal" consumers. The delay in pushing consumers through these stages shows up in the initially slow build-up of disloyal purchasers. There is a still longer delay before we see the first signs of consumers becoming loyal to our product (i.e., they stop buying the rival at all).

Our sales volume to disloyals is calculated from the number in that stock, multiplied by our (increasing) fraction of their purchases and the average monthly purchase rate. To this is added the sales volume to our rising stock of loyal consumers (top right), to arrive at our total sales volume (bottom right). The heavy advertizing spend of our initial market entry is soon paid back with rapidly escalating sales, and cash contribution becomes strongly positive.

Once again, though, the competitor is unlikely to take such an attack lying

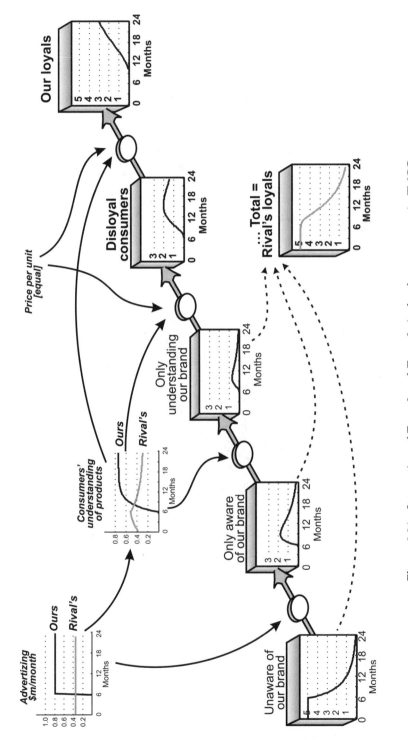

Figure 8.21   Interaction of Type 2 and Type 3 rivalry for new entry in FMCG.

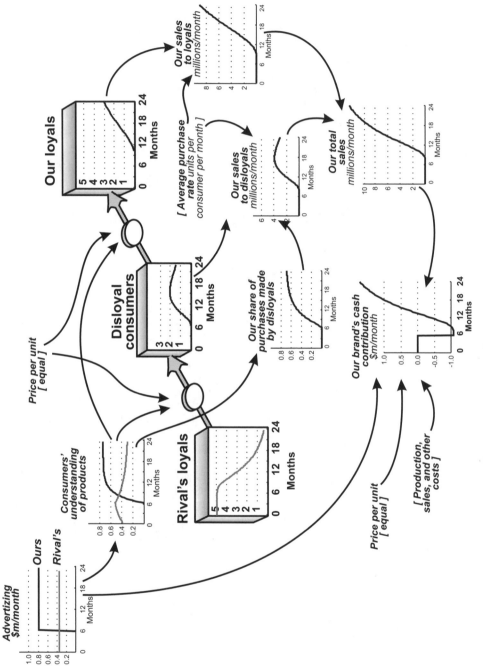

Figure 8.22 Sales and cash-flow consequences of Type 2 plus Type 3 rivalry in FMCG product launch.

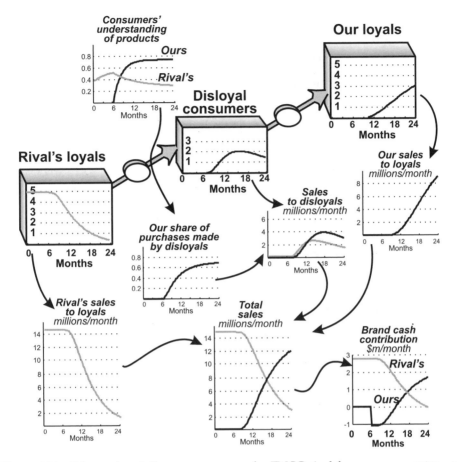

Figure 8.23 Sales and cash-flow consequences for FMCG rival from our new entry—no retaliation.

down, so a possible retaliatory response can be played out. Figure 8.23 starts by examining the damage done to the incumbent (tinted lines) by our original launch, when they take no retaliatory action. Note that their total sales derive from their stock of loyal consumers (initially all 5 million) plus their share (1.0 minus ours) of sales to disloyals. With modest advertizing and a 100% share of the market, their financial results are initially very strong, but soon are severely damaged as we take their sales.

A strong incumbent like this is likely to retaliate on a number of dimensions, including efforts to win distribution and prominence in retail stores, which we are not currently considering. Consumer promotions will also feature, as may various public-relations tactics such as creating doubt in the minds of consumers and stores alike as to the efficacy or even safety of the new entrant. Such tactics are increasingly employed because they can be far less costly than the obvious responses—price and advertizing. This high cost is powerfully illustrated by

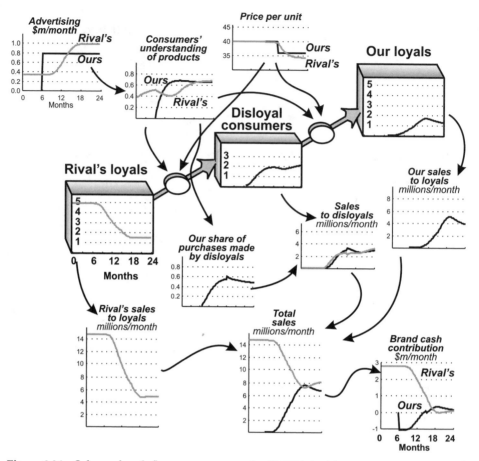

Figure 8.24 Sales and cash flow consequences for FMCG rival from our new entry—with retaliation on both advertizing and price.

playing through a price and advertizing response by the incumbent in this case (Figure 8.24).

In this case, the incumbent responds with increased advertising as soon as consumer disloyalty is detected. This slows down our progress, both in winning disloyal consumers from our rival and in building up loyal consumers of our own.

In a desperate attempt to sustain our momentum, we cut the product's price— a move to which the incumbent also responds. Consequently, although we manage to hold up our consumer-acquisition rate for the short time when we have a price advantage, this soon dissipates and we end up on a trajectory where we are losing consumers.

Although the incumbent's response succeeds in sustaining its sales rate, as compared with doing nothing (Figure 8.23), the financial cost of their retaliation is severe. Our profitability is destroyed by their actions (and our own!). The

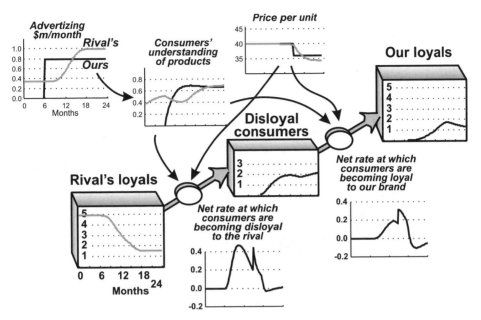

Figure 8.25 Increased clarity of performance dynamics provided by focus on resource flows in the FMCG rivalry case.

incumbent's own situation is a little more complex. By Month 24, they are little better off than when they did nothing. However, in the previous case, the *trajectory* of their cash flow was in decline at this time. By responding, their cash-flow situation is at least relatively stable.

Before moving on from this discussion of Type 3 rivalry, it is worth noting one final observation that has arisen before. Most firms' performance-tracking systems do a fine job of recording the financial outcomes, various ratios, and the *levels* of key resources—numbers of staff, customers, stores, and so on. However, since resource levels can only be changed by altering *flow rates*, these are the critical items that will inform management of underlying performance changes. They also provide much sharper insight into the consequences of their own actions, or those of rivals. To illustrate, Figure 8.25 shows the same consumer numbers as Figure 8.24, but now includes the data on net flow rates.

The net consumer flows shown in the two charts to the lower right of Figure 8.25 show much more clearly than any information in Figure 8.24 exactly why and exactly how fast consumer behavior is changing than any insight that could be gleaned simply by looking at the headline numbers. So . . .

> . . . *always focus on resource flows, and always devote effort to understanding how these flows are being driven, whether by your own actions, by rivals, or by exogenous forces.*

Simplifying multi-competitor dynamics: Strategic Groups

All three types of rivalry can become unmanageable in industries with many competitors (e.g., car manufacture, Internet service providers, law firms ...). Fortunately, it is often unnecessary to assess separately the prospects for every competitor. Mercedes may need to evaluate carefully the interplay with BMW, Jaguar, and other premium manufacturers. However, it is impractical and unnecessary for each of these firms to track in detail their competitive interactions with every one of the low-cost manufacturers who are also involved in the wider car market. For most purposes, this group of rivals can be safely dealt with collectively. For example, they may collectively develop car ownership in emerging economies, into which Mercedes and close rivals will later compete to sell luxury vehicles. Naturally, when such a firm makes a strategic move to compete more directly with these firms—as in the case of the Mercedes A class—then more attention may need to be given to the specific low-cost suppliers whose sales are going to be under threat and who might therefore be expected to retaliate.

This is an example of an approach to simplifying multi-rival competition, already established in the strategy field and known as strategic group analysis. By seeking systematic differences between the resources and policies of rivals, it is often possible to clarify exactly how groups of firms differ, and produce an *industry segmentation*. Though there is a connection between this concept and "market segmentation", the two should not be confused. Market segmentation seeks differences between the characteristics and needs of subgroups of customers and channels. Industry segmentation, in contrast, seeks differences in the characteristics and policies of competing firms—choices that may, of course, include selection of which market segments to serve. In addition, though, industry segmentation seeks differences in the internal characteristics of rival firms, not simply in the markets they seek to serve.

Much uncertainty remains about the importance, or even the existence, of strategic groups. However, many executives know that clusters of rivals do indeed pursue similar behaviors, even if these differences are not observable from financial or performance ratios—which is where much research effort focuses in the hunt for strategic groups. But, it is entirely plausible that two firms could be committing similar fractions of revenue to marketing or R&D, for example, while possessing totally different sets of resources and pursuing entirely different policies on, say, pricing. It is also completely plausible that these two quite different firms might achieve very similar financial results, when expressed as return on sales or return on assets. Conversely, it is quite possible for two firms, possessing similar sets of resources and pursuing similar policies (which would put them in the same strategic group), to achieve very different financial performance outcomes in spite of these strategic similarities.

While much work has been done to refine these ideas, an adequate start-point comes from Porter (1980), who defines a strategic group as, "... *the group of firms in an industry following the same or a similar strategy along strategic dimensions*". The concept of strategic groups developed significantly over the following few years, and, together with extensive references, more recent discussion of the concept can be found in most current strategy texts (see for example Grant, 2001, chapter 4).

This chapter has already illustrated how the concept of a strategic group can be used to simplify an otherwise complicated multi-rival situation—the issuing of licenses to new entrants in the Chinese telecoms market. Here, the clutch of new entrants were treated together, and their impact averaged out to understand the possible impact of their collective attack. If it were known that specific firms among those new entrants would likely follow significantly different strategies in some way, it would be possible to divide the group further. However, for the intended purpose—the effect on market development rates and subscriber capture that might arise from the entry of several rivals, who might plausibly pursue price leadership—this clustering was adequate.

The resource-system perspective offers a systematic means for specifying distinct groups of firms in an industry. This involves addressing three questions:

Strategic groups in aircraft manufacture

Very few world-scale manufacturers survive in the technologically demanding industry of aircraft manufacture. Yet, perhaps surprisingly, several firms continue to seek a toehold in this intensely pressured activity. Activity is focused on the 85–110 seat segment (slightly smaller than the Boeing 737), for which there seems to be increasing demand from short-haul, low-fare airline operators.

The major manufacturers (Boeing and Airbus) are seeking to develop this segment from strong positions in markets for larger aircraft. They bring substantial resources to this effort, both tangible (airline customers, manufacturing facilities, skilled staff) and intangible (reputation for fleet support, customer confidence in future business viability).

Smaller manufacturers include Embraer (Brazil), Bombardier (Canada), and Fairchild-Dornier (Germany), have entered this battle without the resources of the majors, but also without some of the consequential costs. Moreover, these smaller players can make up for their lack of accumulated resources with a competitive responsiveness that the majors find difficult to match.

I am grateful to Antares Reis for permission to report this case.

- *Do firms differ significantly in the **resources** or **resource attributes** they have at their disposal?* In the car industry case, Mercedes differs significantly from, say, Honda in both the number and affluence of the consumers who own its cars, as well as in the number and location quality of its dealer outlets. In clothing manufacture, firms will differ in their choice regarding the number and location of their manufacturing facilities, and in the retail distribution outlets through which they sell. They differ, too, in their choice as to whether or not to own these facilities themselves. (*Recall the fundamental principle, explained in Chapter 1, that firms' strategic architectures frequently utilize resources that they may not own, but to which they merely have somewhat reliable access.*)
- *Do firms differ significantly in the **architecture** of their resource system?* In the newspaper and other media sectors, firms differ in the extent to which they leverage readership (or viewership) to win advertizers vs. relying on advertizer numbers and characteristics to attract certain types of audience.

The extreme cases are TV shopping channels and free papers, which are entirely advertizing led.

- *Do firms differ in the **policies** that they pursue?* The holiday industry features firms who offer apparently similar styles of holiday aimed at similar groups of tourists, but, while some firms advertize intensively and maintain a price premium to sustain this cost, others consistently price more cheaply and rely on tourists and channels to discover the better value on offer. *(The concept of "policy" will be examined in more detail in Chapter 10.)*

These three questions help to clarify both the similarities between firms within an industry segment and the key differences they exhibit when compared with rivals in other groups. Naturally, the three distinctions will overlap in many cases (e.g., you can't have a policy toward distributor incentives if, by selling directly, your resource set does not include such channels).

While a substantial exploration of the resource-system approach to dealing with strategic groups is beyond the scope of this book, the necessary principles have largely been covered. These include, for example, all the rivalry frameworks in this chapter, and the basic numerical disciplines of the method, such as ensuring that connected stocks of a single resource are mutually exclusive and collectively exhaustive (i.e., don't allow any individual customer, employee, etc. to appear in more than one resource stock!).

Extending rivalry to resources other than customers

While rivalry is most commonly discussed in the context of fighting for sales to customers, competition arises in any situation where a scarce resource can be fought over, or "contested". Clearly, this condition often applies in the case of staff, especially when they possess scarce skills that would make a substantial difference to the performance potential of competitors' resource systems. *(This is a more meaningful specification than simply describing these staff and their skills as "valuable".)* Media firms also compete to win advertizers, and to win share of spending from any advertizers they share with rivals.

In contrast to other strategy approaches, the resource-system view also clarifies the importance of competitive dynamics in noncommercial cases. Charities engage in often ferocious competition to develop potential donors, to win existing donors away from other charities, and to win "share of wallet" from those donors who donate to more than one good cause. They will also, on occasion, compete for mind share among donors, politicians, and media commentators. Political parties, too, clearly compete for voters, but also engage in the consumer-development chain described in Figure 8.17. So these organizations too are fighting for mind share.

It is apparent, then, that all three mechanisms of rivalry can be found in virtually every commercial and noncommercial context, wherever scarce resources are being contested. The "war for talent"—or the fight for scarce, skilled staff—is a particularly common challenge across commercial and other contexts, so this issue will be used to illustrate how some of these parallels play out over time.

The particular context shown concerns the brief boom-and-bust that arose for opportunities in the dot.com sector. This flurry of excitement hit hard at established career structures for many types of professional, from MBAs who traditionally went into banking or consulting, through to marketing experts and IT specialists. Public-service sectors that have suffered similar, if rather less frenetic, challenges for key staff include hospitals who have lost out to private providers and police who have lost out to private security firms. The situation shown in Figure 8.26 concerns a population of professionals who go through graduate training, become available to be hired, then take positions either with our firm or one of several rivals:

- all staff in the sector are encompassed in this structure;
- the flow of new staff, either to our firm or to rivals is the *net* flow—the stock of potential staff is sustained above the level that might be expected from the arrival of new graduates alone by the temporary availability of established staff not currently committed to any firm;
- direct switching of staff between firms (Type 2 rivalry) also arises, with established staff moving through the vertical flow between rivals and ourselves;
- the data for rivals' hiring, staff, and attrition are presented only as an *average* across several rivals, so the total flows around "potential staff" will not reconcile. *(This inaccurate representation is used here purely for clarity—strictly, the rivals' stock and flows should be shown in total, and the average derived by dividing these totals by the number of rivals.)*

In the base case in Figure 8.26, both we and our rivals are growing steadily, and we are all offering increasing salaries in an effort to staff up to our desired growth. The increasing career opportunities and higher salaries draw in new students at an increasing rate. We match our rivals in growth and salaries, so performance on hiring rates and staff levels are equal.

In the second scenario (dashed lines), we seek to match success in business development by boosting staff numbers quickly. We offer a salary premium for Years 4–6, which not only increases our share of new hires but also attracts professionals directly from our rivals. Even after we return to offering average salaries, our share of hiring is sustained, since we are now a relatively larger force in the employment market.

The following scenario (Figure 8.27) plays through the impact on staff flows arising from the rapid emergence of a new career path, well suited to the skills of this professional population. It is helpful to distinguish between the relative hiring success among potential staff (the three staff flows to the left of the diagram) and the new sector's stealing of staff from our firm and rivals (the pair of diagonal flows entering the new-career staff stock at center-right of the diagram):

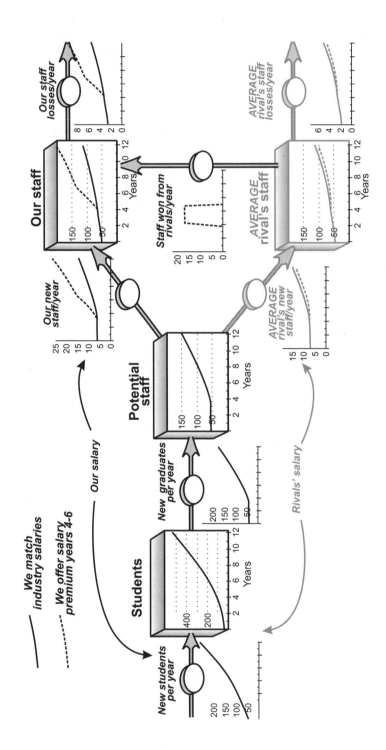

Figure 8.26 The war for talent structure in professional services.

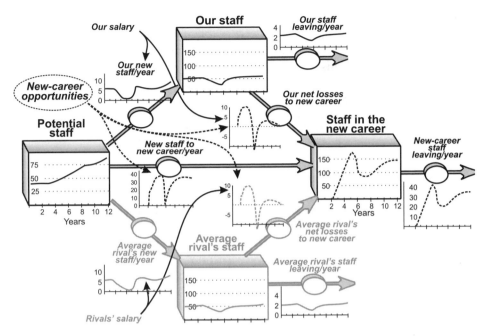

Figure 8.27 New-career impact on the war for talent in professional services.

- The number of staff needed by the new firms is large in comparison with both the annual graduation rate and the current employed population.
- In an effort to capture the staff they need, the new-career firms offer substantial employment terms—not simple salary, but stock options and other benefits (not shown). This not only draws in the vast majority of newly graduating students but also steals established staff from both our firm and our established rivals. The collapse in hiring success for the established firms may appear unrealistic, but during the height of the dot.com frenzy, professional firms who regularly hired many MBAs from top business schools saw actual hiring drop to near zero.
- The drain on these professionals continues for as long as the new-career firms are short of the number of staff they need—far more than the number they actually succeed in hiring.
- The boom in new-career opportunities is short lived, however, with many firms failing, and those that remain becoming more cautious in their hiring. Consequently, by Year 6, salaries in the new sector drop sharply (not shown), and hiring rates drop also. The drop in salaries and reduced career prospects leads to disillusion among the professionals who rushed to the new sector. Consequently, both we and our rivals experience a rehiring of staff from the new sector—the negative section of the two charts showing losses of staff to the new career from our firm and from rivals.

Note that, although our hiring picks up once more from Year 6, our firm becomes desperately short of the staff it needs in the few years before this recovery, and never manages to recover its former scale. Given equivalent lack of response by our rivals, they find themselves in the same position.

Now, it will not come as a surprise to those in the affected professional service sectors that the dot.com boom did severe damage to their previously reliable hiring and staffing policies. Most have successfully lived through this episode and continue to survive, albeit as a pale shadow of their former status. However, a number of issues arise that rarely receive adequate attention:

- As soon as the shock hits the system, evidence starts to build up as to the scale of its impact—"we expected to hire 5 from this source, as usual, but only attracted 2." This makes it possible to anticipate the likely time-path of the early damage.
- Furthermore, it is possible, by tracking back further into the system, to estimate the timing and severity of turning points. In this case, the net formation rate of dot.coms was highly public information, and thus the dissipation of hiring pressure could be anticipated.
- Finally, although survival is welcome, those with a stake in these firms' performance, whether public investors or partners, might reasonably ask how they *might* have performed had the firms responded appropriately and promptly in the light of strong insight as to the trajectory of the system in which they are competing.

(This last observation is becoming increasingly common in Strategy Dynamics studies. Few organizations give much thought to the question of "what might have been". This question is of more than mere curiosity value. The recent performance path has arisen from the policies actually pursued, whether explicit or not—the path that might have been achieved under **alternative** *policies contains important clues as to the opportunity for the future.*

One international mining company going through an organizational transition appeared to be making reasonable progress. However, deeper consideration of critical staff flows revealed that its hiring and staff-development efforts were out by a factor of 3–4, due to a blind spot about interactions between hiring, training, and attrition rates. Now, had the firm continued on its path, change would have happened, albeit too slowly, and the firm would have survived. Three years into the future, no one would have thought to ask what might have been. Yet the reality is that a massive opportunity would have been foregone.)

To illustrate the consequences of an anticipatory response to the new-career threat in Figure 8.27, Figure 8.28 shows the impact of our firm reacting with a simple salary hike to the very first signs that hiring difficulties are being caused by the new-career phenomenon. *(Various time charts have been left out that are relatively unchanged from Figure 8.27.)* Our firm's defensive move impacts on two critical flows:

- our own hiring of potential staff recovers to a strong rate;

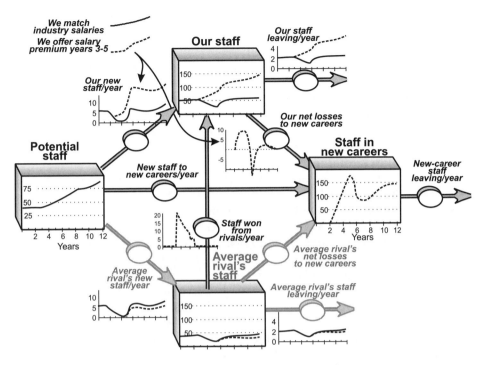

Figure 8.28 Strategic response to the new-career impact on war for talent in professional services.

- we once again draw considerable numbers of established staff from our rivals.

Interestingly, however, we make no impact on the success of the new firms in attracting the staff they require (the "*staff in new careers*" chart is unchanged). The attraction of the new-career path is so strong that this opportunity simply draws a greater proportion of new hires away from our rivals. Nor do we make much difference to the rate at which we lose our own staff during the boom phase. Indeed, we later find we are losing staff at a faster rate, simply because we were more successful at sustaining our numbers through the worst of the attack.

Naturally, the reality of winning and keeping staff in these sectors is more than a simple issue of salary, encompassing a host of considerations from lifestyle to dress codes! Nevertheless, these illustrative results are consistent with actual events. Even the strongest firms suffered staff losses to dot.coms during the boom, in spite of substantial changes to rewards and conditions of employment. Such firms did, however, manage some recovery in their hiring success rate—the pain was suffered disproportionately by weaker recruiters. Many of the best staff in these weaker firms moved on. Finally, the stronger firms were able to continue growth after the episode faded away. Unfortunately for the weaker firms, the evaporation of the dot.com hype subsequently caused a collapse in demand for their services.

It is worth noting a further implication of this war for talent illustration that arises at the industry level. As the Chinese telecom case discussed, firms' strategies not only alter their own performance but can also transform the industry's entire progress. The same observation applies to the human resource dimension. For certain skills, the dot.com boom had the effect of diverting prospective students away from their planned degree courses and straight into the new career. In some cases, even current students dropped their studies to take the opportunity while it lasted. As in the case of the recruiters, the strongest institutions suffered least from this problem. Subsequently, the collapse of the new-career path led to a resurgence in the stream of new students.

The war for talent structure is widely applicable (*not* the specific results, remember—the dynamic implications of any structure are always case dependent). For example, the widely differing availability between countries of health-care staff and other public service professionals is readily traceable back to long-term relationships between employment conditions in these sectors and alternative careers available to well-qualified youngsters. As in the case above, the present stark contrast between countries is an accumulation of relatively modest divergences over sustained periods. Here, too, the question of "what might have been" is critical. The policy dilemmas now facing politicians in solving major shortages of skilled staff can only be resolved if the debate is informed by fact-based understanding of the structural relationships between staff flows. Their own history, and those of comparable cases, provide valuable clues to these relationships, and hence to the building of sound strategy for the future.

Summary

This chapter has explained how, since performance through time depends on building and sustaining resources, rivalry must play out through the battle for resources. Since most research into business performance has focused on competition in commercial product markets, attention has been dominated by concern over customers. However, since organizations' performance reflects the effectiveness of their entire *system*, an adequate method for tackling rivalry should address the process of winning and keeping any contested resource. Three rivalry mechanisms cover all cases:

1   As new potential customers develop (or staff, etc.), rivals fight to win them for their own business. Fighting to capture new customers depletes the remaining stock of potential customers, and slows rivals' ability to build *their* business. Competitors, collectively, also seek to develop this potential pool, a process that is enabled or constrained by external factors such as economic or social conditions. Although Type 1 rivalry is most evident in emerging markets, it continues to arise wherever new potential customers are developing—which is the case in the vast majority of situations. The rate at which customers choose one firm over another reflects the benefit vs. price that they expect from each, but moderated by financial and other costs they have to incur.

2   Competitors also battle to steal resources that have already been developed and are controlled by their rivals. At the same time, they fight to prevent their own resources

being stolen. The rate at which customers choose to leave one firm for another reflects the change in benefit vs. price that they expect from changing, but moderated by financial and other switching costs they will incur.

3   The first two forms of competitive dynamics arise whenever customers commit exclusively to one supplier, rather than its rivals. In many cases, though, customers (and others such as advertizers and investors) share their favors between several firms. In these cases, firms fight to win share of attention. Since switching costs are generally near zero in such cases, share of business can swing between rivals quickly. Firms also, then, compete to pull customers into their rivals' stock of exclusive clients.

Organizations commonly identify with one or two key competitors, with whom they are most directly engaged in the battle for resources. Where rivalry is occurring among multiple competitors, thinking through the dynamics of customer flows becomes too complex. This challenge can be simplified by identifying groups of similar competitors, and treating them as a single rival. Organizations may be similar to each other (and different from firms in other groups) in their strategic architectures and in the strategies they pursue. Any single firm's dynamic performance therefore reflects the rate at which it wins and retains resources vs. individual rivals of its own type, and vs. whole groups of other competitors.

Most cases feature a "war for talent" in attracting and retaining good staff, but, depending on the context, investors, dealers, suppliers, advertizers, and other resources are fought over. As in the case of rivalry for customers, organizations' efforts can stimulate the development of potential resources (e.g., young people choose careers in promising industries)—a process that is also enabled or constrained by the external environment.

The performance of nonprofit organizations such as charities, governmental, public service, and political entities is also fundamentally dependent upon their success in winning and keeping resources, so they too will benefit from understanding and tackling the competitive processes described in this chapter.

9

Building the Capability to Perform

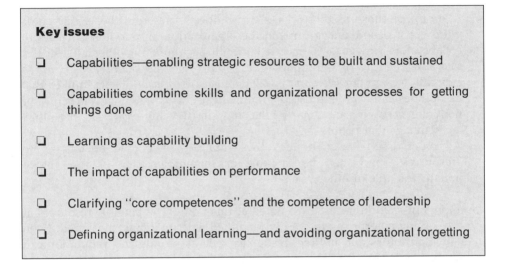

Key issues

❏   Capabilities—enabling strategic resources to be built and sustained

❏   Capabilities combine skills and organizational processes for getting things done

❏   Learning as capability building

❏   The impact of capabilities on performance

❏   Clarifying "core competences" and the competence of leadership

❏   Defining organizational learning—and avoiding organizational forgetting

Chapter 2 commented on the need to distinguish "resources" from "capabilities". While this distinction may seem of only academic interest, confusion of terms is a major reason why strategy concepts fail to help management improve business performance. We start, then with a brief discussion to clarify these terms, and the related concept of "competence". There is no absolute rightness about the definitions offered here, or in any other source—we simply offer meanings that are largely consistent with how other writers use them, and that can be applied reliably in the resource-system approach. Any inconsistency with others' use of the terms is for reasons that are important to this purpose.

Chapter 2 suggested that "resources" are useful *items* that the organization owns or to which it has access, whereas "capabilities" are *activities* that the organization is good at doing. That basic distinction needs to be clarified:

●   Resources, capabilities, and competences are all categories of what are known as "asset stocks". This phrase simply means that these items behave like the bathtubs that have featured throughout this book. The distinctive, indeed unique, feature of asset stocks is that their level at any time is not "related" to anything, but is instead identically equal to everything that ever flowed into it, minus everything that ever flowed out. *Every* item that shows this behavior (whether in business or any other field) is an asset stock—every *other* item is not (see the Appendix for a brief discussion of the theoretical implications).

- Businesses and other organizations own, control, or have somewhat reliable access to certain of these accumulating asset stocks—remember that organizations often use things they don't own. "Somewhat reliable" means simply that there is a good chance that any asset stock you can use today will still be available to you tomorrow.

- A group of those asset stocks—"capabilities"—describe the effectiveness with which people and groups in the organization or its wider network of collaborators achieve tasks that are critical to accumulating other asset stocks. *Chambers' Dictionary* definition of capability is *"the ability for the action indicated, because provision and preparation have been made"*. This implies that capabilities must be expressed grammatically as a language participle or nonfinite verb element—market-*ing*, product develop-*ment*, pric-*ing*—they are activities that people *do*.

- All other asset stocks, besides these abilities of people or teams, are "resources"—and may be tangible or intangible, easy or difficult to imitate, tradable or otherwise.

An important caution needs to be noted at this point. The tangible resources at the core of any enterprise are readily identified, specified, and measured. Even intangible attributes and indirect resources such as morale and reputation can usually be measured with some degree of confidence. In contrast, capabilities are ambiguous and indistinct, so always pose great difficulties of measurement and management. Nevertheless, they are clearly important contributors to performance through time, so some attempt must be made to grapple with them.

One source in the strategy field (Amit and Schoemaker, 1993), as well as offering a definition of strategic resources that is largely consistent with the argument above, defines organizational capabilities as, *"a firm's capacity to deploy resources, usually in combination, using organisational processes ... that are firm-specific and are developed over time ..."*

Although this definition is helpful, it does not make clear for what purpose the firm is actually undertaking this deployment of resources. Since we already know that performance can be largely calculated at any moment from the firm's resources and some external factors, capabilities must somehow contribute to building and retaining resource. A more capable organization will be able to build resources *faster* and hold resource losses to a rate that is *slower* than a less capable organization. To ensure these two organizations are being compared fairly, each needs to have the same availability of other resources that might be needed. This leads to the following definition:

> *A resource-building capability is the relative rate at which the organization is able to build a specific strategic resource, for any given availability of the other resources needed for that task.*

Table 9.1 Capabilities associated with illustrative resources.

Tangible resource	Associated capability	Indicators of strong capability
Staff	Hiring	Success rate, retention rate, suitability of new hires
	Training	Average skill levels, retraining requirement
Customers	Selling	Customer acquisition rates, quality of the customer base
	Customer service	Fraction of customers lost per month
Products	Product development	Speed of product development, users' ranking of product functionality
Manufactured product quality	Production engineering	Reduction rate in reject fraction
Engineering contracts	Pricing	Rate of contract success, profitability of contracts won

In practical terms, this treatment of capability means that each important resource has one or more closely linked capabilities, as illustrated by the examples in Table 9.1.

The concept of capability can be illustrated for a multiple retailer, concerned to build its estate of retail stores. This initially small firm has just three people devoted to the site-finding task, and they have been given the freedom to acquire as many sites as they can that meet the business needs. The team does all the work itself, rather than subcontracting to outsiders. They believe that, if they were completely successful, the total work of assessing and processing each site would limit them to acquiring a maximum of 0.5 sites per person per month. Together, then, they would be able to sign up a maximum of 1.5 new sites per month.

"Completely successful" implies that every aspect of the task happens with the minimum conceivable effort on their part, and with 100% reliability. The team recognizes, though, that their inexperience puts them way off this ideal, finding sites at only 30% of the best rate possible. Looking around at more established competitors, though, they see teams who, they estimate, are about twice as effective as themselves. These competitors therefore have an estimated capability of 0.6.

The result, given no change in this team's capability, is that the firm would expect to win sites at the rate of 0.45 sites per month (3 people * 0.5 max. * 0.3 capability). Starting with just 10 sites, 5 years of growth would build a business with 37 sites. If only the team could be as effective as its competitors, then they could grow at 0.9 sites per month, and expect to have 64 sites after 5 years (Figure 9.1).

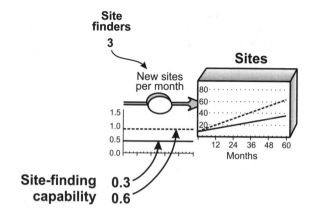

Figure 9.1 The impact of capability on finding retail sites.

Measuring capabilities

The idea that firm capabilities determine performance might appear tauto-logical—a more capable firm performs more strongly, but you can only detect superior capability by finding differences in performance. However, this is analogous to claiming that a gymnast's capability is only observable from her medals, and her medals depend on her capability. We can recognize a highly capable gymnast because she performs complex moves, reliably—and this would be observable, and measurable, even if she had never entered a competition for medals.

The assessment of strategic capabilities relies on two crucial points:

- Given certain external conditions, performance is largely accounted for by resource levels, rather than capabilities. For example, everything else being equal, a firm with double the number of customers will enjoy twice the sales rate. Similarly, double the number of staff will incur twice the salary cost.
- The rate of resource building at any moment depends on the existing quan-tities of resources needed for that task, by mechanisms that are generally feasible to estimate (e.g., our hiring rate reflects quite closely the number of people spending time on that task, the firm's reputation in the employ-ment market, and the employment conditions we are offering).

These conditions make it feasible to estimate capability, independently of bottom-line performance. Our focus on the *relative* rate of resource building in the definition of capability suggests that like many intangible resources, capabil-ities will be measured on a 0–1 scale:

- Zero capability implies that, no matter how much other useful resource the team is given, it would not succeed in building the resource for which it is responsible. If their task is to retain a resource against loss, then its outflow continues at the rapid rate that would occur if the team did not exist.

● Capability of 1.0 is the maximum performance that can be imagined, or that is possible, given absolute limits.

Three common reference points add some precision to these measures:

1   *a maximum rate of resource building*—a sales team's capability would be 1.0, for example, if every sales call won a new customer.

2   *the resource-building rate of outstanding groups within the firm itself (e.g., "If all our plant management teams were as effective as those running the French factory, how high would productivity be?")*. This benchmark may not be 1.0, if we can imagine productivity being still higher than this team is achieving, but gives us a sense of how close to 1.0 each team might be.

3   *the resource-building rate of an exemplary firm in a comparable sector* (e.g., if we believe that no marketing team could do a better job than the people at Coca-Cola, we could ask how fast *they* would build consumer awareness if they had *our* product and marketing budgets to work with).

Our team's capability is, then, the ratio between the rate at which they are *actually* building the resource and the best rate that we can *imagine*, given one or other of the benchmarks above.

While these principles enable management to achieve some grasp of the important concept of capability, the precision should not be overstated. Since capabilities are bound up with messy issues of personal skills and judgments, organizational processes, interpersonal relationships, and communications, they are never going to be pinned down as precisely as the resources that constitute the hard core of the firm.

Nevertheless, it is possible to bring capabilities into sufficient focus to guide management action. For example, our firm in Figure 9.1 is consistently under-performing on its site-finding task, relative to what might be expected from comparison with its rival. Management can then ask what exactly it is about its rival's approach to the task that accounts for their superior performance. If this comes down to differences in availability of *other* resources (e.g., cash, staff morale), or differences in *policy* (e.g., the price offered per site), then these differences can be eliminated. If there is no difference on these factors, the staff skills and processes within the site-finding team can be examined and improvements sought.

Capabilities vs. individual skills

There is a potential minefield here—Chapter 7 discussed "skills" as though they were resources, whereas the argument above insisted on distinguishing resources from capabilities. A strong connection between skills and capabilities will be built shortly, but for now (checking Chambers dictionary once more) skill is defined as "*expertness . . . aptitudes and competencies appropriate for a given job*".

This definition not only implies that a skill is held by an individual but also that a *set* of skills may be needed to suit a person to a specified job. For our purposes, then, we will use the following definition:

> *Skills are the aptitudes for individuals to accomplish defined tasks, so a certain set of skills is required to cope with a complete job.*

This is largely consistent with the meaning implied when skills audits, used to assess training needs and the effectiveness of training interventions, are carried out.

Learning as capability building

We have established that capabilities are "asset stocks", so the same principles identified for resources apply once more:

- the level of capability today is the sum of all capability ever won, minus all capability ever lost;
- the *level* of any capability can only be changed by some new quantity of capability flowing in, or by some existing capability flowing out;
- inflows and outflows of capability depend on the current levels of existing asset stocks, *including the current level of that capability itself.*

Colloquially, an increase in capability sounds like learning and, for our purposes, we can set out a formal definition:

> *Learning is the current rate at which a given capability is being increased.*

This definition has a number of implications:

- It applies equally to the accumulation of individual skills—which we can term "individual learning"—as to collective capabilities or "team learning".
- The definition is only concerned with the *inflow* of new capability, whereas skills and capabilities are quite often lost. Gains and losses can occur simultaneously, when a group gets better at certain aspects of their task, while losing their edge on other parts. As was the case for resources, though, different mechanisms commonly drive outflows vs. inflows. This loss of capability—or forgetting—therefore needs separate attention, which will be given later in this chapter.
- Earlier chapters established that, since performance depends on resource levels and these levels can only be altered by means of the flows that fill or drain them over time, management attention should focus on these flows. Similarly, if "learning" is the inflow rate to a capability, this too should be the focus of attention, along with the outflow that drains the organization of its capability.
- As discussed in Chapter 7 in the case of skills, since capability of 1.0 implies perfection, there will be diminishing scope for further improvement, as a team becomes better at its role.

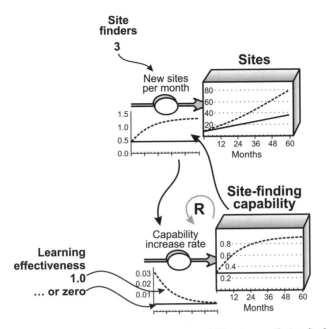

Figure 9.2   The impact of learning on capability in retail site finding.

Returning to our retail site-finding team, then, what might cause an increase in capability? With no changes in personnel, the obvious driver for capability building is "experience", which seems to be manifest in the rate at which this team is acquiring sites. To generalize this point, capability building is driven by the inflow rate to the resource for which the team is responsible. This inflow rate is itself dependent on the current level of capability, so the observation that learning depends on existing capability levels creates the likelihood of tight reinforcement—the better we are, the more we learn from each event.

Figure 9.2 replays the site-finding case, starting with a capability of 0.3, but now allowing the team to learn from each occasion on which it acquires a new site. In fact, if such a team is effective at learning, its capability will *also* be increased by insights that it gains from sites it tries, but fails, to acquire.

Capabilities not linked to resource building

We have thus far asserted that performance reflects resource levels, and that capabilities can affect performance only indirectly through enhancing resource-accumulation rates. However, a small group of capabilities may influence current performance directly.[1]

---

[1] This observation is a revised position, compared with earlier articles, notably: Warren, K. (2000) 'The softer side of strategy dynamics', *Business Strategy Review*, **11**(1), 45–58. I am grateful to Scott Rockart for bringing this to my attention.

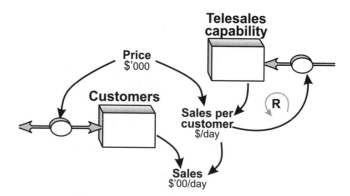

Figure 9.3   Capability not linked to resource building in telephone sales.

In certain cases, particular capabilities can be found in selling and price setting that impact directly on current profitability. Selling was listed above as a capability that drives customer acquisition (i.e., linked to resource building). However, many firms operate intensive sales teams, who drive revenue, minute by minute. A newspaper has an advertizing salesforce, for example, whose task is to win advertizers to include this newspaper in their portfolio of advertizing options. There is also, though, an intensive telephone sales team, whose task is to call these advertizers and persuade them to place advertizements day by day. This team's capability is reflected constantly in the newspaper's current rate of revenue and profitability (Figure 9.3).

Price-setting capability, too, will impact customer acquisition and loss rates, but can again drive profitability on an hour-by-hour basis. The power generation industry offers a particularly vivid example. Firms compete to supply certain quantities of power by bidding prices for short time windows (typically half-hourly). The lowest bids are accepted, up to the point where the total demand in any half-hour is met, and all higher bids fail. Clearly, if a firm bids low enough, it can expect always to win the right to supply, but its costs will make this business unprofitable below a certain price level. Such firms therefore rely on a strong capability to set prices that balance the chance of winning the right to supply against the margin that will be made (Figure 9.4).

In both these examples, the firms' capabilities will accumulate—they will learn, through time, from their successes and failures, and get better at selling or price setting.

Capability that is separated from resource building also arises in many purchasing situations. Buyers for retail store chains accumulate information and negotiating power that assists them to build up a portfolio of the best suppliers and products. However, their ability to negotiate the best supply price at any moment is immediately reflected in current margins and profitability. Buyers of advertizing space in newspapers or TV, too, must both accumulate knowledge of the most effective channels and negotiate immediately the best terms for any advertizement placed (Figure 9.5).

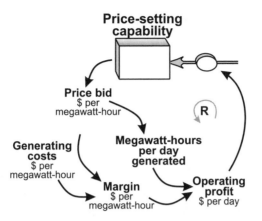

Figure 9.4 Capability not linked to resource building in pricing for power generation.

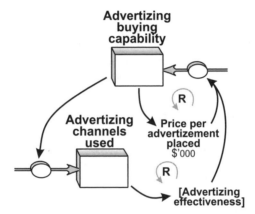

Figure 9.5 Capability not linked to resource building in the buying of advertizing space.

Capabilities, skills, and processes

We now return to the challenge of reconciling the concepts of skills and capabilities. A clue to the connection lies in Amit and Schoemaker's definition of capability given earlier in this chapter, where they referred to the use of "organizational processes". This concept becomes clear and practical when one considers examples of well-established routines used in organizations:

- Franchise businesses control the standards that their franchisees deliver by laying down procedures, processes, or routines by which a wide variety of tasks are carried out. These procedures go beyond just the tasks needed for good customer service, and extend to such issues as cost control, inventory management, and marketing. The franchise manuals constitute a "library" of procedures, each of which contributes to a greater capability than the franchisee might achieve alone.

- Professional firms document procedures for selling, delivering, and assessing the quality of assignments carried out for clients. This allows the inexperienced youngsters that many such firms employ to deliver reliable service to clients. The more devolved such organizations are, and the higher their ratio of juniors to partners, the more they tend to rely on such formalized procedures.

- Banks' lending decisions to both consumers and corporate borrowers are rarely made from first principles on each new occasion. Instead, a set of criteria are applied, derived from past experience, that have proved to provide the best balance between minimizing risk while still giving a good success rate in granting new loans.

- Headhunters and in-company recruiters use simple "rules of thumb", at least in the early stage of assessing potential recruits, to minimize the risk of common hiring errors.

- Call centers research, test, and codify best practise for handling caller enquiries, then train their staff with these procedures. They constantly monitor and review the effectiveness of their procedures, replacing any that have become obsolete or ineffective and adding new procedures to deal with new challenges.

All these processes, and others, have the effect of boosting team capability, whether by increasing the sheer flow of tasks that can be handled, or by improving the probability of success. The key, though, is that each team member is enabled to perform well in excess of what they could manage if they had to rely on their individual skills alone.

Given the potential contribution of such processes to organizations' resource-building effectiveness, it is only to be expected that firms go to some trouble to codify, refine, and update them. It is also natural to protect vital processes against being duplicated or stolen by rivals. Finally, it is clear that codified processes can have a financial value that is reflected, for example, in franchise-fee payments.

If we dig inside this library of procedures, we are likely to find that some contribute greatly to improving the effectiveness of a team, while others have rather less impact. This is reminiscent of the discussion of product-range features in Chapter 7. We are once again in the realm of a key resource (*the list of procedures*) and its attributes (*the contribution to team capability provided by each procedure*). The principles, frameworks, and comments provided to cope with resource attributes will therefore be applicable. The next step, then, is to build this model of a procedure library, and link it to the staff and skills model from Chapter 7:

- Any new business will soon identify the need to proceduralize important, costly, and time-consuming tasks, rather than rely solely on individuals to work out what's best to do on each occasion.

- At first, the opportunities to improve performance by codifying procedures

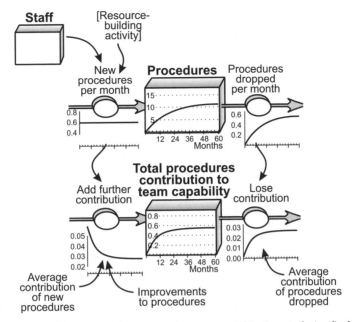

Figure 9.6 Building procedures to enhance capability in retail site finding.

are numerous—simple step-by-step methods each make a large difference to the productivity and effectiveness of staff in different parts of the business.

- Sooner or later, though, further opportunities become harder to find, and those that are found offer less significant benefits, or become more complex to implement. The incremental opportunity from codifying still more of the organization's activities becomes increasingly marginal.
- At the same time, some early procedures become less useful, as changes take place to the business tasks they supported.
- Furthermore, some procedures become obsolete altogether, and are dropped.
- However, new business requirements give rise to continuing needs and opportunities for further procedures.

Because of these mechanisms, the stock of procedures is continually evolving, as is its contribution to the organization's effectiveness. Figure 9.6 shows how this procedure library structure plays out for our retail site-finding team. New procedures for handling the search and scrutiny of new site opportunities are constantly added, as experience exposes new ways to do the job better. For example, demographic and sociological data is often available for very small geographic localities. This analysis can be purchased for existing, successful sites, and any new site can be automatically assessed against these criteria. This method enables the least suitable opportunities to be filtered out in the office, rather than taking up the time of skilled professionals.

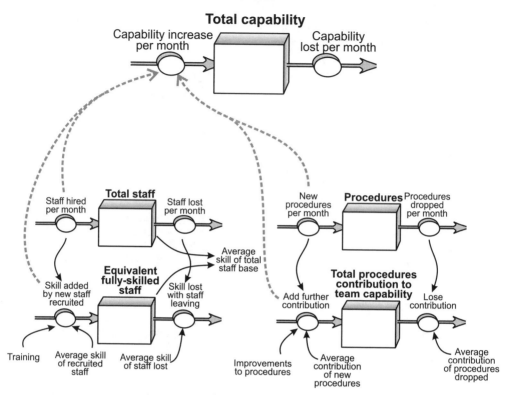

Figure 9.7a The detailed structure behind capability building.

As time goes by, more such procedures are developed, but these do not make such a major contribution to the team's capability as this first trick. Later, the team starts to discover better procedures than it already deploys for certain tasks. For example, the demographic analysis for site localities can be carried out much faster and cheaper with some simple software, so the purchase of data is dropped, and replaced by this new system.

Some cautionary points arise in relation to this representation of procedures and their contribution to team capabilities:

- Organizations never, in practice, seek to codify all their procedures, and could not do so even if they tried. Many routines simply evolve from day-to-day interactions among staff—people get to know "how we do things". An important consequence is that vital procedures can be hidden from view, and the first that management knows of its vulnerability is when key staff move on and things stop getting done properly.
- Codifying procedures can be dangerous. It's a great idea to steer how things are done if procedural rules are well suited to circumstances. But, it's not such a good idea if the procedures are flawed or if circumstances change so as to make them no longer appropriate. Unfortunately, the very act of

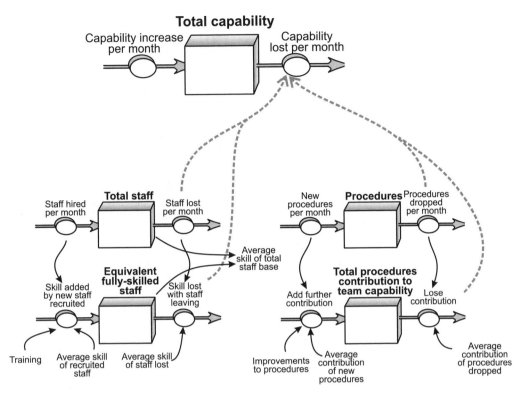

Figure 9.7b The detailed structure behind capability retention.

recording procedures and asking staff to operate by them makes it less likely that they will be challenged or thrown out.

- After a time, some relative stability is reached where the team has implemented most of the procedures that are likely to improve its effectiveness. However, technological and other factors make it likely in most cases that additional opportunities for procedural improvements will continually arise. This has the effect of "moving the goalposts"—the best capability imaginable today becomes superseded substantially by novel methods.

We can now combine the resource-dynamic staff-and-skills structure from Chapter 7 with the procedures structure in Figure 9.6 to provide a formal, generalizable structure for organizational capability building (Figure 9.7a). Figure 9.7b shows the same structure with the links that account for capability-loss rates.

Although these two figures capture nearly all the formal detail behind capability dynamics, simplified structures are usually sufficient to provide policy insight for management. In particular, an adaptation of the skills framework from Chapter 7 can be used, and linked to the resource-building stock and flow (Figure 9.8).

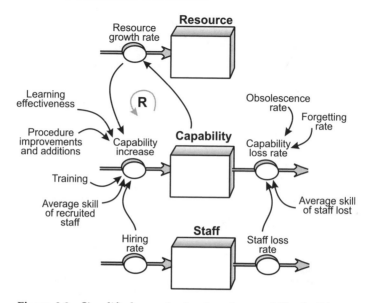

Figure 9.8 Simplified generic structure for capability building.

Multiple capabilities associated with one resource

So far, we have conveniently assumed that a single capability is connected to any one resource, but, frequently, several capabilities are involved.

First, the capabilities needed to *retain* a resource often differ from those that enable its *acquisition*. The retail business described above may need to dispose of poor sites at the same time as acquiring new ones. While general expertise in the property market will be helpful to both tasks, a buying capability requires particular expertise in assessing the business potential from a new location, and in undertaking site development.

Separate capabilities also arise in relation to *developing* a resource. Managing a staff structure requires distinct capabilities in hiring, developing, and retaining people. Similarly, the tasks of winning, developing, and retaining customers each pose different challenges. This division between acquisition, development, and retention is often reflected in the different groups in the organization who have prime responsibility for each activity (Figure 9.9). Difficulties frequently arise when one group is doing a fine job of pursuing its own objectives (e.g., hiring staff or signing up new customers), while their efforts are negated by another group's failures (e.g., poor staff development, poor customer service).

Chapter 5 explained in some detail how such failure can arise from imbalances in the system (e.g., insufficient staff-development capacity or customer-service staff), but an inadequate capability in the organization for undertaking these tasks may also be a source of trouble.

It is also common for a single resource flow to rely on several distinct capabilities. While customer acquisition might be almost wholly due to the efforts of

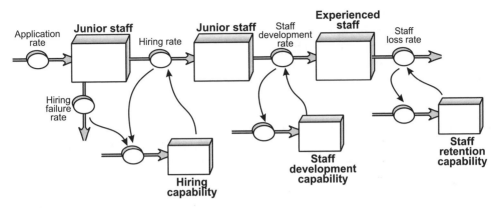

Figure 9.9 Distinct capabilities linked to resource acquisition, development and retention—managing staff.

a salesforce, for example, several groups may play a role in ensuring customer retention. Failures in delivery performance, after-sales support, order processing, and so on may all be involved. These separate contributions can often be identified from information on the distinct reasons why customers leave.

This multiplicity of capabilities driving important resource flows lead to a common difficulty—who to hold responsible. A retail store chain's loss of customers, for example, may be due to:

- the buyers failing to acquire a product range that appeals to the target market;
- the marketing team failing to provide promotional activity that keeps customers loyal;
- the distribution function failing to ensure availability of popular products;
- the store management failing to manage service staff well;
- the personnel team failing to provide sufficient service staff;
- the store-design and maintenance functions allowing the stores to become unappealing or fall into a bad state of repair;
- the real-estate team failing to discard inadequate stores and acquire better sites; or
- the marketing function setting prices that offer consumers poor value for money.

Naturally, the ultimate responsibility for all these possible sources of trouble lies with top management, but this sweeping generalization is unhelpful—top management itself needs to know, first, which of these factors is actually driving customer losses, and, second, what to do about it. We will shortly describe a process for disentangling this diversity of flow drivers, so that management can identify the highest value interventions.

Organizations are often quite clear in identifying responsibility for resource acquisition and development. The capabilities listed in Table 9.1, for example, are readily recognized as lying with particular groups tasked with the job of building each resource—HR drives hiring rates, the salesforce drives customer acquisition, and so on. Even when primary responsibility is pinned on a particular group of people, however, inadvertent assistance or obstruction may arise from others not explicitly identified with the role:

- The HR department may do a fine job of winning good applicants, but if subsequent interviews conducted by line management deter good candidates, the failure to hit recruiting targets is not due to poor capability in the HR function.
- The salesforce may do a fine job of winning customers, but if those customers are not taken onto the ordering system efficiently, disillusion can lead customers to cancel before they actually trade with you. The failure to hit customer-acquisition targets is thus not due to poor salesmanship.

More seriously, strategy dynamics work with organizations suggests that many are far from clear about who is primarily responsible for *retaining* resources. Such distributed responsibility is common, but is rarely specified clearly in terms of scrutinizing and managing resource flows.

This multiplicity of contributions to a single resource flow risks a serious lack of clarity that can be dangerous—if we don't know what capabilities are needed to keep hold of a key resource, let alone where in the organization that capability resides or who is responsible, it is only to be expected that the cause of resource losses remains a mystery. Figure 9.10 portrays the capabilities listed above for our illustrative store chain that is losing customers. Not only are there several capabilities impinging *directly* on the customer loss rate (marketing, pricing, distribution) but several more cause indirect effects, through failure to provide adequate resources to ensure customer retention.

Clarifying exactly the nature of these key capabilities, and the groups within the organization where these capabilities reside, provides a particularly powerful benefit. Many support functions and administrative departments apparently make no significant contribution to the firm's strategic performance. This frequently causes management to treat such teams as "overhead"—cost drivers to be held back to the minimum scale possible. Yet such groups play a vital role in *retaining* resources in the business. Clarifying this contribution, by identifying exactly which resource they support, gives a strong and positive purpose for these groups. Their performance can be identified, measured, and rewarded specifically in relation to the resource flow where their efforts are manifest. For example, if the store chain identified, from customer exit surveys, that their chief source of dissatisfaction was nonavailability on the shelves of listed products, the cause can be traced back either to shelf-replenishment routines or delivery performance. In the case of delivery shortcomings, the necessary scale of improvement can be specified, the required procedures developed, realistic performance targets set, and the delivery team rewarded for achieving them.

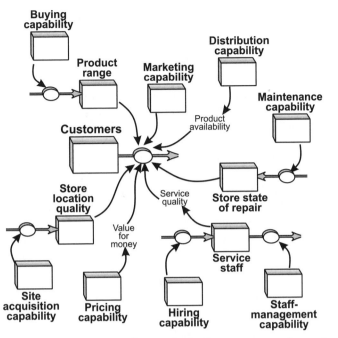

Figure 9.10 Multiple capabilities controlling a single flow—customer losses in retailing.

A process for dealing with capabilities in analyzing performance dynamics

Given the multiplicity of possible causes for the failure of any core resource to develop adequately, it is helpful to have a process for diagnosing the source of problems, identifying where solutions lie, and prioritizing those solutions. The following process assumes that three prior steps have already been taken:

- a problem or opportunity has been identified regarding the organization's performance through time;
- this problem with the performance time-path has been traced back to a resource that is not developing as it should;
- the failure for that resource to develop properly has been identified to lie with either inadequate acquisition of the resource, or else with unacceptable loss rates.

These steps may, of course, discover several resource inadequacies, each of which may feature failures of *both* acquisition and retention. So, the following process should be applied to every such problematic resource flow:

1 *Research the reasons for the problematic resource flow* (for the retailer in Figure 9.10, the loss rate of regular customers). Since we are often dealing with specific decisions that people are making (*"Shall I return to this store or*

not?''), we need to get inside what is often a complex and subtle decision-making process of which individuals themselves may not be conscious. Exit interviews of customers and staff are common, but must be carefully designed to capture the different possible causes of dissatisfaction. We must not only ask what issues matter to people but also how these issues are balanced in their decision-making process. Further care is needed because of reluctance to be honest. Many people, for example, when asked in restaurants if everything is OK with their meal, reply with a simple "yes", when in fact they have been annoyed with some aspect of the product or service. Similarly, exit interviews with departing staff can often miss the true causes of annoyance that led to their resignation. Note, too, the cumulative effect of such irritation (see Chapter 7)—although someone is choosing to act right now, a particular incident may only trigger their decision because of a *history* of poor experiences. Our store customers, for example, may be determined not to return because of a long queue at the checkout *today*, but have become irritated over many months because they often couldn't find the products they wanted.

2   *Connect the reasons for the resource flow to the capabilities or **other** resources whose availability ought to be keeping the flow under control.* While many firms undertake the kind of research suggested in Stage 1, the correction of problems often falls down because of a lack of structural understanding. The list of possible customer losses for our store chain is readily developed into a sound architecture, as in Figure 9.10.

3   *Quantify the **scale** of the shortfall in each resource or capability causing the problem.* The interrelationships between flow drivers are rarely additive. That is to say, for our store chain, that customer loss rates are unlikely to be indicated by adding together customer satisfaction scores for each of these eight items. Some may be "hygiene factors"—assumed to be OK, but highly discouraging if not. Others will be motivators—not missed if absent, but positively encouraging if offered. It is therefore essential to explore how much difference will be made to the target resource flow by a range of prospective improvements to any of the resources and capabilities driving this flow.

4   *Identify, for each shortfall, which of three explanations are responsible*: (a) poor allocation of resources by management (e.g., service staff poorly scheduled vs. the timings of customer demand) or inadequate cash spending on store repairs, (b) inadequate availability of resource that will take time to build (e.g., adding better quality store locations) or revising the product range, or (c) inadequate capabilities such as poor pricing decisions or poorly executed marketing promotions.

5   *Define the scale, timing, and cost of pursuing each contributory solution.* Immediate revision of management policy is quick to implement, whereas rebuilding poor resources is slow and costly. For example, this store chain would be able to raise store-maintenance expenditure quickly, but will need a long time, and considerable investment, to upgrade its store locations. Improvements to marketing capability may take a year or so, but be only modestly expensive.

6   *Estimate the scale and timing of the impact each solution will have on the problematic resource flow.* From intelligence regarding consumers' expectations of store standards, and from comparisons between more or less successful stores, management can estimate the likely impact of improved maintenance standards on consumer loss rates. Similarly, comparison with rivals will enable estimation of the amount by which improved marketing will improve customer retention. Both internal and external comparison of customer loss rates due to poor store location will provide strong evidence for the likely benefits from upgrading the firm's real estate.

7   *Quantify other consequences of each remedy.* Costly remedies, while contributing to improved future performance, will of course damage immediate profitability. However, some policy changes have beneficial effects on the problematic resource flow, at little cost, or even at a saving. Changing the marketing budget to enable short-term promotional activity, for example, will have immediate consequences for revenue, as well as on the problematic resource flow (loss of customers). Relaxing staffing cost limits will have an immediate cost, but will also directly affect revenue and customer-loss rates. In contrast, upgrading store locations will be very costly, and take a long time to impact, though the benefit will be considerable.

8   *Prioritize and sequence these remedies, taking into account their relative costs, benefits, and timings.* Having identified that the principal causes of customer loss are poor product availability, poorly performing marketing promotions, and badly located stores, our retailer can embark on a time-sequenced set of remedies, with some confidence as to their cost, and the likely scale and time-path over which improvement can be expected. They can also implement simple tracking systems to ensure improvements are progressing as expected, and adapt their policy accordingly.

The impact of capabilities on performance of the entire business

We can now examine the effect on performance of capabilities operating across an entire enterprise, taking as an illustration a start-up low-fare airline like easyJet. The principal resources to focus on for this case are:

- the fleet of aircraft;
- the cabin crew and service staff;
- the passengers;
- the number of routes.

Cash would be a vital resource for such an airline, but we can assume that this firm either succeeds and can raise the cash it needs to grow, or fails. The staff resource consists of many additional categories and further teams of people, but this case focuses on those front-line staff delivering customer service. Several ground-based infrastructure resources also arise, including maintenance, luggage handling, reservation systems, and so on.

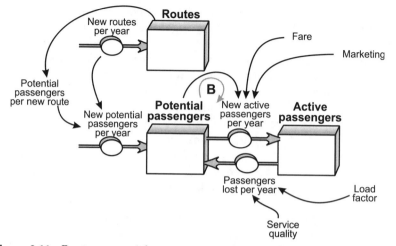

Figure 9.11 Routes, potential passengers, and actual passengers for an airline.

Each decision to start a new route brings the airline access to new potential passengers (Figure 9.11). As a low-fare entrant into a previously high-fare, business-oriented market, this potential passenger base is largely unexploited. The most attractive routes will be taken first, so that the new potential passenger base from each additional route will start high, but then start to fall. Having opened up a route, potential passengers will be won if the airline offers competitive fares and markets its service well. *(The details of fare structures are clearly crucial in winning passengers, but assume here that this airline is simply offering a much cheaper option than incumbents.)*

In spite of the low fare being offered, passengers will desert the airline if its service is poor. Furthermore, if load factors are so high that seats are rarely available, people who would *like* to use the airline will give up, and return to the potential pool.

The core architecture of this airline is shown in Figure 9.12. The firm is subject to at least three powerful balancing constraints:

- Unless sufficient planes are provided, load factors increase to the point that active passengers are lost. Fortunately, this brings load factors back into balance, albeit having lost potential revenue.
- Unless enough staff are available, service quality falls and active passengers are lost once more—another self-correcting, if costly effect.
- As the potential passenger pool in each route market is developed, there is an inevitable slowdown in the rate at which active passengers can be won.

There is also a dangerous reinforcing structure—if staff come under too much pressure, some will leave, increasing the workload on those who remain, and causing more people to resign. This only operates on the downside, since the best that can happen is for staff not to be overstretched, so that attrition is minimized.

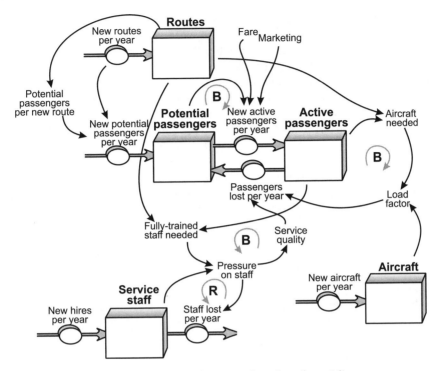

Figure 9.12 Core architecture for a low-fare airline.

Many important elements of such a firm are not covered in this architecture. For example, aircraft acquisition, scheduling, and maintenance are assumed to be perfectly arranged, so that aircraft are always available and fit to fly. Reputation too must be built and sustained, and would be damaged if problems with service quality or load factors were to persist.

Additional sources of reinforcing growth also occur, not just from word-of-mouth effects but also from recycling of cash flows into additional marketing, route development, and aircraft purchase. To this resource system, we can now add relevant capabilities:

- One capability relates to the opening of new routes. This affects both the lead time before each new route can be started, and the potential on each new route. A less capable firm will take longer to open a new route, due to the difficulties of finding and negotiating suitable airports and facilities. Furthermore, they are likely to lose out in the race for the most attractive new routes with the strongest potential market, or make mistakes in estimating the potential.
- The airline needs a strong service capability, to ensure that passengers are well served. This is linked to the service staff teams, who carry that capability.

- In support of the service capability, the airline must be able to hire service staff in sufficient numbers, and with sufficient proficiency in customer service. For simplicity, the distinction between trainees and experienced staff is ignored. Staff may be lost, and take their capability with them, if they are put under too much pressure.
- Finally, we will consider the impact of the airline's marketing capability. Given that it is operating on a route, how rapidly do its advertizing, promotions, and public relations efforts convert potential passengers into active customers?

Figure 9.13 shows how the airline performs, with each of these capabilities at two different levels. Aircraft numbers are taken to match the passenger volume on routes operated. Operating profits derive from the margin per passenger, minus the costs driven by staff and aircraft numbers, plus some overhead.

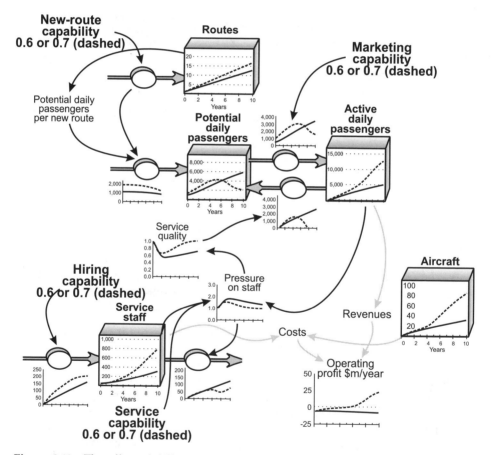

Figure 9.13 The effect of differing capability levels on the performance of a low-fare airline.

In the low-capability case (solid lines) routes are opened steadily, but bring with them only low numbers of potential passengers. Modest marketing capability develops these people into active passengers at a steady rate. Indeed, over the 10 years, marketing efforts bring on *more* passengers (over 20,000) than were ever available in the potential market. This paradox is resolved when the backflow of passengers is considered—from Year 2, the airline again loses nearly as many passengers as it develops.

The explanation for this failure to keep customers appears at bottom left. Although hiring progresses at a steady rate, the airline's service capability is poor, due to failures in staff scheduling and poor processes for ensuring good service standards. The poor service capability and limited hiring success impose heavy pressure on the staff, a large fraction of whom leave each year.

The firm's poor operating performance is reflected in its profitability. Its failure to win and keep customers falls short of providing the revenue and margin to cover the costs of operating an increasing number of routes.

In the high-capability case (dashed lines), new routes are opened up more quickly, and take the airline into markets with more potential passengers. The inflow of potential passengers slows, simply because the best routes are used up first, leaving less attractive routes for later years. *(Note that, for clarity, the steady growth in potential traffic on all routes that is a continuing feature of this industry is not included here.)*

The airline's stronger marketing capability develops active passengers from this potential pool at a rapid rate, but a crucial difference in this case is that subsequent passenger *losses* are short lived. This is due to stronger hiring and service capabilities, which ensure staff are mostly well able to cope with the increasing passenger volumes. There is a short period of stress during Years 2 to 5, but this is never sufficient to push staff attrition into the sustained excess of the first case.

Much stronger passenger numbers on slightly more routes provide sufficient revenues to more than cover the higher costs that come from having many more staff and aircraft, and the airline becomes profitable by Year 5. Once the early difficulties are overcome, profits grow strongly to Year 10.

Core competence

A special note is required on the concept of core competence, since many firms have latched onto this sophisticated-sounding phrase and attempted to apply it to their strategy development. Experience has been mixed, at best. Not only are many efforts to apply core competence strategies confounded by abstract and erroneous use of the concept, it is also applied to situations where it is inappropriate and where a fundamental flaw becomes apparent.

As defined in the seminal article by Prahalad and Hamel (1990), core competence is strictly applicable only to corporate (i.e., multi-business) situations. Its closest connection to the terminology adopted here is as a *capability* originally developed in pursuit of one product-market opportunity, but subsequently leveraged to provide access to others. So, for example, Honda's core competence in four-stroke engine technology during the 1980s allegedly gave it competitive advantages across several markets into the 1990s, from cars and motorcycles to lawnmowers and jet skis.

Practising managers, as well as teachers and management-development professionals commonly look for core competences for single businesses. But, it should by now be clear that firm performance depends on accumulating and maintaining a *complete system* of mutually-supportive resources. If *any* of these is inadequate in scale or quality, the performance of the entire system will suffer—the firm must be capable in *all* resource-building and maintenance activities. Attempts to identify a single capability that will provide sustained advantage are doomed to failure, as a review by the *Economist* (4th July 1998) explained for Honda.

By 1990, a whole array of supposedly *non*-core capabilities were in poor shape—*design* capability to create cars that people wanted, *product-development* capability to get them into production quickly, *production engineering* capability to achieve low unit cost, *marketing* capability to build the customer base, and *accounting and control* capability to translate revenues into cash. The solution to Honda's troubles involved reducing the focus on technology for its own sake, turning attention instead to market research and product design, and moving policy control from the engineering function to the marketing and production departments.

One further point to note is that much written comment and practical application of competence-based thinking focuses exclusively on *customer-facing* capabilities, on the assumption that anything that does not contribute to customer value cannot be important. The resource-system perspective shows this approach, too, to be flawed. Many capabilities drive resources that the customer never directly sees. The HR function seeks to recruit, appraise, and develop staff across many functions, including many who will never be in direct contact with customers. Yet, poor capability in this activity results in a firm having poorly-performing accounting staff, treasurers, systems specialists, and others, who may readily damage the performance of key parts of the system.

To avoid confusion with "core competence", which, as noted above, is strictly only relevant in multi-business firms, the term "core capability" may be more consistent with what many executives and consultants seek—a killer capability that, if only it can be discovered and built, will ensure dominant performance. However, the weakness in the concept of core capability can be illustrated by replaying the airline case with modest capability levels for all resources except one. Figure 9.14 shows the impact of a high capability at opening new routes alone (dashed), as compared with the more widespread, if less impressive, capabilities across all activities (solid). If new routes are opened quickly, and bring with them a rapidly growing stream of potential passengers, even a modest marketing capability develops active passengers quickly. But, this merely serves to increase pressure on the inadequate staff and service resource, so that service quality is devastated, and customers are lost at a very rapid rate. (The charts actually understate the likely problems, by ignoring the reputation damage that would result from such sustained poor service.)

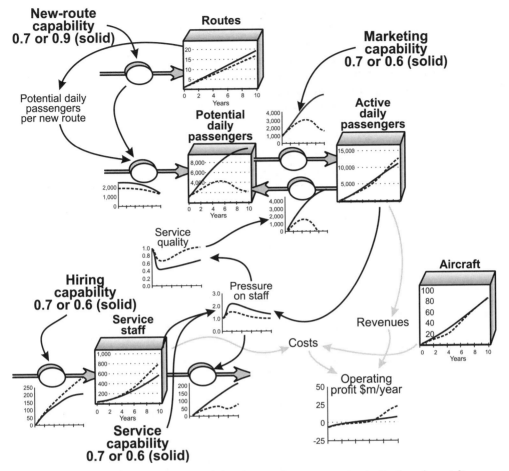

Figure 9.14 Adding a core capability in opening new routes to the low-fare airline.

In spite of the high capability in opening routes, then, the airline struggles to grow operating profits at all, and by Year 10 is in a far less robust situation than if it had ensured a basic adequacy in all its capabilities.

Similar results arise if a core capability is assumed for any one of the other resource-building tasks. In the case of "core capabilities" for hiring and service capabilities, the results are a little less disappointing than Figure 9.14, since these two capabilities at least help relieve pressure on inadequate staff, and customer losses are reduced.

From team learning to organizational learning

This chapter previously introduced the idea of learning as capability building, driven by experience gathered from accumulated successes and failures in teams' efforts to build and sustain resources. This discussion was followed by a detailed consideration of how capability is built by adding and maintaining a library of procedures and methods that enable teams to achieve their tasks more quickly and effectively. The last section showed that relatively small capability differences across several functions have a powerful impact on the organization's overall performance. It is now possible to connect these two insights—multiple capabilities and team learning—to tackle the question of organization-wide learning.

Many firms have devoted considerable effort and care to encouraging learning within their organizations, often with impressive results. Such an organization-wide multiplicity of rapid capability building might reasonably be termed "organizational learning". However, this notion too is most usefully wielded by digging into exactly what is going on, where, and why. From this sound knowledge arises the opportunity to build improved procedures, incentives, and communications that can raise learning rates throughout the organization.

A firm that is genuinely doing well in this effort will exhibit some demonstrable evidence that it is doing so:

- Resource flows will be observably stronger than benchmark organizations.
- These strong resource flows will be traceable to well-codified, or at least widely and commonly understood processes and procedures for getting things done.
- Individual employees will likely exhibit rapid increases in functional skills, manifest in high market value to other employers at relatively young ages or low levels of experience.
- Although the organization may experience staff turnover rates that are comparable with rivals, it will be robust in the face of even quite large staff losses. Critical resource flows will be sustained, even if experienced staff depart.
- There will be evidence of learning from failures, as well as successes. It has become axiomatic that a "no blame" culture encourages risk taking and the opportunity for learning. If this is genuinely in place, there will be evidence that changes in processes and policies constantly arise from identified failures. Moreover, there will be evidence that failures are not repeated, or at least that failure rates are reduced.

The airline example has thus far considered only static capabilities for opening routes, winning passengers, delivering service, and hiring staff. These capabilities can now be made dynamic, by adding learning mechanisms for each:

- *Opening new routes.* The learning structure in this case includes two elements. First, as each new route is explored and negotiated, and the necessary infrastructure is developed, the team learns how to improve this process, so that future investigations, negotiations, and developments take less time. Second, experience with early routes helps the team learn how to assess and configure newly opened routes so as to gain access to larger numbers of passengers (Figure 9.15).

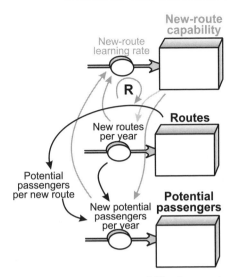

Figure 9.15 Learning to improve capability in opening new routes.

- *Marketing.* Early in its life, the airline is unlikely to choose the best mechanisms and channels for marketing its service and winning passengers. As time passes, though, its success at attracting customers provides continuing evidence as to the most effective choices. These become embedded in the marketing team's knowledge, and uprate the effectiveness of future marketing campaigns (Figure 9.16). The team learns most when significant quantities of new experience arise; so, as the business builds, opportunities for new knowledge fall and the learning rate declines. It does not stop altogether, however, since there will always be some proportion of new customers.
- *Hiring staff.* As the airline gains more experience in hiring service staff, it becomes more adept at finding the people it needs (Figure 9.17). In addition, it is likely to identify people who are better able to deliver good service, and are more suited to working in this firm, so less likely to leave.
- *Service capability.* The service teams' opportunity to learn arises from its continuing experience from actually dealing with passengers—indicated by the ratio of active passengers to service staff (Figure 9.18). In practice, this ratio is unlikely to fall below some minimum value, since the airline will not continue with many more service staff than it needs to serve its current passengers. However, if staff come under *too much* pressure, they have little time to devote to capturing what they have learned about giving good service. Consequently, the feedback around service capability can either reinforce, or counteract, the learning rate, depending on whether staff are working above or below a critical rate.

Figure 9.19 shows the performance consequences if the airline is able to learn from its experience and increase all its capabilities. The firm's progress

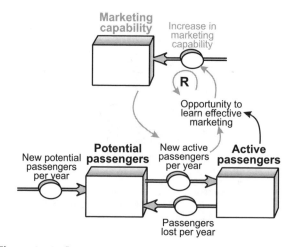

Figure 9.16 Learning to improve marketing capability.

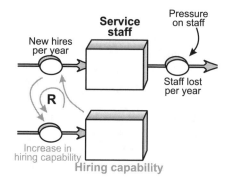

Figure 9.17 Learning to improve hiring capability.

immediately starts to improve, as compared with the no-learning case. This is most evident from the escalating rate of new potential passengers, as better routes are chosen. As this potential increases, though, the marketing team too starts to build a strong capability, and acquisition of active passengers accelerates.

Meanwhile, service staff quickly learn how to deliver better service, and hiring efforts too become more successful. As a result, the early pressure on staff quickly eases and better service quality becomes possible.

The biggest benefit, at least in absolute terms, comes in the later years, when continued learning sustains high levels of capabilities across all tasks. The passenger base grows to much higher levels than before, and this is matched by a large service staff delivering excellent quality. This operational strength is reflected in the profitability of the business.

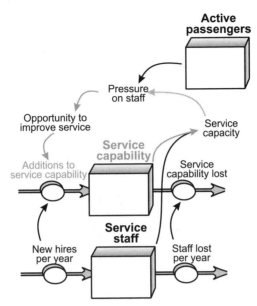

Figure 9.18   Learning to improve service capability.

Organizational forgetting

While much attention has been devoted to organizational learning, the resource-system view encourages attention to outflows as well as inflows—and capabilities can be lost as well as gained:

- the most basic process involved is the simple decay of capability through procedures being ignored or, literally, forgotten;
- in addition, capabilities decay through procedures becoming obsolete;
- clearly, staff who resign take with them some of the organization's knowledge, but, as noted earlier, a strong team capability should be somewhat resilient to such losses.

However, in addition to these inevitable processes, organizations can impose capability losses on themselves, due to pressures on management or perverse policies:

- The obsession with reducing cost that has been so prevalent in the last couple of decades can eliminate people, infrastructure, and procedures that together constitute critical capabilities.
- This pressure has in many cases had the knock-on effect of putting so much strain on remaining staff that attrition rates have escalated. This has often institutionalized a tendency for organizations to lose capabilities rapidly, even when staff manage to find the time and space to create new capabilities in the first place.

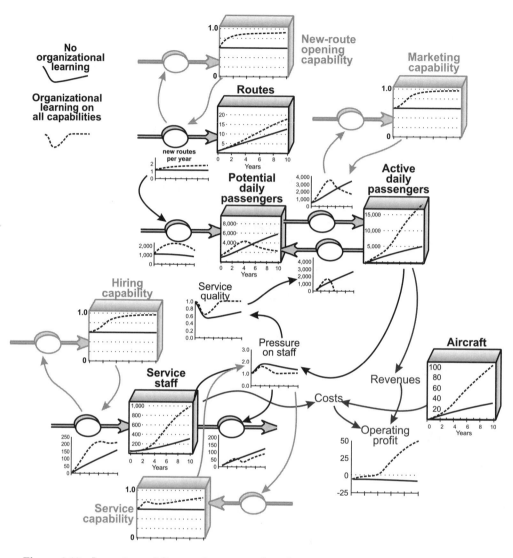

Figure 9.19 Impact on airline performance of moderate rates of organizational learning across all capabilities.

- A parallel obsession with constant reorganization or, more excitingly, "organizational transformation", has also caused firms to throw out critical capabilities.
- Outsourcing has been another potentially dangerous fashion. There is often real potential to benefit from the capabilities developed by the outsource supplier. Indeed, the best outsourcing partnerships include mechanisms to enable further learning to take place. However, firms must be alert to the risk

that the organization loses its own capabilities, as well as potentially foregoing future learning opportunities.

Finally, the investment community bears a heavy responsibility in relation to organizational learning and forgetting. An excessive focus on quarterly-earnings reports inevitably drives management to bear down on people, activity, and cost that do not quickly show up in profitability. Not only does this eliminate the organizational slack that provides the space for capability to develop and future performance to grow, it may also push management into destroying the firm's existing capabilities.

The most serious illustration of this danger arose during the early 1990s' fashion for "downsizing". As so often, a proportion of executives were seduced by a simplistic slogan, rather than trusting their own experience and judgment. The damage, particularly to corporate America, was considerable— and not repaired when the most vociferous advocate of the policy (a Wall Street analyst, rather than anyone with management experience) admitted to having "got it wrong". Investors, and the analysts who advise them, should ask themselves a simple question when considering how strongly to push management to perform—would we prefer 15% return on equity for the foreseeable future on a static or declining business, or 10% return with the prospect of strong, sustained earnings growth in the medium term?

It has become axiomatic that the life-time career is dead, and that any self-respecting professional will from now on move from job to job—not at Egon Zehnder International it hasn't! (Zehnder, 2001).

In contrast to many professional firms, this executive search agency has stuck to a remuneration policy that gives partners equal shares of profit, adjusted only for length of service. No attempt is made to track or reward individual performance.

The immediate result on the professional staff resource is, surprisingly, that the firm attracts outstanding individuals, but also, crucially, keeps them (partner-level attrition is well under 5% p.a.). The more subtle effect, however, is that this reward policy has built an awesome capability in understanding clients' needs and matching them with well-suited candidates.

The result is both a culture and system that has institutionalized a very low rate of "organizational forgetting"—which also explains why the firm has among the highest rates to be found of repeat business from its clients.

The importance and potential damage arising from organizational forgetting and carelessness can be illustrated by repeating the airline's learning scenario from Figure 9.19, but adding two effects:

- a continuing forgetting rate across all capabilities;
- a step increase in the forgetting rate on service delivery, caused by a new managerial decision to downsize service staffing in Year 4.

The scenario is played out in Figure 9.20 (dashed lines).

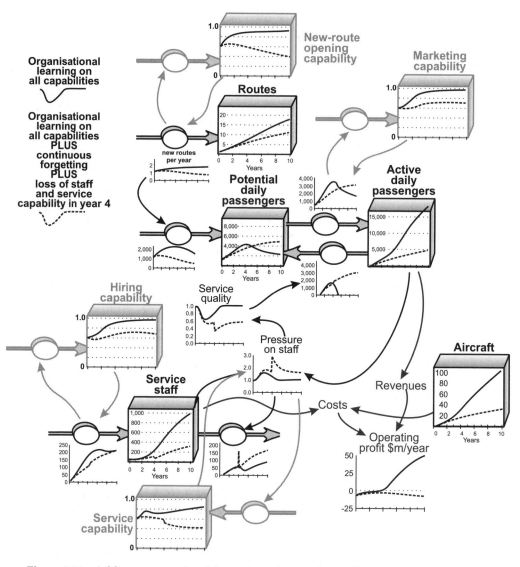

Figure 9.20 Adding organizational forgetting, plus service-staff downsizing to a low-fare airline.

The situation in the very earliest months is quite promising. There is much to learn regarding opening routes and delivering good service. However, the slow rate of progress fails to reinforce learning across all capabilities, and forgetting processes take over. An exception is staff hiring, where the need for continuous high recruitment rates after the first year serves to build increasing capability. By Year 3, the hiring efforts are providing sufficient staff to reduce the work pressure they are suffering, and hence rebuild service quality.

Unfortunately, it is at exactly this time of recovery that management switches to lean staffing, by shedding a large fraction of service personnel. This knocks back service capability, steps up the pressure on remaining staff, and triggers an increased forgetting rate on service delivery. Just when staff are beginning to cope with the number of passengers being served, work pressure is raised and staff attrition, which was on the point of falling back, instead escalates to new, higher rates.

Leadership team competence

In an attempt to offer some clarity, this chapter has defined both skills (held by individuals) and capabilities (held by groups) in a careful and prescribed manner. The term "capability" has already been reserved for the combination of individual skills and organizational processes that enable a team to build or sustain a resource. In the course of this clarification, it was also necessary to examine how the phrase "core competence" is commonly (if erroneously) used.

Two other terms are commonly used interchangeably with some of those above, resulting in widespread confusion:

- *competency* (note the "-y" ending) is most often used to mean the same as "skill";
- *competence* (note the "-e" ending and the absence of the "core" adjective) is the term that seems to be in the most widespread use among strategy professionals and writers.

"Competence" is often implicitly used to refer to higher organizational levels than a functional team, describing instead the ability of senior management to orchestrate the system as a whole. This orchestration ability encompasses several different levels:

1 At its most basic, *senior management competence shows up in sound operational decision making, with consistency across functions, resulting in strong performance through time, given the existing strategic architecture.* A management team facing customer service problems and signs of damage to reputation responds with coordinated decisions on sales effort and staffing. A business with an overextended product range requires coordinated changes to product development priorities, the focus of marketing and sales efforts, and rationalization of production resources. (The formulation of policy and decision making will be explained in Chapter 10.)

2 Above and beyond (but not replacing) this first competence, *a highly competent senior management is able to design and create a strategic architecture for the organization that has the potential to perform strongly.* The low-fare airline, for example, is competently led if its senior management make near ideal, and consistent, choices as to which routes to open, which planes to acquire, which customers to target, what fare structures to adopt, what services to offer, and so on. In addition, they develop strong processes to maximize the

firm's chances of succeeding in each of these tasks, as well as effective and consistent policies for guiding decision making on each. Whether the organization actually *does* perform strongly relies on the management team possessing the first kind of competence, above.

3   Finally, since it is critical for strategic architectures to adapt and preemptively exploit opportunities for improved performance, *a strong senior management competence is manifest in adaptations, additions, and deletions to the architecture that continue through time while remaining near ideal for evolving circumstances.* The airline's management exhibits strong competence at this level if it is aware of, and can articulate, changes in its operating environment that either threaten the appropriateness of the existing architecture or open opportunities for stronger performance than that existing architecture will permit. They will also be able to redesign, perhaps radically, the organization's resource system to enable it to cope with those challenges. This redesign will encompass choices of which resources to build, which to own, outsource, or obtain from partners, and whether any should be dropped or replaced. The redesign will also identify new capabilities and processes that must be developed, and new policies for steering and coordinating decision making under the anticipated conditions. Our airline will need to adapt to the emergence of new competitors, pursuing different strategies, to anticipate growing or changing needs of travelers, to identify new opportunities, and to design and implement new strategies. For example, it may become both feasible and necessary to alter its initial hub-and-spoke route network by adding point-to-point routes, a change that will require new configurations of ground-based support and management.

A useful analogy for distinguishing these three types of senior management competence is to think of a Formula One racing team. The first type of competence reflects the driver's ability to win races, given the car that is available. The second competence is the ability for a new team to conceive of, design, and construct a potentially race-winning car. The third competence is analogous to an established team anticipating new track conditions, new design regulations, or new technologies that may become available, and constantly adapting the car's design so that it continues to offer the best performance potential.

If you want to practise the art of "system redesign", you could pose for yourself the challenge facing record companies in 2001 from Napster, the online service that enabled the public to download music from the Web.

Record companies have grown up with a business model that assumes they sign up promising musicians, record and copyright their content, then package and sell this content through retailers to the music-buying public. The system is intrinsically costly, due to the many players in the value chain who seek to make a return on their expensive assets like retail stores. Pirate copying has therefore long been a threat to this business model, though, through succeeding generations of technology, the actual impact on original product sales has not in fact been particularly severe.

While most record companies reacted to Napster by pulling up the drawbridge and issuing lawsuits, Bertelsmann saw that such services could provide the engine of growth that the industry needed at a time of stagnant sales. Not only did the firm work with Napster to put together a proposed new service that would return some royalties to copyright owners, it took an option on the success of this new business architecture through a loan to Napster that was convertible to equity.

In the event, the legal action by the music publishers forced Napster to retreat, but in early 2001, this was by no means a certain outcome. So, what business architecture would *you* design for a music publisher operating in a world where online access to music becomes the norm? And how would you keep your options open, so as to prosper in either scenario?

Before this last section on competences, we already pushed the potential for fact-based assessment and management of resource and capability-based strategy about as far into the swamp of messy challenges as is reasonable, given today's understanding of the mechanisms that connect complex organizations. Indeed, some of the frameworks and methods have probably strayed too far onto unsafe ground. This criticism might quite reasonably be levelled at certain parts of Chapter 7, on intangibles, and this chapter's treatment of capabilities and processes. Nevertheless, practical experience suggests that these frameworks are of real help in evaluating the scale and speed of change to the more subtle elements of organizations, together with the impact of these changes on the more tangible parts of the system.

Although the observations above may help clarify the nature and challenge of senior management competence, it seems unlikely that we will ever be able to apply a similar level of quantitative, fact-based analysis to these competences themselves. Whether any organization is led by a strongly competent senior team will become apparent in its continuing possession of a coherent architecture of resources, capabilities, processes, and policies that delivers strong performance at all times, as compared either with its rivals or with the best that might be conceived as possible. A critical observer would be unable to identify anything that the organization could have done differently that would have likely led to better performance than it is currently achieving.

Summary

This chapter has explained how, since performance through time depends on building and sustaining resources, capabilities must operate through enabling resources to be built and sustained (though a few special cases arise where capabilities contribute to immediate business performance). Capabilities capture how effectively teams in an organization get things done, and come about from the combination of individuals' skills and carefully designed procedures and processes. These processes are built up over time, and, since people carry their skills with them, capabilities accumulate and deplete in just the same way as resources do.

Any one resource may be dependent on several capabilities, so it is important to distinguish these, and follow a careful process to identify the order, scale, cost, and performance outcomes from potential improvements.

Since the business depends on the entire resource system being in good shape, performance is strongly influenced by the strength of all capabilities throughout the organization's architecture. Consequently, the quest for what many refer to as a "core competence" (a magic bullet that alone will ensure success) is doomed.

Team learning is measurable as the rate at which any capability is building through time—a process that arises through feedback from experience at tackling the task of building, developing, or sustaining a resource. This learning occurs through accumulating better procedures, whether these are codified or merely habits that the team adopts. Learning, when it occurs across all critical capabilities, has a powerful impact on the organization's resource levels over time, and hence contributes to growing strong, sustainable performance. However, there are powerful mechanisms that drive organizations to forget—many of which have been inadvertently chosen in response to investor pressures.

"Competence" is a term reserved here for senior management's ability to design a sound strategic architecture of resources, processes, and policies, to adapt this architecture in the light of emerging problems and opportunities, and to steer performance once the architecture is in place.

10

Keeping the Wheels on the Road—Steering the Dynamics of Strategy

> **Key issues**
>
> ❑ Goal-and-control structure of managment policy
>
> ❑ Diagnosing causes of changes to performance
>
> ❑ Limits to decision-making abilities
>
> ❑ Interference between goals and policies
>
> ❑ Building on the balanced scorecard and value-base management

We now have a near comprehensive set of frameworks for a fact-based diagnosis of an organization's historic performance, current trajectory, and likely prospects under alternative external conditions. We also have a means of assessing the speed and scale of consequences that may arise from changes that impact the organization, whether from its own choices or from elsewhere. Successful strategic *management*, though, requires a further component—a means of understanding how decisions and policies (i.e., decision rules) can be best *informed* by the present trajectory of the organization's performance, then *designed* so as to bring about a strong future.

The term "strategic", when applied to decision making, conjures up images of grand, bold moves such as mergers, entry to new markets, or disposals. However, if "strategic" implies having a significant impact on the organization's medium to long-term performance, then many such supposedly grand moves are of rather minor importance, and other apparently routine, mundane decisions can be critical.

A headline-making move of marginal importance is exemplified by the entry by some major airlines into the low-fare travel sector. Several such business units have been started, as a protective move against focused low-fare airlines of the kind discussed in Chapter 9. In few cases has this had any significant impact on the core business of major airlines, nor has it had substantial repercussions on the air travel market as a whole. Conversely, seemingly minor, tactical moves in local markets during the introduction of 64-bit hand-held games consoles caused sales and income outcomes that led to upheaval in the relative competitive positions of the main suppliers: Sega, Sony, Nintendo, and latterly, Microsoft.

Management therefore needs a means of understanding and designing policy that works at all levels, from the apparently minor choices devolved to low levels in the organization, to the bigger decisions made by senior executives themselves. The key difficulty in all this is that, since policies steer decisions on factors that are dispersed around an integrated business architecture, these policies will inevitably interfere with each other. This chapter, then, builds up through the following levels of complexity:

- specifying the structure and behavior of mechanisms for directing development of a single resource;
- dissecting the performance information that lies beneath the interference between conflicting goals and policies;
- balancing between mutually conflicting performance outcomes, taking account of limits to our ability to handle complex decisions;
- widening the perspective to deal with interference between policies, to build strong, sustainable performance.

Managing a single resource—the "goal and control" structure

Management's need to control the firm system comes in two flavors:

1 *Enabling growth to flourish.* The reinforcing processes described in Chapter 4 provide the essential elements to serve this first need. The more resource the firm has, the more it should be able to generate further resource flows, notably cash. But, life is rarely so simple.

First, remember that reinforcing feedback can go into reverse, so any shrinking of the firm's cash flow or vital resources can lead to collapse. A policy of spending a fraction of revenue on marketing is fine, so long as that fraction is high enough and revenue is growing. If something were to knock the firm's revenue back, the policy implies that marketing spend must be cut, which may reduce revenue. *(See the cautionary notes regarding reinforcing feedback in Chapter 4.)*

Second, most of the resources in the system are cost drivers, so the immediate effect of adding to these is to reduce net cash flows, rather than increase them. Only when the necessary time has elapsed for these costly resources to stimulate growth in customers will the additional revenue be available to spur the next round of growth.

Finally, since investors ultimately seek free cash flows to emerge from this money-making machine, there is generally a tension—how much cash should be ploughed back into growing the resource system, rather than being distributed?

2 *Keeping resources from getting out of balance.* We have already dealt with the basic structure by which firms control resource growth—the balancing

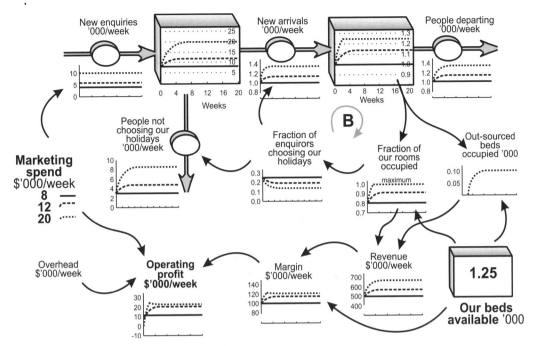

Figure 10.1 Marketing and capacity constraints affecting demand for a holiday company.

feedback mechanism. Chapter 5 described how balancing feedback acts as a constraint, with some limiting factor obstructing growth. For example, a limited number of service staff constrains a firm's ability to cope with more customers. However, it was also pointed out that balancing feedback could be beneficial, preventing one part of the firm growing beyond the ability of the rest of the system to cope.

This positive role of balancing feedback provides management with the means to take control. Rather than have business growth constrained by problematic imbalances, with all the knock-on difficulties this can cause, management chooses its own target and controls growth accordingly.

Figure 10.1 shows a holiday company, needing to decide on marketing expenditures. The firm has enough rooms to provide holidays for 1,250 people at a time, and all holidays last one week.

In the base case (solid), the company spends $8,000/week on marketing to persuade tourists to consider its holidays in preference to alternatives. This steady spending rate attracts 4,000 people/week to enquire and, after considering their choice for 2 weeks, 25% choose our company for their holiday. This fraction is limited by the current occupancy of rooms—the more rooms are occupied, the less choice remains, and the lower the fraction of people who find a holiday that they want. This is a balancing mechanism that increasingly acts to stop the business growing beyond its capacity. (*In practice, of course, there is*

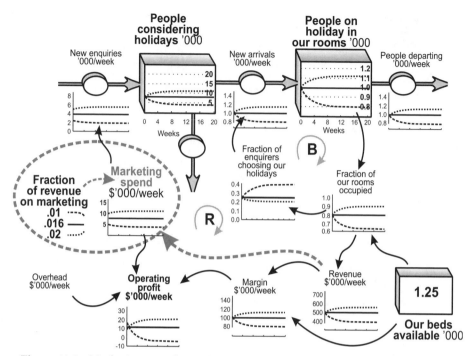

Figure 10.2 Marketing spend as a fixed fraction of revenue for a holiday company.

a much longer elapsed delay between booking the holiday and actually taking it, but, for present purposes, we can assume that once the booking is made, the room is sold, regardless of how many weeks later that week is actually taken.)

In an attempt to drive more revenue, this company could raise its marketing spend. If it spends $12,000/week, new enquiries rise to a rate of 6,000 per week, and the number of people considering a holiday starts to climb (dashed). With still reasonable room occupancy, 25% of this increasing number book holidays, so that the number of people on holiday also rises. With only 1,250 beds available, occupancy rises to over 90%, and the fraction of enquiries that result in bookings falls to under 20%, bringing the system back into balance once more.

Finally (dotted), if the firm really boosts marketing spend to $20,000/week, enquiries come in much faster, and bookings take off. Soon, all the company's own rooms are occupied, so it has to outsource some rooms from other hotels at its holiday destinations. This is costly, so the company makes a loss on these excess bookings. The combination of this cap on margin and the ineffectively high marketing spend stops operating profit being much better than in the second case.

Figure 10.2 examines the implications of the most basic kind of "policy" for steering strategy. Our holiday company wants to grow, but recognizes that it can't spend extravagantly, so it spends a fixed fraction of revenue on marketing. This should work pretty well. Start with enough spending to get demand growing, then the more revenue we win the more we should be able to spend, and the more we spend the more we should grow. Management might expect this policy to generate exponential growth—after all, they have constructed an apparently powerful reinforcing feedback structure.

The outcome is not so simple, though. First, the chosen fraction of revenue to be spent on marketing has to be sufficient to initiate growth. In the base case (solid), this fraction is 1.6% of revenue, which is only sufficient to sustain an inflow of new enquiries and bookings that just matches the rate at which holidays are ending. The firm has to spend a larger fraction than this (blue) if it is to stimulate growth. Any lower fraction (dashed) and the business actually shrinks.

Second, the performance path shows no sign of the exponential trajectory that reinforcing growth is supposed to generate. This is due to the very powerful counterbalancing effect of room occupancy. As soon as the higher marketing fraction wins more bookings (dotted), this occupancy rises and the fraction of successful enquiries drops. Similarly, the too-low spending policy should trigger a total collapse—less marketing equals fewer bookings and less revenue, leading to reduced marketing and still lower bookings and revenue. However, with increasing vacancies, the fraction of enquiries resulting in actual bookings climbs sharply, once again counterbalancing the reinforcing process of management's policy.

A generic structure for decision-making policy

The decision-making approach described in Figure 10.2 may seem too trivial to warrant the grand title of "policy", but it illustrates nearly all the essential elements:

- some controllable feature of the business architecture (*here, marketing spend*);
- certain variables, whose value is immediately altered by the decision—either performance measures or other items (*new enquiries per week and operating profit per week*);
- certain information on the state and trajectory of the business that management select as relevant to the item on which they need to decide (*in Figure 10.2, the holiday company uses only current revenue, though it is clearly common for management to use several items of information*);
- a somewhat stable rule that management applies to the chosen information to guide their decision from time to time (*in this case, "increase or decrease marketing spend to match the chosen fraction of revenue"*).

This crude policy, though, is missing a crucial fifth element that is normally needed, namely:

- a target against which the current state of the business is compared. (*In this example, it doesn't matter what state the business itself is in—whether bookings are coming in fast or slow, whether rooms are busy or empty, whether profits are growing or declining—the fixed fraction of revenue will always be spent.*)

A helpful analogy is to consider how you control the accelerator pedal when driving a car—without automatic transmission! With no traffic, no sharp bends, and no steep hills, holding the pedal at a fixed position will work. *(This is an even simpler rule, more analogous to Figure 10.1.)* The car will accelerate to a steady speed, and gradually slow down if it comes to a gentle uphill gradient. Provided that the hill is not too long, the car will not stop altogether, and a downhill slope will see the car speed up once more.

A closer analogy to the policy in Figure 10.2 is for the car driver to press down on the accelerator as the car speeds up, and release it as the car slows down. This would clearly be perverse. On the upside, the car would accelerate to its maximum speed—a speed limited only by friction and wind resistance. On the downside, the car would decelerate to a standstill. This is equivalent to our holiday company with new bookings constrained by an upper occupancy limit, but with no compensating boost from higher bookings when occupancy is low.

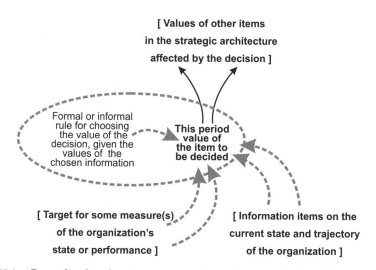

Figure 10.3 General policy function structure to guide organizations' decision making.

Although it may seem rather foolish to operate without a target, such policies do have the advantage of simplicity, which can be appealing to managers confronted with great complexity. Furthermore, a simple policy might be adequate when conditions are favorable and do not vary too much.

These components come together to form a generic structure for the managerial policies that guide decisions, shown in Figure 10.3, from Forrester (1961) and Morecroft (1985). This view of the structure of decision making has important implications when seen as part of the firm's strategic architecture:

- many choices that management deem to be important have immediate, direct effects on performance metrics (*a decision to raise marketing spend hits operating profit immediately*);
- *strategically important* consequences of the decision (i.e., those that make a

significant difference to performance beyond the short term) arise from impacts on resource flows (*in the holiday firm, the change to the new enquiry rate*);

- there will often be consequences *other* than on the item you most wish to influence, which may be evident or hidden (*the holiday company's marketing spend could affect staff motivation and cause changes to the company's reputation level*).

Furthermore, policy functions are not restricted to the boundaries of the organization, either in the information that influences them or the consequences that arise:

- managers commonly take account of information on exogenous items (*increased consumer income and competitors' marketing efforts will affect this holiday firm's choice of expenditure*);
- the decisions that emerge from the policy function influence exogenous items, as well as impacting within the firm itself (*the firm's marketing spend causes tourists to divert income temporarily into savings, rather than spending that income on other items*).

Adding these extra influences on, and consequences of, the organization's decision making, produces the following definition and the broader perspective on the place of policy in the organization and its environment shown in Figure 10.4:

> *A policy is a somewhat stable rule, either formal or informal, explicit or implicit, for guiding a decision that affects the organization's performance. The policy is* **informed by** *data deemed relevant by decision-makers, both on the current state and trajectory of the organization's performance and resources, as well as on external conditions. The policy* **affects** *both the organization's own performance and resources, as well as external conditions, these effects including both immediate consequences and longer-term outcomes arising from changes to accumulation rates of the organization's resources and external asset stocks.*

Such policies are often described as "rules of thumb", or the more sophisticated-sounding term, "heuristic". (*This is not strictly accurate—"heuristic" actually refers to how the search for information is guided, rather than how a decision is made.*)

The definition above recognizes that policy is often implicit and informal, rather than explicit and formal. However, there is an inescapable reality—*policy is an integral component of the organization's strategic architecture.* If we are to understand and direct the organization's performance, then, we have no choice but to make explicit the significant policies that are operating, and identify their impact on the system's performance. We can now return to the holiday firm, and consider how some more sophisticated policies might operate.

Policy example 1—control marketing spend to sustain high sales. A basic policy that makes sense for this firm is to seek a marketing spend rate that builds sales, while making sure it's not overbooked. So, if rooms are occupied less than it would like,

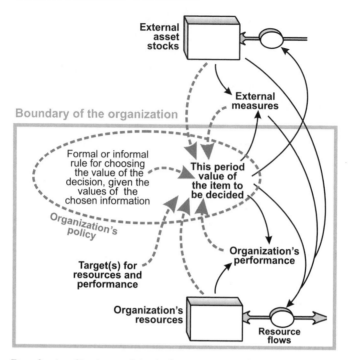

Figure 10.4 Broader implications of the influences on, and consequences from, an organization's general policy function.

the firm raises marketing spend, while overbooking will cause spending to be cut. The five components of this policy, then, are:

- decision item to control—*marketing spend, $'000/week;*
- affected flows and other items—*new bookings per week and current operating profit;*
- chosen information—*the current fraction of rooms occupied;*
- target state of the business—*fraction of rooms occupied—say 95%;*
- somewhat stable decision rule—*if occupancy is below target, raise marketing by a certain fraction, and if above, reduce it by a fraction. For now, take the fractional adjustment to be the same for both increases and decreases.*

The policy is therefore:

> *For each week that room occupancy is above or below our target of 95%, decrease or increase marketing spend (respectively) by a fixed fraction, x.*

All that remains is to specify what that adjustment fraction should be, which is part of the rule itself. Figure 10.5 shows the consequences of changing marketing spend by ±5% and ±10% in response to under or overbooking.

If management adjusts marketing spend by the quite modest fraction of 5% in each week when occupancy differs from target (solid), the actual spend builds

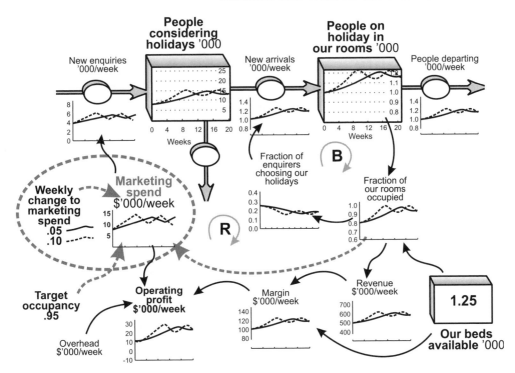

Figure 10.5 Policy of adjusting marketing spend to build and sustain a high, but not excessive room occupancy.

slowly to the rate that achieves the target. There is some overshoot—occupancy rises a little above the target—before management sees evidence of overbooking, and reverses the marketing increase to bring occupancy down again. This is the classic behavior of balancing feedback with a delay (see Chapter 5).

With the more aggressive adjustment of 10% for each week when occupancy differs from target (dashed), there is naturally a shorter period of underachievement. Occupancy hits a peak by about Week 9. However, both the overshoot and subsequent cyclicality are more extreme. If management is still more aggressive (e.g., change marketing spend by 20% whenever occupancy differs from target—not shown), the speed of adjustment is very fast, but the overshoot and cyclicality is so high that the firm is often overbooked to the extent that it has to use outsourced rooms.

It is not difficult to come up with a more thoughtful rule. Two alternative adjustments might work:

- Since hitting the occupancy target suggests that marketing spend is close to the ideal, the *decrease* fraction for overbooking could be set at less than the *increase* fraction for underbooking. For example, *"For each week that room occupancy is below our target of 95%, increase marketing spend by a fixed*

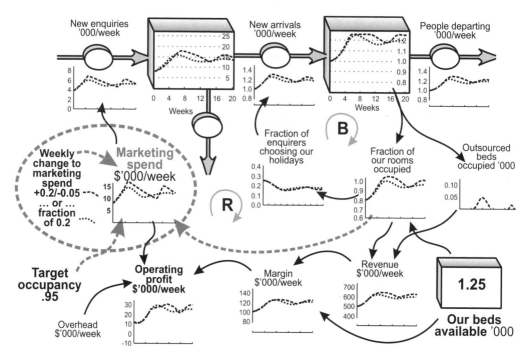

Figure 10.6 Fast (dashed) or varying (dotted) adjustment of marketing spend to reach target room occupancy.

fraction 20%, and for each week it is above target, reduce spend by one-third of this fraction, about 7%."

- The adjustment fraction itself could be changed in response to the gap between current occupancy and the target. For example, *"For each week that room occupancy is below/above our target of 95%, increase/decrease marketing spend by a fraction—this fraction being 20% if the occupancy shortfall is 10% or more, but reducing in proportion as this shortfall is under 10%."*

Figure 10.6 shows the result of these two policies. As expected, the fast initial increase in marketing of 20% each week drives enquiries, bookings, and occupancy upward very quickly. But the first, linear rule (dashed) keeps going until the number of people on holiday is well beyond the number of available rooms. Remember that this firm has no foresight—it is simply reacting to the data it sees at any moment. The overshoot arose because it kept increasing marketing at a time when high marketing was already delivering more bookings than it would be able to accommodate.

In the varying-adjustment case (dotted), the firm still has no foresight, but is moderating the strength of its adjustment in line with the size of the discrepancy it is trying to close. The initial adjustment is rapid, but progressively weakens as the goal is approached. Such thoughtful adjustment produces a more easily managed business—there is no overshoot, and adjustments are progressive rather than rapidly switching from plus to minus. Although the operating profit is no better, it is not exposed to the practical risks that would arise because of the stresses in the first case such as pressure on staff and damage to quality and reputation.

The second policy, of progressively varying adjustment, may seem unrealistically complex—surely no one writes down such subtle and complicated rules for deciding on a simple number like marketing spend. But, it is an entirely normal human reaction to make stronger corrective decisions when things are a long way from being as we want them, and to make less strong adjustments when things are closer to our goal.

This is crucial! Executives are often skeptical that the subtlety and sophistication of their decision making can be laid bare in this way, and can also feel threatened by what may seem a challenge to their authority and skill. However, *decisions are critical features of the strategic architecture, and must be being made* **somehow**—*all we are asking is to lay them out clearly so we can see how they affect the system's performance.* In most cases, the clarity that emerges for the team's collective understanding of why the business is performing as it is, and the potential for substantial improvement is more than adequate to overcome individuals' anxieties.

Periodic decision making

One feature of the decision-making examples so far that *is* unrealistic, however, is the continuous nature of the adjustments. This firm, for example, would be most unlikely to scan its performance constantly and make fine-tuning changes to its marketing spend every day or every week. More probably, it will decide on a spending rate that seems a good balance between improving the situation and not risking a big error, then see how events turn out for a while before considering a further change.

Figure 10.7 repeats the varying adjustment policy from Figure 10.6, but with changes to marketing spend only being made every 4 weeks:

- During the first period, management is learning that their current spend is enough to sustain enquiries and bookings, but not sufficient to build toward its goal. The team therefore makes a step increase in marketing spend.
- During the second period, evidence comes in of an increased enquiry rate, a brief surge in the new-arrivals rate, and an increase to a new plateau of room occupancy, but this is still below target, so a further but smaller increase in marketing is made.
- During the third period, business builds once more, but, after a further 4 weeks, it has grown to be too high, so the next decision point sees marketing spend reduced somewhat.
- The fourth period sees a brief drop in the rate of new enquiries and bookings, and room occupancy settles down to match the target.

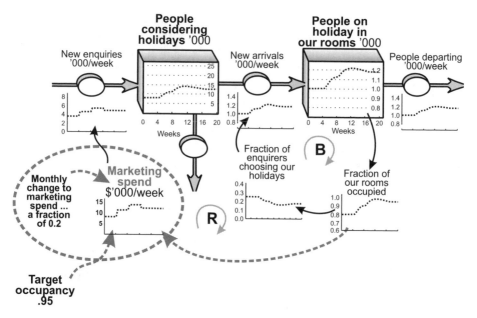

Figure 10.7 Periodic adjustment of marketing spend to reach target room occupancy.

This periodic decision-making approach not only has the obvious practical advantage of avoiding the need for constant effort to scan information and decide, it also turns out to be more useful in one important respect. When decisions are being constantly adjusted, the consequential effects are continuous and small, which makes it difficult to detect and understand what is going on. In contrast, stepwise adjustments are more likely to have effects that are detectable and amenable to being isolated from other events (see, for example, the significant changes to the rates of new enquiries and new arrivals in Figure 10.7). Management therefore receives, paradoxically, *more* information about critical policy relationships from making *fewer* decisions, provided, of course, that they make efforts to collect that information!

Policy example 2—set pricing to grow profits. The single policy issue that causes most anxiety for management is the setting of price. Yet, in spite of its critical importance, the pricing decision too is often guided by rather unsophisticated rules of thumb.

The decision on advertizing spend was, compared with pricing, relatively uncomplicated. More advertizing would probably, up to a certain rate, raise sales volume and revenue, so it would be straightforward to estimate the point at which a further increase in spending would not be worthwhile.

In contrast, the consequences of price changes are often ambiguous. Certainly, higher price will increase margins, but at the same time it will probably reduce sales volume. For any given state of the business, then, it is most unclear whether a price increase will raise or lower profitability, even in the short term. Add to this dilemma the observation that pricing will affect customer *gains and losses over*

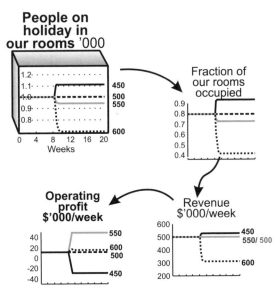

Figure 10.8 Effect of price change on holiday sales, revenue, and operating profit.

time, as well as their purchase rate, and it perhaps becomes clearer why management finds this decision so tricky.

To illustrate, let's switch attention to the holiday firm's pricing choice. Apart from the direct and immediate effect on margin, we'll assume that its only other effect is on the fraction of enquiries that convert into bookings. There is a simple, but unknown, demand elasticity—the booking success fraction falls with rising price, but to an unknown degree.

Figure 10.8 shows the effect of a one-off price change in Week 8, as compared with a base price of $500 per person week:

- the number of people in our rooms and fractional occupancy show, unsurprisingly, that more holidays are sold at a lower price, and fewer at higher prices;
- revenue, though, is virtually unchanged between prices of $500 and $550;
- consequently, operating profit is highest at $550 (grey line), since the margin is greater by $50/person than for the base-case price. At the lowest price (solid), the margin lost is far too great to make up for the extra number of holidays sold. At the highest price (dotted), the extra margin is almost completely eliminated by the far lower number of holidays sold.

This response of the customers to price is not actually known to management, so must be discovered by experience. The puzzle at the start, though, is "*Which direction to move price?*" On the one hand, occupancy is low, so if a modest price cut filled a lot of empty rooms, profits might rise. On the other hand, raising price increases margin, so if customer bookings only fall by a small rate, profits might improve from that alternative. In either case, the company

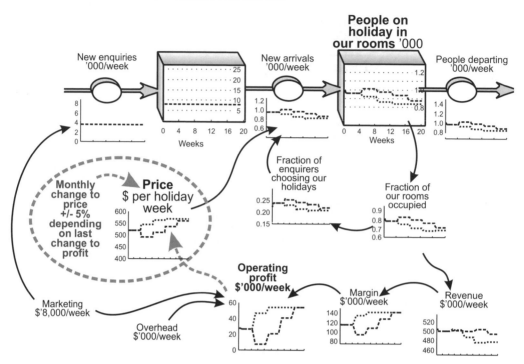

Figure 10.9 Periodic price change policy on holidays to move towards increasing profits.

will need to wait long enough after each change to see the effect come through to profits.

These two options correspond to a policy like: *"Cut (or raise) price by 5%, and, if profits rise over the following 4 weeks, repeat this change, otherwise reverse it."* The scale of price adjustment and the review period can of course be changed. In particular, management is likely to moderate its pricing change if they seem to be moving toward an optimal price level. Figure 10.9 shows the progress of sales and profits if this policy is pursued, from an initial price of $520, depending on whether the first move is to lower price (dashed) or raise it (dotted).

It is apparent that an initial price *cut* is an expensive option, since the increased bookings fall far short of the lost margin. Nevertheless, over the following 16 weeks, the policy pulls price back to a level very near to the optimum.

Dissecting interference between policies

Thus far, we have been making three important simplifying assumptions:

• management has one clear and unequivocal goal;

- only one decision variable is being moved in order to pursue this goal; and
- the firm can take any time necessary to move toward the goal.

None of these conditions applies in most practical cases. Depending on the context, management may be under pressure to hit goals for earnings, return on capital, sales growth, market share, capacity utilization, shareholder value, or a host of other measures. To hit these goals, management generally has a bewildering array of decision levers to pull—pricing, marketing, sales effort, capacity investment, hiring, and so on. Finally, the time horizon for the various goals ranges from weeks (''We've got an earnings announcement next month, so pull that advertizing!'') to many years (''We can move our share of this mature industry from 15% to 35% over the next 8 years by targeting our product development efforts at squeezing out the weakest competitors.'')

Some of these issues can be illustrated with a case concerning a specialist manufacturing business that supplies measuring equipment for major producers in process industries—chemicals, food, and drink, etc. The equipment, though relatively simple and inexpensive, is a common feature of all such production plants, having replaced manual measurement methods several decades ago.

The industries using these devices are all relatively mature, so customer numbers are rather stable. The equipment has a limited useful life, so sales, averaging 50 units/month per customer, mostly reflect a replacement demand. The small fraction going into newly constructed process plants more or less balances the loss of sales as customers close old plants.

The market consists largely of about 250 major customers worldwide, and this firm has around 40% of the market, the rest being shared between a principal competitor and some smaller rivals for whom this equipment is a less important business.

Costing around $1,000 per unit, the equipment is not a major expense compared with the large and costly production facilities of its customers. Buyers therefore tend to favor one supplier at any time, since this makes it easier to service the devices. However, the total purchases for any one customer add up to a significant overall cost, so high pricing both makes it harder for the firm's salesforce to acquire customers and also accelerates loss of customers to rivals.

Being a mature technology, large price changes are uncommon. The rate of customer migration is relatively slow, as competing salesforces circulate around the process industries in an attempt to influence the senior engineers responsible for purchasing these devices. There is a small degree of demand elasticity among customers, whose equipment budgets can justify purchasing more units for marginally useful purposes if prices are lower, or defer such purchases at higher prices.

The main costs for the business are:

- Unit production costs of around $500, plus some fixed capacity costs.
- Sales and customer support staff, who support other product lines for the company. Salesforce time is allocated between product lines on the basis of

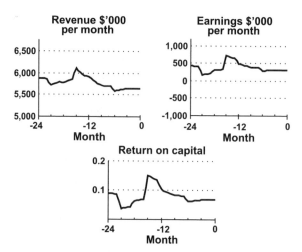

Figure 10.10 Recent performance of measuring devices manufacturer.

sales opportunities, and support staff reflect the installed base of equipment at customer sites.

- Marketing expenditure is needed for literature and trade-press advertizing. The firm also takes stands at trade shows, which occur in the major industrial regions of the world on a more or less regular basis throughout the year.

Before developing policies for the measuring devices firm, management faced a difficulty that confronts most organizations—its history included continuous choices on multiple decisions that affected overlapping performance outcomes. Specifically, changes had been made to both pricing and marketing expenditures, and both of these had caused changes to several performance outcomes, including customer numbers, sales, and earnings. The first task, then, was to tease out from the firm's recent history some insight regarding the separate effect of price and marketing.

At the time of the study, the division had been losing customers slowly but steadily. Its earnings were falling, and return on capital was disappointing (Figure 10.10). This poor performance had put management under two conflicting pressures:

- the need to retain customers and sales implied keeping prices down and marketing spend high;
- the need to support and improve profits required higher prices plus cost savings, including cuts in marketing spend.

In an effort to build sales and profitability, management had pursued a variety of marketing and pricing policies, but with little sustained benefit (Figure 10.11). These decisions were typically agreed at quarterly meetings of the management team.

Management had already tried to understand what was going on, and to find

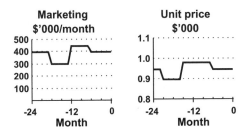

Figure 10.11 Recent marketing and pricing decisions.

relationships between their decisions and the business performance. By putting these charts together, though, the team had seen little pattern, apart from the obvious: that profits increased for a short time when price went up, or when marketing was reduced. But, the effect was unsustained, and it clearly made no sense to keep raising price and cutting marketing spend.

To seek further understanding, they had also looked to see if revenues or earnings were correlated with marketing and price (Figure 10.12). For reasons explained in Chapter 3, these analyses told them little of value. These charts implied that revenue was *lower* at higher rates of marketing spend, which did not seem to make sense, and that revenue was lower at higher price, which at least seemed plausible. Earnings did not seem to be related to marketing spend in any systematic manner, and the relationship between price and earnings

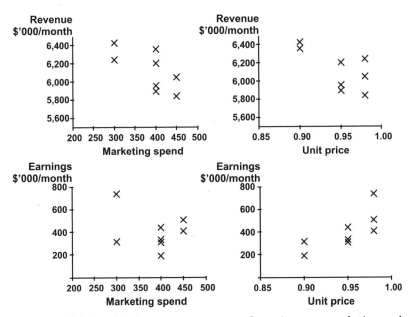

Figure 10.12 Relationship between revenues and earnings, vs. marketing and price.

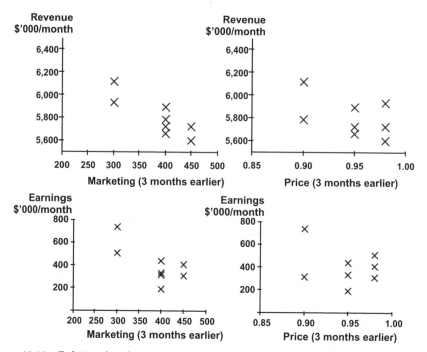

Figure 10.13 Relationship between revenues and earnings vs. marketing and price, 3 months earlier.

suggested nothing more than the obvious—that higher price gave higher margins.

Recognizing that price and marketing might take some time to have an effect (they estimated about 3 months), the team also wondered if *current* revenues or earnings were more strongly related to *previous* marketing expenditures and price (Figure 10.13). But, these comparisons made little more sense than the simultaneous relationships.

To truly understand what was happening in the measuring devices business, then, required a sound picture of its strategic architecture. This is shown in Figure 10.14, together with the firm's last 2 years' performance.

Management then set about picking apart this experience to look for some understanding of the drivers of business performance:

- The clearest part of the picture concerned price and sales per customer. It was no surprise to see unit sales to each customer fall sharply when a substantial price increase was implemented in Month −15. It also seemed, though (Month −12), that marketing affected current sales to each customer.
- The critical insight, however, came from studying the flow of net customers won. (*As noted in earlier chapters, separating customer gains from customer losses would have been more valuable still, but this information was not readily available.*) The sharp switch to net customer losses in Month −15 was particularly clear,

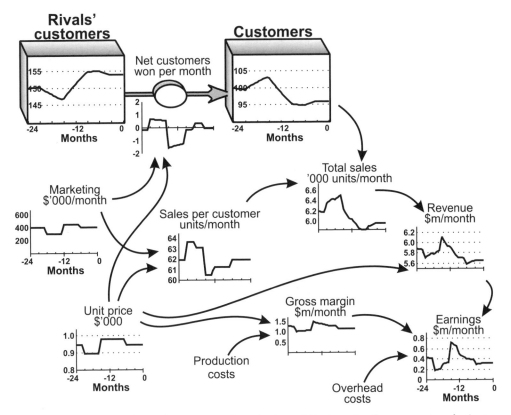

Figure 10.14 Historic performance and strategic architecture for the measuring devices firm.

which explained why the earnings jump at that date had lasted for so short a time. At an earlier time (Month −21), a price cut appeared to have triggered a net inflow of customers, though the drop in earnings that this price cut caused undermined management's confidence, and led to the later hike in price.

- Marketing also seemed to affect customer acquisition quite strongly. Management knew that marketing would take some time to work, as increased visibility and promotion needed subsequent sales calls to turn customer interest into actual sales. The marketing increase in Month −12 did seem, by Month −9, to have stopped customer losses. Also, the most positive period for customer acquisition (Months −21 to −15) seemed to have followed a period of sustained marketing spend of approximately $400,000 per month.

The next task was to assess the likely future for sales and earnings under alternative policies. First, since the net customer flow at Month 0 was zero, it seemed that the current price and current rate of marketing spend were likely to result in

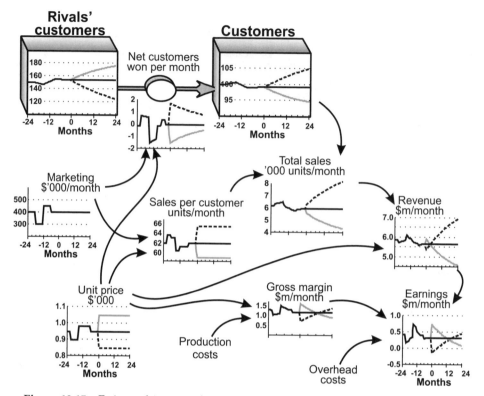

Figure 10.15 Estimated impact of new price levels for the measuring devices firm.

stable performance. So, what would be the likely long-term impact of a step change in price or marketing spend? Each was thought likely to trigger *both* an immediate change in customer purchase rate *and* a persistent shift in the net rate of customer acquisition.

On price, historic evidence suggested that existing customers would change their purchase rates substantially, while customer win rates too would shift. However, although this assessment produced an optimistic view of potential growth in sales volume and revenues, the cost in lost margin due to the price cut needed to achieve any gain would be considerable (Figure 10.15). Hence, the sharp drop in earnings for the price-reduction option (dashed) would take some time to be recovered through customer acquisition. Incidentally, there was no evidence to suggest that customers were relatively more sensitive to price increases vs. decreases, or vice versa.

Management's estimate of the response to marketing spend is shown in Figure 10.16. Like price, marketing seemed to affect the customer acquisition rate quite strongly, though, as noted above, there was thought to be a 3-month delay before increased marketing brought in new customers. The historical evidence suggested that the rate of sales per customer changed only modestly

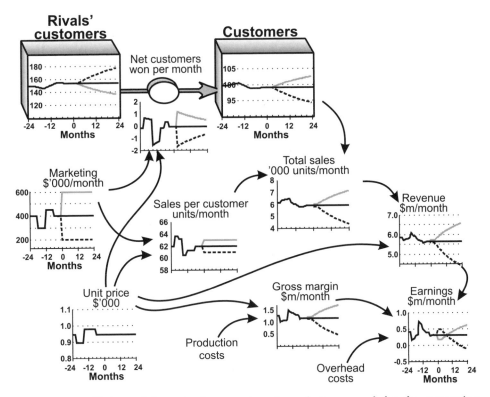

Figure 10.16 Estimated impact of new rates of marketing spend for the measuring devices firm.

in response to any marketing change. This seemed reasonable, since existing customers already knew about the firm's products.

Taken together, the faster customer acquisition rate and increased sales per customer looked likely to drive strong revenue growth, though, again, the early cost of increased spending would hurt earnings for some time before additional profits flowed in from a higher sales rate.

Management was now in a position to develop policies for price and marketing spend, but with an important precaution. The estimated impacts of these decisions on sales and earnings are exactly that—estimates—though apparently consistent with recent history. Actual market responses might well turn out rather differently from these, so policy would have to be flexible enough to adapt as information on customer acquisition and sales came in.

At least four performance indicators might be used here to guide policy on price and marketing:

● The volume of *total sales* ('000 units/month) seems to be a useful indicator if, as is common in many cases, management takes the view that "market share is all-important—profitability will follow". If a given change in price or marketing results in growth of sales volume, then the change would be repeated, otherwise the change would be reversed. Since neither a price *increase* nor a marketing *decrease* is likely to grow sales, this policy is likely to keep driving price down. Price decreases or marketing increases would likely continue, until no more customers were motivated to switch or to increase their purchase rate.

- Using *customer acquisition* (net customers won per month) to inform decisions appears likely to have a similar effect, again driving price down and marketing up until customers stopped switching.
- Since these first two performance indicators risk driving price down and throwing away margin, management could look at changes in *revenue* ($m/month). This indicator, too, would probably result in persistent increases in marketing spend, but its impact on pricing decisions is less certain. A price decrease ($/unit) would both increase sales per customer and customer win rate, but could move revenues either up or down, depending on whether the fractional increase in sales volume was higher or lower than the fractional drop in price. Moreover, the *timing* of the comparison would be important—since the price decrease would trigger an *inflow* of customers that would persist for some time, the net effect on revenues might be positive or negative, depending on when management chooses to make the comparison.
- The firm's *earnings rate* ($m/month) appears to be the ultimate indicator. After all, it is the outcome on which investors will judge the firm's management (there's no significant capital investment going on here), and it should reflect the longer-term net effects of changes to customer numbers, sales rates, and margins.

Conflicting goals

Having separated the impact of policies that interfere with each other, at least to some degree of confidence, we now turn to the second source of complexity that must be taken into account in formulating those policies—the simultaneous pursuit of conflicting objectives.

Let's first look at the marketing spend decision for the measuring devices firm, and compare two policies:

- pursuit of earnings; and
- pursuit of sales.

First, since earnings seem the best overall guide to the wisdom of its decisions, the firm could change its marketing spend, then 3 months later look at how earnings have changed. An increase in marketing would probably increase customer acquisition, and perhaps boost sales per customer, so it should simply be a question of comparing the extra margin from these increased sales against the cost of higher marketing—if there's a net increase, try a further boost to marketing for the next quarter, if not, cut spending back once more.

However, we already know that marketing will trigger an *inflow* of customers, so it is probable that, just 3 months after the decision, earnings will be on an upward trajectory. We should, then, look at what earnings will *grow to* if the increase continues. In total, the evaluation of earnings, 3 months after the last decision to increase marketing spend, should reflect the sum of four items:

- the initial and continuing cost of the higher marketing spend rate;
- the increase in earnings up to the third month that has arisen from any additional customers won;
- the *projected* increase in earnings after the third month that will arise from a continuing gain in new customers; and
- the further earnings increase arising from higher sales to all customers, including those expected to be won after the third month.

The dilemma is—how far into the future to project gains in customers? The firm's trading history hints at customer acquisition continuing for at least 6 months after marketing spend is increased. But, market responses may be different in future, and it is also possible that our revised policy will take marketing spend to levels we have not experienced before, so it might be wise for management to assume no more than a further 3 months of persistent customer gains from any increase in marketing.

This earnings-driven marketing policy can be compared with a pure pursuit of total sales, which, as explained above, is likely to result in continually increased marketing spend until customers cease to respond to further increases. Table 10.1 summarizes these two contrasting policies.

Figure 10.17 plays out these two policies, based on the relationships estimated from the firm's historic experience. As expected, the sales-driven policy (solid) progressively raises marketing spend, which creates a continued positive acquisition of customers, as well as an increase in sales per customer. By Month 24, though, the first signs of diminishing returns to marketing are beginning to show—with the net customer acquisition rate starting to fall. Within a further 12 months, therefore, the firm might expect to see customer acquisition cease, even if it were to continue to raise its spending.

The customer base, total sales volume, and revenue also rise progressively during the following 24 months. In the medium term, the firm suffers a reduction in earnings, to pay for the increased marketing. However, after each quarter, the previous increase in marketing spend has just about brought in enough additional business to pay for itself, so earnings hover around $300,000/month. By Month 12, though, the accumulation of new customers is beginning to be felt, and the increased sales/customer on a rising customer base more than pays for the higher spend, and earnings start to rise.

In contrast, the earnings-driven policy (dashed) favours reduced marketing spend over the 24 months. The first step (an increase in marketing) at month 0 is costly, and even projecting the pace of earnings growth 3 months later is not sufficient to give management the confidence that increased marketing is good for earnings. Consequently, marketing is then cut back to $400,000/month. This boosts earnings, which encourages management to repeat the cuts. Only twice

Table 10.1 Policies for deciding on marketing spend in the measuring devices firm.

Sales-driven policy	Earnings-driven policy
Decision item to control—both policies	
Marketing spend, $'000/week	
Affected flows and other items—both policies	
Customer-acquisition rate	
Sales per customer per month	
Earnings per month	
Chosen information	
Total sales (units/month) this month vs. 3 months ago	Earnings ($'000/month) this month vs. 3 months ago, plus 3 further months of the current rate of increase
Target state of the business	
Sales rate higher than 3 months ago	Earnings rate, plus 3 months projected increase, higher than 3 months ago
Decision rule	
If sales are higher than 3 months ago, raise marketing by $50,000/month, otherwise reduce by the same amount	If earnings plus 3 months' projected increase are higher than 3 months ago, raise marketing by $50,000/month, otherwise reduce by the same amount

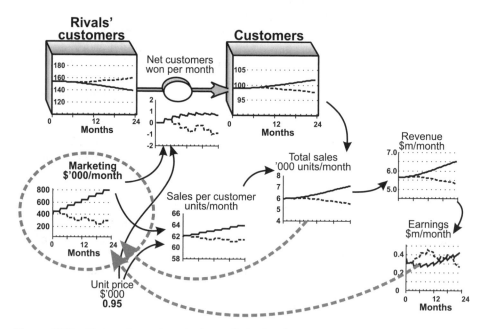

Figure 10.17 Comparison of marketing policies for the measuring devices firm, in pursuit of sales (solid) or earnings (dashed).

during the 2 years (Months 12 and 21) does the increase in earnings seem insufficient to justify a further cut in marketing. However, in both cases, the earnings hit that results from the subsequent increase in marketing reaffirms management's belief that marketing is too costly, and the firm resumes its cost-reducing strategy.

The most interesting feature of this comparison, of course, is that the sales-driven strategy actually results in *higher* earnings by Month 21 than the more allegedly earnings-driven strategy. It should by now be clear that this is an inevitable consequence of the "history matters" principle. By Month 21, the firm is reaping the rewards of the increased rate of sales and revenue that comes from the accumulated increase in customers. It is not hard to see why a company held to account for quarterly earnings statements, and hounded by analysts projecting earnings increases, could lose its nerve during the first three quarters of its marketing-driven strategy and switch to cost cutting.

It would be tough to refute a challenge from an outside observer looking at the firm in Month 9, who charged that the marketing strategy "isn't working". Ironically, if management *did* succumb to such pressure, the firm's earnings would indeed jump sharply—the saving of $200,000/month in marketing expenditure would flow through to the earnings statement, and there would be no apparent damage to sales or earnings. The analyst's criticism would thus be graphically vindicated, and only over the next 2 years would the damage from renewed loss of customer flow be felt.

The choice of performance outcomes also arises in deciding the price for the measuring devices. Table 10.2 sets out policies for pricing that parallel those used for deciding on marketing spend.

Management decides on an initial price increase in Month 0, before once again reviewing the situation 3 months later and making further adjustments. The standard price adjustment is $25/unit, or about 2.5%. Figure 10.18 plays out the consequences that arise from deciding price on the basis of sales growth (solid) and earnings (dashed), respectively.

As might be expected, the policy of setting price to pursue increasing sales volume persistently pushes price down. As a result, customer acquisition, sales per customer, and total sales volume all rise. However, sales *revenue* does not rise over the first 9 months, since the volume increase is more than countered by the reduced unit price. As the purely volume-driven policy is rather ill-advised, pursuing revenue growth might be a more sensible option.

In contrast, driving price decisions from earnings growth appears to work rather well. Price increases persist until Month 9, when customer losses and reduced sales per customer offset the margin gained from the price increase to $1,050/unit in Month 6. This price increase is therefore reversed, and price hovers around $1,000–1,050 for the next few quarters.

It seems, then, that using earnings growth to steer pricing decisions is a sound policy for this firm. But, by the end of the period, there are worrying signs that earnings make a poor choice of performance indicator, just as it was for the decision on marketing spend. Between Months 9 and 18, earnings fall as customer losses continue. The earnings recovery that occurs in each quarter

Table 10.2 Policies for deciding on marketing spend in the measuring devices firm.

Sales-driven policy	Earnings-driven policy
Decision item to control	
Unit price $'000	
Affected flows and other items	
Customer-acquisition rate	
Sales per customer per month	
Earnings per month	
Chosen information	
Total sales (units/month this month vs. 3 months ago)	Earnings ($'000/month) this month vs. 3 months ago, plus 3 further months of the current rate of increase
Target state of the business	
Sales rate higher than 3 months ago	Earnings rate, plus 3 months projected increase, higher than 3 months ago
Decision rule	
If sales are higher than 3 months ago, raise price by $25/unit, otherwise reduce by the same amount	If earnings plus 3 months' projected increase are higher than 3 months ago, raise marketing by $25/unit, otherwise reduce by the same amount

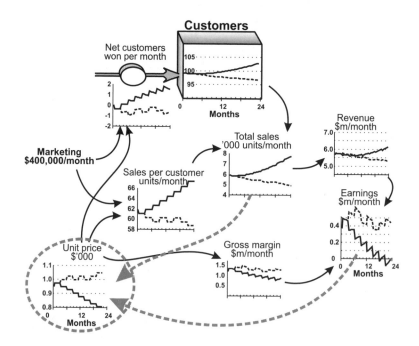

Figure 10.18 Comparison of pricing policies for the measuring devices firm, in pursuit of sales (solid) or earnings (dashed).

that a price increase is reversed is never sufficient to justify continuing with this reduction, and price is increased once more. Unfortunately, by Month 18, the customer base has fallen sufficiently that a *further* price increase more than offsets any immediate drop in sales. Given the recent history up to Month 18, then, management is likely to choose further price increases, in spite of the damage this did to the customer base a year previously.

Balance between conflicting performance outcomes

An obvious solution to the disadvantages of driving decision making by sales or earnings alone is to use a balance of the two. Such compromises are frequently adopted in practise, not just regarding marketing and pricing, but across a wide range of decisions. The outcomes being traded off can also be more wide-ranging than simply whether to favor sales growth or near term earnings. For example, the simple marketing decision in this case could reasonably be expected to affect salesforce motivation, and management may fear that the pricing decision will trigger a response by competitors. Decisions on everything from hiring to product development to financing always require management to balance priorities between conflicting objectives.

While a compromise decision in such cases might seem to imply indecisiveness on the part of management, a more thoughtful assessment suggests a fundamentally sound rationale for avoiding one-dimensional decision making. Earlier chapters have explained, in various contexts, how performance can be kicked out of balance, due to a substantial change in just one resource. By using a mix of performance indicators, management reduces the risk of creating such imbalances.

It would be entirely reasonable, then, for the measuring devices firm to base pricing and marketing decisions on a balance between the outcomes for both sales volume and earnings. Figure 10.19 shows the result if management pays equal attention to these two performance measures when deciding on either marketing spend (Figure 10.19a) or price (Figure 10.19b).

When marketing spend was set by reference to the earnings outcome alone (Figure 10.17, dashed), a series of spending reductions were made, which resulted in loss of customers and sales over the 2 years. When sales volumes, too, are considered (Figure 10.19a), higher spending is pushed through, and both customers and sales increase. However, the continued attention to earnings moderates the spending increase.

The pricing decision (Figure 10.19b) is considerably more reasonable, when informed by the balance between sales and earnings, than it was when either indicator was used alone. An initial increase in price boosts earnings, but the loss of customers and sales by Month 6 encourages the firm to reverse this decision—a pattern repeated in Year 2. Although earnings do not hit the high earnings rates achieved, albeit briefly, when this objective alone was pursued (Figure 10.18, dashed), the firm avoids undermining its core customer base.

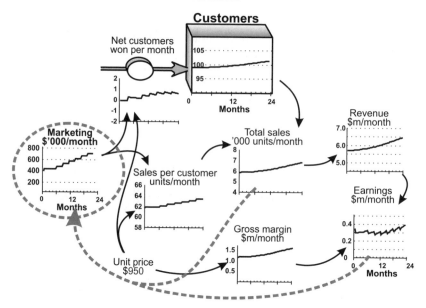

Figure 10.19a   Using a balance of earnings and sales volume to set marketing spend for the measuring devices firm.

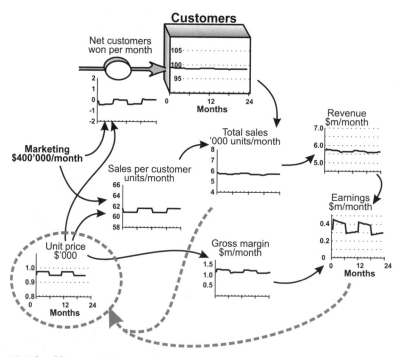

Figure 10.19b   Using a balance of earnings and sales volume to set price for the measuring devices firm.

Limits to human decision making

The latest example has only concerned two rather simple decisions affecting a few rather simple outcomes in a rather simple business architecture. Yet, we already find ourselves needing to grapple with complex and interacting outcomes, and define complex decision rules in order to cope. And these rules look unrealistically formulaic and contrived, compared with the routine and effortless decision making that executives carry out every day.

How, then, does management cope with the complexity of real decisions, without suffering a mental breakdown at the vast array of potentially relevant information and the multiplicity of consequences that may need to be considered? A single decision on marketing spend may, in reality, be informed by current sales, market share, customer research, rivals' expenditures, imminent product launches, product availability, targets for sales, customer acquisition, market share and profitability, and the state of the department's budget.

A behavioral view of decision making suggests that people cope by not even trying to take all these issues into account. Instead, they surround themselves with filters, selecting only a very few items of information on which to base their decision (Simon, 1976). These filters, whose operation is shown in Figure 10.20, include:

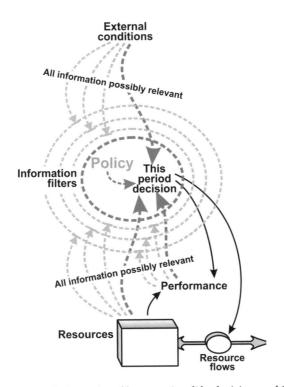

Figure 10.20 Information filters to simplify decision making.

- cognitive limits—"*I can't take **that** into account too*", or "*I don't understand what this piece of information means*";
- operating goals and incentives—"*My bonus depends on hitting a market share goal, so I'll ignore information on profits*";
- measurement limits—"*I can't trust the information on competitors' marketing activity*";
- organizational or geographic constraints—"*The sales report from the North region is always out of date, so I won't take that into account*";
- cultural problems—"*I don't care if there's no stock to fulfill the sales forecast; my job is to sell the stuff*".

In contrast to the rational decisions often assumed in economic models, managers exhibit bounded rationality in their decision making—a reasonable effort at good-enough decisions, within the constraints they face. Nor could we expect much to change, even if managers had limitless information-processing capability. Because *others* are also making boundedly rational decisions, considerable uncertainty will always surround both the information available to us, and the outcomes of our decisions.

The clarity provided by a sound picture of the resource system that managers are steering may help improve decision making, while recognizing these limits to human decision making. We have already explained that resource flows are the *only* places in the business architecture where strategic performance can be altered. Furthermore, Chapter 9 explained how teams typically have primary responsibility for one or two key flows. We also saw how one group may, often inadvertently, influence further flows beyond their direct responsibility. This makes it possible to simplify decision making and the information supply on which it depends:

- clarify the key resource flows for which a manager or team is responsible;
- identify other resource flows that this manager or team is also influencing;
- focus their performance goals on achieving the resource flows that are their primary responsibility, while supporting, or at least not damaging, others that they may influence;
- concentrate their information reporting, analysis, and performance incentives on these same resource flows;
- where interference arises between goals and policies pursued (whether within or between teams), use resource-system analysis on this part of the organization's architecture to resolve the interference and make appropriate choices.

Interference between goals and policies

It might seem that we now have a simple means for resolving the interference between different policies such as that between marketing and pricing for our measuring devices firm. But, this problem is not so easily dismissed—for a very simple reason. Where two or more decisions act on the same resource flow or

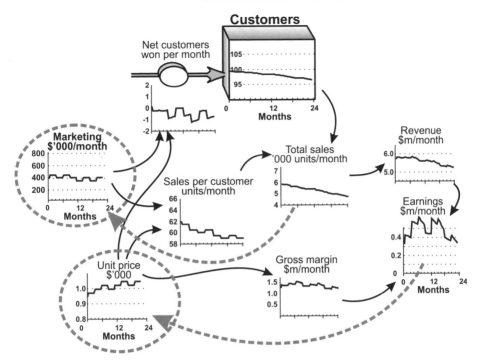

Figure 10.21 Interference between marketing and pricing decisions that influence common outcomes.

other factor, it is difficult to identify which decision is responsible, to what degree, for any particular outcome.

In our case example, price and marketing both impact on three items:

- the net win rate of customers;
- the current purchase rate of customers;
- current operating margins.

Of these, only the third is readily calculated—operating margin is reduced by an increase in marketing, and by a reduction in price. In contrast, if marketing and price are *both* moved, it is impossible to separate by analysis the extent to which each is responsible for any subsequent change in customer win rate or purchase rate. Figures 10.15 and 10.16 represented *estimates* of these effects, but we can't be certain that those estimates are right, or that they will persist into the future.

To illustrate, Figure 10.21 shows what happens if the measuring devices firm tries to decide on both price and marketing each month, using the following rules:

- if our last price change was followed by an increase in earnings, repeat the decision, otherwise reverse it; *and*

- if our last marketing decision was followed by an increase in sales volume, repeat the decision, otherwise reverse it.

Clearly, price is interfering with the sales-volume information being used to decide on marketing—increases in marketing spend are followed by a decrease in sales volume, so the increase is reversed. Decreases in marketing spend are favored, and marketing spend will interfere with the earnings information we are using to decide on price. So, how do we overcome this difficulty of policy conflict?

First, we must be careful only to carry out analysis that is safe, given the accumulations involved and the interconnected architecture of other arithmetic relationships. Chapter 3 explained the weakness of correlation methods to elucidate performance outcomes such as sales or earnings. However, statistical analysis *is* safe, provided that no accumulating stock lies between the independent variable (in this case, our marketing and pricing decisions) and the variable we are trying to explain. This suggests the guiding principles in Table 10.3.

Table 10.3 Principles for analyzing the consequences of managerial decisions.

Guiding principle	Examples for the measuring devices firm
1. Focus attention on closely connected relationships	Sales per customer vs. marketing spend Sales per customer vs. price (*not* revenue or earnings vs. marketing or price)
2. Seek, in particular, immediate drivers of resource flows	Net customer win rate vs. marketing spend Net customer win rate vs. price (ideally, we should try to explain gains and losses separately)
3. Statistical analysis must *never* be applied to explain any asset stock	Current customers vs. marketing spend Current customers vs. price
4. Great care must be taken that *no* asset stock can arise between independent and dependent variables	Current sales volume, revenue, or earnings vs. marketing spend Current sales volume, revenue, or earnings vs. price

The firm we are considering here is extremely simple, so there may seem little danger of falling foul of this last problem. However, there are in practice several asset stocks that could go unnoticed. Increasingly uncompetitive pricing progressively damages salesforce morale, especially if the devices are part of a wider product range. The architecture of the situation suggests a correlation between sales per customer and price, but the hidden intervention of morale makes any findings quite unsafe.

The second task we must undertake to allow for the interference of decisions about one factor on the decisions we take about another is to adjust the information we use:

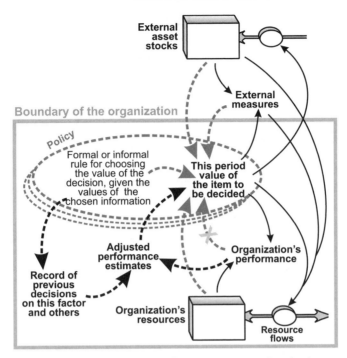

Figure 10.22 Adjusting the general policy function to recognize the impact of previous decisions.

> *For all information items used in a decision, estimate the dynamic consequences today of decisions taken previously, including both decisions about the factor itself and about others that may have affected those same consequences.*

This implies adding a mandatory element to the generic "goal and control" structure described earlier (Figure 10.22).

Figure 10.23 plays out a determined marketing-led strategy for our case example. *Previously*, the strategy would have played out as follows:

- the increase in marketing spend would damage earnings;
- the earnings drop would have triggered a sustained increase in price;
- the price increase would have cut sales/customer and sales volume;
- so, the increase in marketing spend would have been reversed; and
- the positive acquisition of customers would have stalled.

This time, before making its pricing decision, management adjusts the change in earnings to allow for its last decision on marketing spend. It also makes more cautious changes to price. The story in Figure 10.23, then, is:

- the initial increase in marketing spend damages earnings;
- correcting this damage to earnings before making the price decision, though, allows management to tolerate a small price cut;

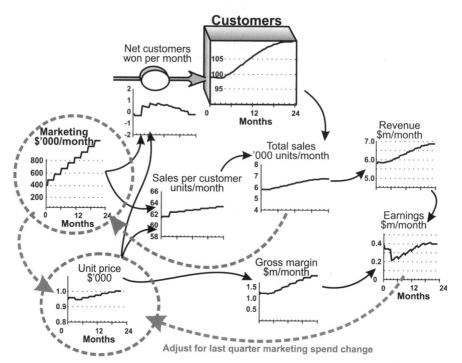

Figure 10.23 Adjusting the price decision to reflect the impact of marketing spend on earnings changes.

- sales/customer and sales volume therefore rise, as the marketing spend and price cut work through;
- which permits management to continue the increase in marketing spend;
- so, the firm continues a positive net acquisition of customers; and
- customer numbers, sales, revenues, and earnings climb persistently.

Goals, controls and the Balanced Scorecard (BSC)

The Balanced Scorecard is an integrated and holistic approach to performance measurement and management that has been adopted with success by many firms (Kaplan and Norton, 1996, and see also www.balancedscorecard.org). The method recognizes that financial factors alone provide inadequate targets and incentives, so adds measures relating to:

- customers—satisfaction, retention, market share, and share of business;
- internal performance—quality, response times, cost, and new product introductions;
- learning and growth—employee satisfaction and availability of information systems.

Only if these additional factors are in good shape will the firm deliver strong financial performance. The BSC offers important advances over traditional reporting approaches, both in recognizing the interconnectedness within the business and the importance of measuring and managing soft issues. Increased training of staff about products, for example, will improve sales effectiveness, which will in turn improve sales and margins. Both Richard Kaplan and David Norton have long advocated a systemic approach to business management and performance measurement, and there are clear connections between the main sectors of the BSC and the strategy dynamics approach.

1. *Scale, timing, and interdependence.* The first contribution offered by the resource-system perspective is to clarify *which* measures matter, how much they matter, how strongly they are connected, and over what timescale they change. Chapters 1 to 6 laid out exactly how the strategic architecture of firm resources can be identified and quantified, and showed where the critical control points lie—at the resource flows. Sound business processes work to ensure that all the important resource inflows are running strongly, that resource development is progressing as planned, and that outflows are under control. Crucially, the firm's strategic architecture can be brought to life with time charts of all important measures, while at the same time ensuring that these data are consistent and their interdependence clear.

A powerful feature of BSC reporting is that it highlights a link between actions, decisions, or initiatives and the performance item on the scorecard that this response is expected to correct. However, it has been shown throughout this book that accumulation and feedback processes combine to disrupt and confuse the hoped-for clarity of such causal connections. In addition to the clarity that the strategic architecture brings to the interdependence within the business system, this chapter has offered an approach to specifying goals and controls that should improve the confidence, reliability, and internal consistency of decision making.

2. *Intangibles.* The next contribution regards the measurement and use of intangible factors. Traditional financial measures pose little trouble in this regard—the most important ones such as staff costs and margins clearly *are* most important because any change makes a large difference to earnings. This clarity is lacking for many soft factors. If morale improves from 0.6 to 0.8, for example, traditional approaches offer little guidance as to the impact on earnings or other performance measures. Chapter 7, though, has described how intangibles can be specified, quantified, and managed.

3. *Learning and growth.* Chapter 9 offered some formal and reliable structures for capturing capability and learning. Capabilities arise from the firm's accumulated experience at resource building and development, and are manifest in the combination of staff experience and business processes. These formal structures provide exactly the metrics for capability and learning that are needed for informed policy.

4. *Competition.* The resource-system approach extends a competitive dimension to BSC measures (Chapter 8). Not only should we be in control of our own customer gains and losses, staff hiring and retention, and so on, but we

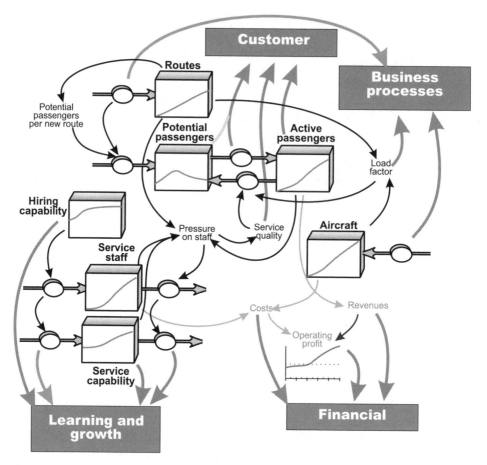

Figure 10.24 Contributions to the Balanced Scorecard arising from a sound strategic architecture.

should also understand how this performance is interacting with that of rivals. In addition, we should be anticipating how broader exogenous forces are changing our operating environment, both posing new challenges and opening up new opportunities for business development and the building of new resources and capabilities.

With the exception of the competitive frameworks, these contributions are illustrated in Figure 10.24 with the architecture developed for the low-fare airline.

A final contribution we offer concerns the practicality and process of performance measurement and management. Integrating a sound strategic architecture with BSC principles leads to a scorecard that is not only balanced but compact, joined up, and dynamically sound. Ideally, boardroom walls should have a white, erasable surface, on which is sketched one or more high-level resource-system maps (such as Figure 10.21 and others illustrated throughout this book). Each week or month, the time charts should be updated with actual information from the business, and the team's agenda should include a thorough review of policies and decisions.

Meeting spaces for the main functional teams, too, should feature resource maps—subsidiary diagrams of the main architecture that expand the detail of critical parts of the architecture. For example, the HR team room might feature diagrams such as the staff development chain (Figure 7.19) or the organizational change structure (Figure 8.18). The corporate development team would benefit from a map of the competitive industry evolution such as Figure 8.10 and industry-level rivalry (Figure 8.14). The marketing team should be using real-time maps of customer development such as Figure 8.17 and changes in customer annoyance (Figure 7.8). Similar submodels can support the needs of R&D, product development, sales, service, and finance groups.

Crucially, though, each submodel will highlight two vital features—the links *to* other groups' maps that show the health of the team's contribution to the rest of the system, and the links *from* those other groups that show the team how they depend on others.

The resource-system approach once again offers a rigorous, fact-based, coherent picture of how the factors that constitute the business itself connect, both to each other and to financial outcomes. The strategic architecture that can be elucidated for any organization provides a clear and easily communicated road map that shows staff exactly what matters and why, and how their actions and decisions affect performance in the medium to long term.

The only remaining problem is to get the organization to *stop* reporting, monitoring, and acting upon measures that don't matter! One senior partner in a major consulting firm estimates that, once a dynamically sound strategy is supported with properly-chosen initiatives and reporting systems, most clients should simply drop two-thirds of their existing activity and reporting efforts. This excess is often not just irrelevant, but positively dangerous, encouraging staff and management to pursue inappropriate ratios with ill-chosen policies and initiatives. Unfortunately, old habits die hard, and most managers cling to the comforting measures they have always used, in spite of their demonstrated failure.

Illustration of valuing a strategic initiative

We started, in Chapter 1, pointing out the critical importance to firm valuation of a sound understanding of the time-path of future earnings. Figure 10.25 offers a small example of how resource-system analysis can help in providing a firm foundation for evaluating a strategic response by management to a challenging situation. To grow its fleet of aircraft, our low-fare airline must employ additional capital. Deducting this cash outflow and making other adjustments causes the free cash flow to be sharply lower than the operating profit.

In the base case (solid), the airline has strong capabilities on all resource-building activities, and grows routes, passengers, and staff strongly. However, its success in the marketplace soon creates more demand than its staff can cope

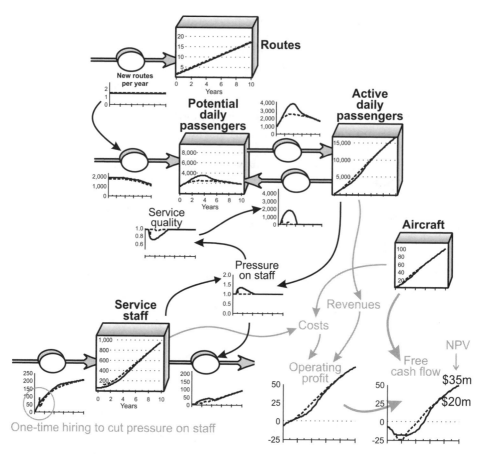

Figure 10.25 Valuing a one-off hiring decision for the low-fare airline.

with, which has two effects. First, service quality suffers, and the rapid acquisition of passengers is counterbalanced by a period of sharp passenger losses. Second, the work pressure causes significant staff attrition, which leads to the pressure and service difficulties continuing for 2 years.

In the alternative case (dashed), the airline experiences the same early growth and pressure from too much demand, but is fortunate in being able to hire in Year 1 a number of already trained staff from a competitor whose business has failed. The staff pressure is immediately relieved, service quality is repaired, and staff attrition reduced. Passenger losses too are cut, so that the firm's passenger base sustains a stronger growth. Operating profits are somewhat higher between Years 2 and 5. However, since the firm is now able to continue growing its fleet during Year 2, there is a brief period when free cash flow suffers from faster growth of the fleet. This is quickly compensated, though, by stronger operating profits from the middle of Year 3, and, in addition, the firm is not making the catch-up aircraft purchases of the base case. Consequently, free cash flow is much stronger in Years 3 to 6.

The result is a net present value for the firm's strategy of $35m, rather than the $20m of the base case, so that the one-off hiring decision has a strategic value to shareholders of $15m.

Summary

Management directs performance by comparing (whether explicitly or implicitly) the current state and trajectory of certain measures against goals or targets for those same items. "Policy" consists of somewhat simple guidelines for decisions that seek to close this gap between the actual and desired state of affairs.

To ensure that policies are sound and mutually consistent, management faces a difficult task in disentangling the outcomes that arise when two or more decision items interfere. This can be accomplished by carefully dissecting the resource accumulation and causal effects of each. Use of correlation methods to separate such effects must *never* be used when an accumulating resource arises between the item we wish to explain and possible explanatory factors.

Decision making is far from being perfectly rational, being constrained by unavoidable uncertainties in the information available and its implications, together with ambiguity and conflict between the different goals and pressures on management. However, in making any particular decision, a sound understanding of the organization's strategic architecture enables interference between decisions to be understood. It is therefore possible to adjust current decisions to allow for the consequences of *prior* decisions.

A rigorous portrayal of the strategic architecture, populated with quantified information on the organization's performance through time constitutes a truly dynamic balanced scorecard. This provides a sound basis for continuous and coherent monitoring and revision of strategy, and for the targets and incentives for the organization.

Using the strategic architecture to build an internally consistent projection of business performance and free cash flow outcomes provides a much-needed bridge between business strategy and the financial evaluation of firms, and of the strategic decisions made by management.

11

Further Developments on Existing Strategy Concepts

Key issues

❏ Firm-level, industry-level, and strategy process themes

❏ The dynamic basis of the experience curve

❏ Avoiding dangers from poor development of strategy dynamics, and using advisors

❏ The industry-level perspective, viewed as rivalry between firm systems

❏ Incorporating exogenous forces and building fact-based scenarios for assessing strategic options

❏ Easing the process of strategy development and delivery with a clear business architecture

❏ The further potential from applying a rigorously dynamic approach to corporate-level strategy questions.

Chapters 1 to 10 have built up a coherent, integrated set of frameworks for explaining, anticipating, and directing strategic performance. But, this perspective does not imply that all previous tools for strategy analysis and development should be thrown away. Strong connections can be identified with many existing frameworks, especially those that are fact-based and rigorous. A substantial development could be made to many of these connections, but practical constraints limit this chapter to no more than glimpses of this potential.

Since the strategy dynamics frameworks are built on the concept of enterprise resources, the clearest links identifiable are firm-centered. However, from this foundation, connections with industry-level approaches can readily be built. The strategy dynamics method has little to say, directly, regarding the strategy *process*—the question of how strategy arises and is disseminated. Practical experience, though, suggests that a sound strategic architecture offers indirect improvements to process, by making discussions more factual, less ambiguous, and more integrated.

Earlier chapters have already made connections with existing, widely-used frameworks. Chapter 1 explained the vital importance for valuing firms of a strategically robust, fact-based understanding of likely future earnings, and the well-known limitation of industry-level approaches. Chapter 2 explained how a rigorous analysis of resources and capabilities offers a substantial improvement on the often ambiguous consideration of a firm's strengths and weaknesses (part of the still-popular SWOT analysis). Chapter 3 pointed out the impossibility of reaching the earnings estimates that we require on the basis of commonly used correlation methods. Chapter 4 explained how the value-chain approach can be enhanced, by specifying the costs of holding and building resources and adding a time-path perspective. We will look at one more firm-level strategy tool in particular—the experience curve—and then move on to further discussion of industry-level perspectives.

Other firm-level strategy frameworks

The experience curve

In use since the 1960s, the experience curve is one of the few truly dynamic frameworks in Strategy. Though widely discussed by management in qualitative terms—*"If we cut price and build sales, we can drive down the learning curve"*—the experience curve in its true form is a quantitative tool. It arose from observations by the Boston Consulting Group (1970) that, in many manufacturing firms, the unit costs of production fell by characteristic amounts as *cumulative* output (i.e., "experience") increased. Specifically:

> *each time that cumulative output doubles, unit costs fall by 10–20%, this percentage being lower in the early phase of prototype development, higher as mass production becomes established, then lower once more when the market matures and sales growth slows.*

The experience curve has arguably become so axiomatic for fast-moving manufacturing sectors, and the dynamics of cost reduction so extensively developed by firms in such sectors that it warrants little discussion in modern strategy writing. However, its insights remain valid and important for newcomers to strategy.

The experience curve is in fact tracking the coincidence between two variables that are both changing through time—output and cost. Figure 11.1 portrays the experience of a firm serving a potential market of 2 million consumers with a high-value product costing, initially, $1,000 each to produce. From an initial base of just 20 users, its market grows by 10% each month—a threefold increase each year—until most of the likely users are developed, when only a fraction of this remaining potential are sold to each month.

Unit sales come from this flow of new users, but, in addition, consumers replace their product every 2 years, so that unit sales peak around Year 4, then stabilize as this replacement rate becomes an increasingly dominant fraction of

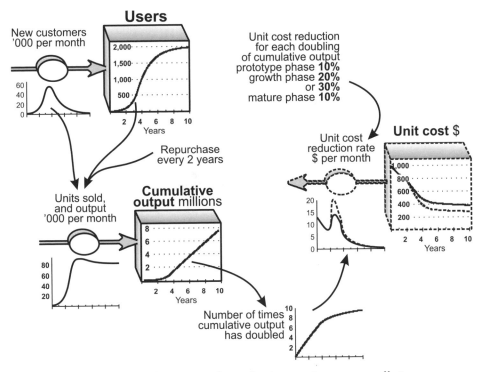

Figure 11.1 Unit costs reduce, due to experience-curve effects.

total sales. Over the 10-year timescale, production output more or less matches sales, resulting in the path for cumulative output shown in the lower-left stock.

The number of times that this record of cumulative output has doubled can be calculated as time passes, and the resulting cost-reduction rate estimated. This illustration compares two cases, in both of which costs fall by 10% for each doubling of cumulative output until this has occurred four times. From this point, the firm gets into its stride, and drives down unit costs by either 20% (solid) or 30% (dashed) for each doubling of output. From the seventh doubling of experience, cost reduction opportunities become harder to find and unit costs once again fall by only 10% for each doubling.

Figure 11.2 traces out the coincidence between unit costs and cumulative output, showing the characteristic three-phase trace observed by BCG. Notice that each marker on the curves represents the situation at each year from the starting point, indicating clearly the progressively longer time it takes to double cumulative output as the market becomes saturated.

Management of firms in industries that exhibit strong experience curve effects have long based their pricing strategies, in anticipation of market development rates, on the expectation of such cost reduction curves. It is clearly tempting, in this example, to price at $500 in Year 1, in order to bring forward the market's

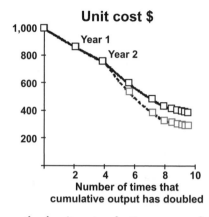

Figure 11.2 The path of unit cost reduction as cumulative output doubles.

development and capture both initial sales and replacement purchases ahead of rivals. However, such strategies are fraught with dangers, notably due to inaccurate estimation of market potential. Mobile phone manufacturers, for example, were caught out by the failure of WAP handsets to achieve more than a small fraction of expected uptake among consumers.

A second common error, though, is to assume that these experience-based benefits arise automatically. In reality, the curves indicate a likely *limit* to the rate at which costs may be reducible. Actually achieving those reductions requires constant, intensive production engineering effort. The "unit cost" resource in Figure 11.1 is a contrivance—there is in fact no such resource stock (hence its dashed outline). Unit cost is simply a ratio between total production costs and monthly manufactured output, so a proper treatment of this concept should track back not only to the genuine resources that are involved, notably employees and production capacity, but also to key intangibles such as plant reliability and yield. For the early part of this firm's history, up to Year 4, these resources develop strongly to enable the growth in required output. Unit-cost reductions in this phase can therefore only result if the costly resources grow less quickly than actual output (e.g., we only need 90% more people to produce twice the rate of output).

Thereafter, cost reductions must imply reductions in staff and other plant operating costs, or increases in yield. A usable resource-system analysis of experience-curve opportunities would therefore break out each of these components and scrutinize their flow drivers in the search for opportunities. In this effort, the accumulation of "capability", in the form of processes and procedures, will feature strongly (see Chapter 9). It has long been common in car manufacturing plants, for example, for production staff to meet briefly but regularly to share what may seem quite trivial cost-reduction opportunities. Crucial to this effort, though, is that these opportunities are collected, accumulated, and shared so that, over time, total costs are inexorably driven down.

Other management tools

Several other management and strategy methods can assist in delivering the strategic performance improvements that a Strategy Dynamics analysis may identify.

Business Process Re-engineering (BPR), when properly applied, is a powerful method for achieving potentially substantial improvements in operational effectiveness. The dynamic analysis will often expose critical dependencies between, for example, staffing and output, or between engineering effort and product development rate. A sound appraisal of processes may well reveal the opportunity to transform efficiency and thus the performance of the entire system.

Benchmarking, too, can be valuable, but requires caution—you are operating *your* business, with its own resources and architecture, not someone else's. It can be positively dangerous to scrutinize firms in other sectors with a view to simply copying their approach to customer service, HR development, and so on.

Many other management tools have grown in popularity over recent decades, only to fade from fashion as more novel concepts are developed. Such fashion cycles are somewhat inevitable, as genuinely better approaches supersede those whose contribution has been exhausted. However, two other phenomena also feature.

First, some genuinely sound and valuable methods fall from favor as a result of being misunderstood, misrepresented, and misapplied. BPR, for example, suffered this fate, resulting in an attitude among many managers of "Been there, done that, it doesn't work".

The problem of misapplication is often brought about by belief in the promise of a quick fix, so often suggested by management books and consultants. The deep and extensive effort required by many sound methods, and clearly spelled out by their originators, is often not committed. The difficulties that arise from superficial application of otherwise quite sound management methods are frequently exacerbated by "initiative overload"—the tendency for top management to instruct their people to make one initiative after another their "top priority", resulting in none being carried out properly, or completed before the next is started.

Avoiding disappointment with Strategy Dynamics

Strategy Dynamics, too, will not survive the damage that can be done by unprofessional application, so, in an effort to head off that risk, we can offer some promises—and some warnings:

- It is possible, even with limited time and effort, to achieve a quantified, top-level understanding of why your business performance is following its current path, and what might be done to improve its future.
- This understanding, though, will only be safe if the discipline of the method is properly applied. The basic rules have been spelled out definitively in the

early chapters, and, if these are not followed, your findings *will* be badly flawed, and you *will* risk making badly mistaken decisions.

- Beyond the top-level view of your strategy, detail becomes important. You will gain some insight by considering, for example, how the dynamics of your overall customer base or staffing are playing out, but, in all but the simplest cases, you will need to dig down into the specific numbers that are playing out for different customer segments and different groups of staff.

- This increasing detail makes the discipline of sticking to the quantitative facts increasingly challenging, but no less important. You *will* have to investigate these facts in some detail.

- The dynamic complexity that arises, both from the detail and, more importantly, from the interdependency within the business system, will quickly give rise to puzzles and counter-intuitive findings. Even the basic interactions through time between the flows and levels of a single resource are nonobvious. You will therefore need to find sound expertise in system-dynamics modeling (SD). Unfortunately, true expertise in this work is, as yet, exceedingly rare. Though a great many consultants claim the ability to build SD models, few do so properly, and the software's power and ease of use encourages the rapid creation of bad models. Don't let the expert out of your sight! Initially, restrict the analysis to capturing critical, small pieces of the architecture such as staff flows or the customer development chain. Only when you are satisfied that these small tasks have been properly accomplished should you work with the modeler to assess the connections between them.

- It is highly likely that much of the information you need has never been collected. Your first option at this point is to give up and not bother to go any further. But, be conscious that important factors such as staff attrition, market reputation or customer annoyance *are* playing out through time, whether you choose to assess them or not. So don't blame the method if your business gets into trouble because you didn't bother to understand these issues. The alternative is to make the best attempt you can at assessing these issues, and start on efforts to understand them better. While you are still uncertain, exercise extreme caution in drawing conclusions or instigating significant policy changes. Look for "no-regrets" moves (i.e., those that promise some upside while not exposing you to serious risks). A good question to keep in mind is, *"What's the worst that can happen here?"*

- Consultants are already offering to carry out strategy studies based on analysis of dynamics, and will do so increasingly. Many of these will claim to solve your problem by working with you on a qualitative diagnosis, and following up by building an SD model. A very small group of elite SD experts can carry this off—most others will simply get it wrong. You will be left with impressive-looking diagrams that you understand only superficially, and confident recommendations that may at best be useless, at worst positively dangerous. Even if they are OK for now, you will soon need to review your performance dynamics—a need that will never go away. *You can't subcontract strategic leadership—so you can't subcontract strategic under-*

standing. Do the work yourself, using consultants as advisors, as additional analytical resource, and as a sounding board for your own insights.

Industry-level approaches to strategy

Industry forces

The dominant approach to emerge from the industrial economics perspective on strategy is the analysis of competitive forces, commonly referred to as "five forces". The announcement in an MBA class that a five-forces analysis of a case study is required will often be greeted with groans of irritation, boredom, or annoyance. However, some important points are worth noting:

- Prior to the emergence of the method in the early 1980s, there was very little substance to strategy analysis—this framework brought considerable enlightenment to what had previously been a dark and mysterious world.
- In spite of the cautionary comments above regarding the limited explanatory power of industry conditions, the forces that the framework captures can be seen playing out in sector after sector to this day. It is therefore worth reviewing the contribution of this important framework and seeking opportunities to improve on its insights by adding a rigorous dynamic perspective.

The approach can be understood by building on the notion, explained in Chapter 4, of the firm as a value-adding entity between the costs of its inputs and the price it can charge for its outputs. Extending the value-adding principle backward and forward throughout an industry structure leads to a network of supplier and customer firms, each of which must make this margin over its costs. The result is a picture of the "value system" offered by the industry supply chain. Figure 11.3 shows a simplified value build-up for book supply through a conventional distribution chain. Essentially, analysis of this value build-up answers the question, *"Where does the money go?"*

Within this broad description of an industry's system, the analysis of competitive forces focuses on the pressures that compete away the profitability of firms at one specific place in the chain. The more profitable the activity, the more tempting it is for other firms to try to capture some of that margin. Generically, this pressure comes from five directions—customers, suppliers, current competitors, potential new rivals, and substitute products or services.

Although five-forces analysis has featured widely in strategy for two decades, there is widespread misunderstanding about the question to which the framework provides an answer. Most often, a review of these forces concludes, for example, that rivalry is "quite strong", buyers "very powerful" or the threat of substitutes "very weak". Properly carried out, however, this analysis should explain:

- *the profitability of this stage in the industry structure*—for example, the average return on sales and return on assets in airlines are very poor, because many

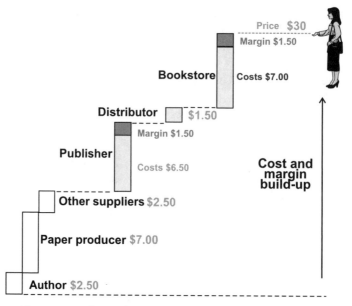

Figure 11.3 Simplified industry value system in books.

rivals compete for the same business, customers are both motivated and able to switch to better-value providers, and there is little to stop new firms entering the industry (a full analysis is, of course, more fine-grained than this brief summary);

- *the variance of that profitability among the population of rivals at any moment*—for example, profitability does not differ widely among supermarket firms, because any opportunity to be more profitable than average is readily copied by rivals, whereas profitability among restaurants is more widely distributed, due to the difficulty of identifying and replicating the reasons that allow some firms to command higher margins;
- *the variance of profitability over time*—for example, profitability in paper supply cycles strongly, due to changes in the balance of power between producers and customers as the balance between supply and demand changes; profitability in the supply of novel PC peripherals declines quickly after their initial development, because many rivals can copy the products.

From a sound understanding of how these forces determine profitability at any stage of the supply chain, management may be able to use the framework to guide important strategic choices. For example:

- Is there a market segment of buyers who value our products or services sufficiently that they will pay more than industry-average prices?
- Are there sufficient barriers (like specialist know-how) to prevent rivals from providing products and services of comparable value to our own?

- And, if rivals *could* copy our offering, do there exist (or can we create) barriers to keep our customers from switching away from us?
- Can we ensure that our business is sufficiently independent of specialist inputs that we can avoid losing our profitability in higher prices to our own suppliers?

and so on. Note the prevalence in this framework of various forms of ''barrier''. The more profitable is our industry or segment, the more it is worthwhile for one of these five groups to invest in overcoming whatever barriers keep them from getting their hands on our margin. The bigger those barriers, though, the more defensible is our higher-than-average margin.

Although the poor explanatory power of industry-level factors, noted in Chapter 1, limits the value that can be extracted from the industry forces approach to strategy development, the framework continues to provide explanations for important phenomena. For example, the boom-and-bust of the dot.com era was a classic illustration of the five forces at work. By eliminating substantial costs of conventional supply chains, e-businesses could create high-margin value propositions. It was anticipated that buyers would face few switching costs in taking up these alternatives (e.g., online access was widespread in chosen markets). By getting very big, very fast, the new providers would establish considerable buying power over their own suppliers, and erect substantial barriers against rivals or would-be entrants. The established suppliers constituted the substitutes, whose bricks-and-mortar legacy assets would be so difficult to unwind that they would be unable to compete away the margins available to the new business model.

Unfortunately, the five forces also describe quite neatly why most such initiatives were doomed to failure. Buyers who were able to switch *to* the new offering faced very low barriers to switching *away from* any one firm to another, and did so even for the smallest financial incentive. The new business model was often quite transparent, and required little investment in assets, so rivals and new entrants could copy the offering quickly. Worst of all, since so many enterprises saw the same opportunity for the same high returns from the same business models, there was a rush of new entry. In anticipation of great future profits, many gave away more than the margin that they ever expected to make, in the hope that, as the last survivor, they would be able to recapture margin in later years.

To this story can be added the gross misestimation of the potential offered by many markets, hopeless optimism regarding the attractiveness to buyers of often low-value service offerings, and the considerable value of certain legacy assets to bricks-and-mortar firms (e.g., their long-established reputation with customers). Finally, as in other episodes of new business opportunity, everyone thought that *they* would be the survivor, and all industry margin was given away to buyers in record time.

To understand how industry forces play out through time, it will be necessary to raise the resource-system perspective from the firm level to the industry level. Figure 11.4 portrays a simplified generic resource-system for an entire industry or industry segment. At top right is the shared resource of all segment customers, which is made up of the customers served by all the firms who seek to provide similar products or services. Those customers provide the industry with its

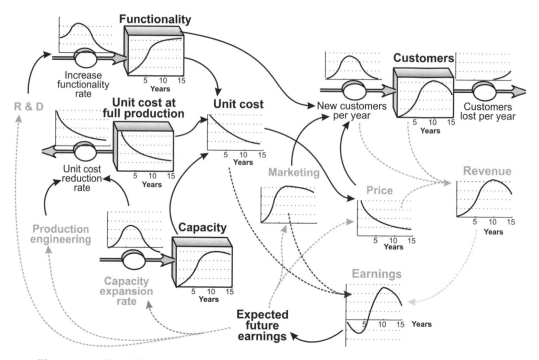

Figure 11.4 Simplified, generic industry resource system (note that each resource quantity is the total for all firms, and does not represent any one firm or any average).

revenues, through their purchase rate at current prices (i.e., total revenues reflect the *specific* prices charged by *each* supplier to *its* customers, not some abstract industry average). Customers are won to this industry from previous alternatives by the success of suppliers at offering improved functionality and lower prices. Eventually, a further industry emerges that offers still-greater benefits, and customers move on to that alternative, by flowing out of the top-right stock.

At left are highly aggregated summaries of the supply-side resources being developed by all the firms involved. These supply-side resources drive the industry's fixed and variable costs which, deducted from the revenues from customers, accounts for the industry's earnings stream at bottom right. Managers of both existing and would-be enterprises develop an emerging expectation of *future* earnings opportunities, which drives their efforts and investments in the industry via the mechanisms described in Chapter 10. These responses stimulate improvements in the supply-side resources—products or services with better functionality, lower unit costs, and increased capacity.

Certain points about this structure deserve noting. First, it shows neither the source of potential customers nor the subsequent industry to which they are lost—these arise at either end of the customer-flow chain at top right. Second, much of the feedback is not structural or programmed in, but depends on expectations and policy choices of management in the industry's firms. So, for example, the product's price is influenced by, but not a defined function of, current unit costs. Third, depending upon the product in question, sales will be driven either by the inflow of customers (i.e., the installed base for durable products), by the current resource stock of customers in the case of consumables, or possibly by both flow and stock, as illustrated in Chapter 4 by the elevator industry.

Next, note that unit cost is affected not just by the firm's production engineering efforts but also by capacity increases (giving rise to economies of scale) and by the product's functionality (unit costs are higher for a more functional product). Finally, note that, though we are rehearsing this story implicitly for a physical product, analogous arguments also describe the evolution of service products.

The industry's entire life cycle plays out as follows:

- At first, no firm is able to offer a product that is sufficiently functional to be useful to potential customers—the functionality resource is virtually empty. Furthermore, the unit cost is prohibitively high, so that, even if a functional product existed, firms could not afford to offer it at a price that would appeal to a significant number of customers. The industry's customer base remains empty, and the inflow of customers is zero. *Consider the example of flat-screen TVs that, in 1998, were so large, heavy, inefficient, unreliable, and costly as to be nonviable as a consumer product.*
- Even at this early stage, however, the promise of future sales and earnings is sufficiently clear to encourage investments in R&D to improve functionality and unit cost. There

Industry dynamics can have widespread effects

Titanium is tough and light, in many ways an ideal structural metal for many purposes. It is also more than five times the price of stainless steel, due to the complex and chemically messy process by which titanium is extracted from its ore. However, a new electrolytic production method promises to be radically cheaper. While the new process is still (at the time of writing) in the development stage, it might feasibly cut the cost of titanium metal by as much as three-quarters.

If this outcome is realized, it will trigger revolutionary dynamics that will ripple through downstream industries, and back up through markets for substitute and complementary products. Initially, the reduced price would simply stimulate modest increases in short-term demand from existing customers, following conventional demand-elasticity principles. However, the titanium industry would also experience major long-term shifts in its architecture. First, the new balance between price and functionality for the metal can be expected to initiate process innovations among metal fabricators. These will accumulate over several years, and will likely trigger competitive gains and losses, depending on the speed at which rival firms respond.

Manufacturers of end-products would then be offered an increasing range of newly functional materials at reducing prices, which would in turn trigger accumulating innovations in end-product functionality. This would encourage additions to end-product capacity, and the arrival of new manufacturers, which should drive growth in final customer numbers and demand for end-products. All of the above would drive further economies of scale in titanium metal production and processing, and trigger further rounds of functionality enhancement and cost reduction.

This scenario would have wider implications for the industries from which demand is captured. Structural steel for high-performance construction applications, for example, would be progressively substituted by the new material, and, as functionality and price improve still further, more and more application segments would be substituted. All assuming, of course, that this wouldn't be the first false dawn for a radical technology shift!

Were the promise of the new process to be fulfilled, the full range of industry dynamics will be manifest in discontinuities to the architectures of the mutually dependent sectors (i.e., several copies of Figure 11.4 will all start to move toward a new configuration).

comes a point, then, at which a viable product *can* be produced, at a cost that enables an affordable price—the product is still very expensive, and does not work brilliantly, but the combination is sufficiently attractive at least to win some early adopters among the potential customer base. The inflow to the customer base starts to run, and sales revenue begins to pick up. Earnings may be increasingly negative, however, due to the rising investment rate by firms whose confidence in a viable business opportunity is growing. Note too that marketing expenditures will be starting, in an effort to bring forward the flow of potential customers. *This industry phase too is exemplified by the flat-screen TV sector that, during 2000/1 saw increasingly viable and affordable products reach the market, and increasingly frequent advertizing. In this case, the "customer" sector should include the retail distribution channel, as well as consumers.*

- With further improvements in product functionality, unit cost, and affordability, customer growth takes off, at a rate that reflects the value offered by *this* product as compared with alternatives that either existed before the sector's birth, or else are developing in parallel. Firms continue to invest, not only in improved functionality and cost reduction but also in increased capacity. As described in Chapter 8, this dynamic will also be susceptible to exogenous factors such as changes in social and economic conditions.

- Gradually, progress for the entire industry slows down, as each resource hits limits to further progress. Opportunities for further improvements in functionality become smaller, and increasingly hard to find, and the removal of costs slows to a trickle. Furthermore, the industry runs out of new customers, as all those who might have found the product useful have been won over. Sales volume and revenues may continue of course, either from continued purchase in the case of consumable goods, or from replacements in the case of durables.

- Finally, this industry sector, too, is overtaken by a new upstart, whose innovative product becomes more attractive than that offered by the firms in our sector. Customer outflows start to run, further limiting both the potential for continued improvements and the managerial incentive to seek them. Capacity may be reduced too. This, together with the ending of resource-building investments and the lack of appeal to new-entrant firms, can make the later phases of an industry's life surprisingly profitable. This stands in sharp contrast to the often ferocious scramble for share in a growing industry and the heavy investments that go with this race.

We can now consider the implications of this industry-dynamic perspective for the five-forces framework.

The power of buyers to drive down prices and margins reflects both their ability and incentive to switch between the firms that make up the resource system in Figure 11.4. The mechanisms driving buyer switching were discussed in Chapter 8, which focused on the *rate* of switching through time. This switching rate is a consequence of the balance that customers perceive between the value (utility vs. price) of alternative products and the switching costs they experience in changing from one firm's product to another. Note, though, that Chapter 8 assumed neither perfect rationality among buyers, nor instantaneous switching at the moment when a perfectly rational decision to switch would be indicated.

Competition among rivals to capture revenues and earnings from each other reflects the policy choices on pricing, marketing, and resource development represented around the lower part of Figure 11.4. The early phases of the industry's life clearly provide the temptation to reduce price in anticipation of future cost reductions, a temptation driven by managerial perceptions of anticipated future earnings (see established economics texts on pre-emptive pricing and game theory). Rivalry for contested resources other than customers was also covered in Chapter 8, and is subsumed in the unit-cost resource.

A further important mode of behavior by rivals is their tendency to exit from the industry if profitability is poor. Again, the policy-response frameworks in Chapter 10 make no assumption that this question is addressed rationally. The worse the expected earnings at the bottom of Figure 11.4, the more pressure builds on management to leave the industry—"exit" implies shutting down the fraction of the industry's supply-side resources held by the particular firm, or else selling these to rivals or new entrants. However, the policy choice to exit will be subject to great uncertainty regarding future earnings. Since firms' business plans are expected to represent the positive outcomes of management's striving for strong performance, the sum of all business plans of all firms in most industries most certainly adds up to an implausibly optimistic view of the future. There is thus an inbuilt bias against exit.

The threat from substitutes is readily captured. A substitute is some alternative product or service that fulfills the same purpose for buyers as the product or service offered by the firms in the industry in question. A substitute for certain business air travel customers, then, might be videoconferencing. This pressure on the industry's profitability is represented by a second industry-level resource system, but this time capturing the supply-side resources of the firms offering the substitute. The relative gains and losses for the two industries arise from the three standard types of rivalry for customers discussed in Chapter 8.

The threat from new entrants arises when an industry's expected profitability is sufficiently attractive to make it worthwhile for new firms to consider entry. In addition, though, for the threat to be substantive, it must be feasible for such firms to assemble a complete system of resources. Once again, we are not stuck with having to treat entry as an on-off question, where either (a) entry has not occurred, so incumbent firms can enjoy strong profitability, or (b) entry has occurred, and profitability has been competed away. Instead, we can capture:

- the *rate* at which new firms enter the industry;
- the rate at which those firms accumulate the resources to compete;
- the consequential success that they enjoy in capturing contested resources, especially customers, from incumbents;
- their boundedly rational evaluation of earnings prospects and resulting decision making; and therefore
- the resulting rate of change in industry profitability.

The power of suppliers to extract margin from the industry by charging higher prices for its inputs does not seem to be encompassed by the industry resource system in Figure 11.4. However, in this case, the firm is, itself, within the "customer" resource stock for each of its *supplying* industries. Management therefore requires a quite separate picture of the resource system of upstream sectors for which it is one of many potential customers.

It may often be important to evaluate, dynamically, the upstream industry for which your firm is a customer, since firms often make commitments of their own on the assumption of a certain trajectory by their suppliers. This can clearly be dangerous. The entire product category may never achieve sufficient appeal to enough end-consumers, as when, for example, car dealerships are left with unsold stock of novel vehicles that their suppliers expected, wrongly, would appeal to car buyers. A more substantial example concerns the quandary facing consulting firms as to whether they should invest in skills development to support emerging information-systems services under development by hardware or software vendors. One such firm, for example, diverted a large proportion of its effort to providing IT consulting services in e-business just one year before the demand for these services, promoted with much optimism by vendors, collapsed.

A second purpose in analyzing the resource system of a supplying industry is to ensure that your own firm is not missing opportunities for advantage that arise from the dynamics playing out upstream. It is common, for reasons discussed above, for firms to make commitments on the basis of *expected* profitability, rather than current returns. As a customer to an industry, therefore, it may be to your benefit to evaluate whether any upstream firms or new entrants are offering pricing or functionality on such a basis, and to exploit such windows of opportunity. However, it will be equally important to ensure that their prospects are not so endangered by their strategy that they put your business at risk as well as their own.

Generic strategies

An early insight offered by the wielding of five-forces analysis on various industries was the observation that successful firms tended to pursue one of two contrasting positions:

- One route to superior profitability seemed to arise from pursuing cost leadership, where attention focused heavily if not exclusively on stripping out costs.
- The alternative route was to pursue differentiation, where the firm would selectively add costs to activities that promised to capture a more than compensating margin from customers.

A sophistication of this concept arose from recognizing that firms need not attempt to serve the entire market with one of these two alternatives, but could, instead, focus on the particular needs of a market segment.

Certain industries were found to offer few opportunities for differentiation. These were recognizable colloquially as "commodity" industries such as petrochemical raw materials or electrical power. Other industries offered far more extensive opportunities for differentiation.

This view of generic strategy choices is now regarded as far too simplistic. In particular, differentiation opportunities are typically both found and exploited in many allegedly commodity industries. Indeed, pursuit of this, or any other simple strategy choice is exceedingly dangerous. As has been emphasized throughout, the details of *your* strategic choices depend on *your* circumstances, not on generic findings from other cases. It is worth considering the basis of such simplistic advice, so that managers can recognize when they are again being urged to pursue one-dimensional strategies.

Many suggested explanations for strategic performance arise from efforts by researchers to explain profitability variances among large groups of firms. The data for such analysis typically arises either from databases of financial reports lodged by firms when they report their periodic results, or from a wide variety of survey services. Researchers also issue questionnaires to managers in order to capture further measures that they wish to evaluate. Great care is taken to ensure that the data used is reliable. However, two puzzling issues arise regarding the analysis that is then done with this data. Both concern the performance measures that are scrutinized.

In many cases, powerful statistical regression tools are applied to the data, to test for correlations between variables that are thought to explain performance as specified by some measure of profitability—typically, return on sales, on assets, or on equity. However, all these performance measures are *entirely* explained by the factors from which they are calculated. Return on assets is, by definition, the firm's operating profit divided by the value of its assets. So, it is not clear that other possible explanatory variables can improve on what is already a perfect explanation.

If the performance ratio is found to be well correlated with some other explanatory variable, it would have to be the case that either or both of the numbers from which that ratio was derived is also well correlated with the explanatory variable. The analysis would therefore be cleaner if a search was made for correlation between the explanatory variable and each of the components of the performance measure. If we think, for example, that the amount spent on marketing is a good determinant of return on assets, then it should also be the case that marketing spend is well correlated with operating profit (and/or with assets employed, though that would seem less plausible). However, operating profit is, itself, the difference between the cash gross margin and operating costs, so, again, we should expect marketing spend to be well correlated with gross margin, and so on.

Pursuing this logic, as suggested in Chapter 1, we ultimately get back to one or more asset stocks, where we might expect marketing spend to correlate with numbers and size of customers, but, as has been fundamental throughout this book, the current quantities of these asset stocks are not "correlated" with anything—they are identically equal to the sum of everything ever added, minus everything ever lost. *Not only is it impossible for simple correlation methods to explain usefully the current quantity of any accumulating asset stock, it is therefore also impossible to explain any value that depends upon that asset stock—which includes all financial performance measures.* There is thus no possibility that strategic rules, guidelines, theories, or frameworks built on regression analysis can offer more than a passing, coincidental resemblance to reality.

The second puzzling question concerns the performance measures themselves that research seeks to explain. As Chapter 1 noted, it is well established that financially-oriented investors seek sustained future streams of cash flow. And as any modern finance text will explain, free cash flow is neither the same as, nor well indicated by, profitability measures such as return on sales (ROS), on assets (ROA), or on equity (ROE). Neither investors nor management are typically so foolish as to fail to realize that cash distributed in earnings today is cash *not* reinvested in future growth, whether in marketing, training, or capacity expansion. A firm declaring operating margins of 15% while comparable firms are achieving 10%, will therefore come under careful scrutiny by investors and analysts, who will want convincing evidence that this higher margin is not being achieved at the expense of future cash flows.

One plausible consequence of this observation is that, to some degree, the failure of firms to sustain superior profitability, is a self-fulfilling inevitability. There is no reason to suppose that firms generating the strongest stream of free cash flows over many years will happen also to achieve the highest rates of return for all, or even for *any*, of the individual reporting periods during those years. We therefore have a curious situation, where strategy research hunts for statistical explanations for performance measures that shareholders do not value, and toward which managers do not strive.

PEST analysis

Chapter 8 explained how industry development is subject to the influence of exogenous forces falling into four categories—political, economic, social, and technological—these four initials providing the acronym for "PEST analysis". To be useful for strategic decision making, the scanning of these exogenous forces needs to be fact-based, time-based, and connected to the resource developments of firms in the industry. An accurate, quantified resource-system representation of these firms and their industry makes this aspiration feasible, by the rigorous identification and evaluation of the relevant asset stocks, especially (but not only) customers, channels, and staff.

Chapter 10 pointed out that policy responses by executives within firms will spill out to influence the accumulation and depletion of exogenous asset stocks such as consumers' savings levels or suppliers' production capacity. Note that these groups, and others, will enact policy responses of their own. A full exploration of these wider interactions between firms and exogenous asset-stock accumulations and policy responses is beyond the scope of this book. However, the principles explained in detail in Chapters 1 to 6, together with important concepts from Chapters 7 (intangibles) and 10 (policy) provide the basis for accurate evaluation of PEST factors on a firm's prospects and for developing the range of promising strategic responses.

Scenario-based strategy development

The dependence of firm performance upon exogenous factors has long made the forecasting of market and industry development a regular component of organizations' strategic planning processes and consulting firms' methods. However, the poor reliability of forecasting approaches has led many firms to adopt "scenario planning" approaches—attempts to describe plausible future states of the world, in order to test, at least qualitatively, the potential and robustness of alternative strategies (see, for example, de Geus, 1988; van der Heijden, 1996).

It is possible, though, to improve substantially on this qualitative approach by adding means for estimating the factors determining the scale and pace of change of industry evolution. Figure 11.4 already provides the basis of a coherent framework for the building of scenarios for an industry and its environment. That industry representation already captures explicitly, not only the influence of factors outside the direct control of the firm (customers, potential resources, and the resources of rivals) but also the factors that drive change in those exogenous resources. The opportunity to formalize a generic model of evolving industry scenarios therefore emerges from the observation that . . . *industry development arises from processes of **mutual** accumulation and depletion between demand-side asset stocks and the supply-side resources of all firms participating in the industry.* We already observed, in connection with Figure 11.4, that these interdependencies typically play out over the history of the industry sector in a characteristic manner. Where, then, does the opportunity for *contrasting* future scenarios arise?

Although the industry-dynamic structure has the potential to play out a characteristic life cycle, its likelihood of doing so, and the scale and timing of its principal phases, are highly uncertain. The contrasting fortunes of Japan's iMode and Europe's WAP phone sectors have been remarked upon before. Both markets featured consumers making choices to take up the service and purchase handsets, both involved service providers building Web-based service mechanisms to serve those consumers, and so on. Their contrasting outcomes arose from significant differences in the exogenous factors involved in each case, especially the usefulness of alternative mechanisms of service provision and the penetration of online PCs. There was always going to be a limit to the certainty with which firms could anticipate the consequences of these contrasting conditions between the two markets.

Such uncertainties are the norm rather than the exception, especially in emerging industries and sectors, so the resource-system perspective provides an integrated framework where the interplay between such uncertainties can be rehearsed. This rehearsal will generate many scenarios for the future, each with its own coherent story, its own contingencies, and its own degree of plausibility. Management can then make various uses of the model and its alternative scenarios:

- The variety of industry outcomes often suggests certain *"no-regrets" moves and options* that the firm can take, to preserve its access to opportunities while minimizing its exposure to a disappointing industry development. Microsoft, Intel, and others have developed some mastery in making relatively small commitments to a range of possible products, services, and solutions in the IT industry, enabling them to "step on the gas" fast when evidence seems to suggest that one alternative is proving successful, and withdrawing at little cost from others.

- The industry framework exposes *high-impact interdependencies* that will determine the likely path of development. Banks considering whether to switch their consumer credit cards to new chip-based technology could be wasting their money if too few retailers install the terminals to make use of the new cards' facilities. Any one firm can monitor this uptake of terminals by retailers, in order to judge the timing of its own conversion.

- The industry framework will also *identify critical flow rates* that suggest the sector is embarking on one or other path into the future. The major aircraft manufacturers, Boeing and Airbus, face high uncertainty as to whether the air travel market will move in a direction that would make the provision of super-jumbo aircraft viable. Both are watching carefully the patterns of passenger flows into alternative route patterns (notably hub-and-spoke vs. point-to-point), together with the accumulating rates at which airlines are changing the provision of these alternatives and the rate of development of new airport locations. In a different context, the rate of improvement in certain technologies such as voice-recognition and solar-energy capture are progressing along well-understood trajectories through time. These trajectories will, in due course, make these technologies feasible alternatives for a progressively increasing range of applications. The rate at which products embedding these new technologies are developed will provide strong evidence as to whether specific sectors are embarking on a switch to a new business model or not.

- It is also possible to go beyond the resource flow rates themselves and *seek leading indicators* in the factors that are likely to stimulate those flows. In the case of WAP and iMode phones, handset and infrastructure suppliers should have kept closely in touch with consumers' use of, and satisfaction with, the pre-existing alternatives. If this usage and satisfaction were low, then a novel alternative with demonstrable advantages could be expected to enjoy rapid uptake. A more fine-grained examination would have extended this research across contrasting groups of consumers, in order to check whether early uptake was the start of mass adoption or merely an experimental whim by early adopters. In another case, car manufacturers, concerned to judge the likely adoption by consumers of more fuel-efficient vehicles, are monitoring carefully the attitudes of young adults toward environmental issues.

- We have repeatedly pointed out that an understanding of the resource system for a firm does more than simply prepare management for what may happen—it offers a powerful tool for altering that future to the firm's advantage. The same applies to the industry-level models that provide a rigorous basis for exploring alternative scenarios, since they may *highlight powerful leverage points where the firm itself may direct the industry's future.* Returning to the example of the switch to chip-based credit cards, it is probable that certain influential banks will be able to drive the industry's migration by careful choice of whether selectively to subsidize retailers' adoption of new terminals, and, if so, when, how, and how strongly to do so. In the case of fuel-efficient cars, a manufacturer committed to taking the high ground has the option to choose a deliberate series of actions, including specific timing and scale, in order to precipitate exactly the transition in the wider market that is in its own interests. Such actions may be extremely extensive such as educational initiatives, political lobbying, dramatically symbolic acts, and other public relations devices.

The strategy process

This book has had little to say about issues in the so-called "process" agenda of the strategy field, which covers such topics as strategic leadership and commitment, the strategy development process, the link to organizational structure, cultural and political conditions within the firm, and the special issues that arise when firms attempt to change strategy or transform (Mintzberg and Quinn, 1997).

A central observation regarding the nature of strategic management is that many firms appear not to *have* an identifiable strategy—at least not one that is made explicit. However, we have taken it as axiomatic that it is both possible and advisable for management to seek, deliberately, to identify and pursue better strategic options rather than less promising alternatives. While there is no dispute that many firms and their leaders adopt an "emergent" stance (*watching what seems to work, then doing more of the same while cutting back on less successful initiatives*), powerful firms in many sectors evidently both make deliberate *ex ante* choices, and commit strongly to those choices, and enjoy strong, sustained, and growing earnings from having done so.

It is also apparent, though, that other firms make equally strong commitments to pursuit of strategies that are far from optimal, or even disastrous. Our aim, then, has been to load the odds in favor of management making the former, better choices rather than either making poorer choices or else making no choices at all.

With this purpose in mind, early evidence suggests that the resource-system approach, helping teams build a picture of their strategic architecture and a time-based appreciation of their situation and prospects, offers a significant contribution to the strategy process:

- A sound strategic architecture provides a firm foundation for the mission and vision statements that adorn boardrooms, offices, and reception desks in many firms. Clarity of purpose, evident in a strong strategic intent and commitment, is clearly preferable to confusion and indifference. Leaders, executives, and other staff find the enthusiasm to support their organization's efforts more readily when its purpose is clear. The diagrammatic depiction of the enterprise offered by the strategic architecture brings that purpose and direction into sharp focus.

- At the same time, we have already warned of the danger that, by being tightly specified, strategy can get frozen into a state that risks becoming inappropriate for changing environmental and competitive conditions. Strategy must be encouraged to evolve, or emerge through time, which is only possible if experimentation takes place around the central stream of progress. Chapter 10 highlighted the need for all organizations to retain some margin for reinvestment in developing the resources and capabilities needed for the future. Blind pursuit of optimal "returns" destroys any slack that this process requires. However, that chapter's emphasis was on the need to reinvest in resources for the *current* architecture. If an organization is to evolve, it also needs sufficient slack to experiment with *novel* resources, *adaptations* to its current architecture, and possibly complete *alternatives*. Once such experimentation produces some outcomes, its potential contribution to future strategy and performance is readily evaluated by using our architectural diagnosis.

- We have not attempted to develop any strong connection with considerations of organizational structure. However, Chapter 9 suggests that aligning staff groups with resource flows may be advantageous. This suggestion is supported by the observation that most examples of organizational capability seem to be closely associated with the confident and effective management of gains, development, and losses of resources. Since "capability" seems to be manifest in the accumulation and sustaining of processes and procedures, both codified and implicit, it seems advisable to encourage staff teams to become strong *custodians* of such capabilities. Furthermore, by making explicit each team's custody of critical capabilities and resource flows, the interdependence of each team on the support of others becomes crystal clear.

- We have had even less to say about strategic leadership, or the power and politics involved in the maneuvering that takes place around senior personalities. Yet, strategic choices made by organizations unavoidably reflect those personalities and power relationships. Charismatic leaders, with strong reputations, gain support from their colleagues, and can leverage this support to initiate and sustain commitment to a strategic direction. Things go wrong, though, when that reputation and charisma are ill-founded, or when they drive commitment to ill-advised strategies. Our fact-based depiction of the organization's strategic history, trajectory, and future offer two contributions. First, by clarifying exactly what *has* been achieved and how, it raises the probability that such personal influence is supported by a strong record of real achievement. (*In particular, it should expose the hit-and-run tactics of executives who make spectacular improvements to short-term performance, by actions that initiate the destruction of the firm's essential fabric, before moving swiftly on to another "triumph" elsewhere!*) Second, explicit use of the strategic architecture provides some quality assurance on the new purpose that such leaders attempt to inspire in their people. It is one thing to feel that we trust our leaders—how much better, also, to be able to say, *"Not only do we respect your leadership, we also see clearly where you are taking us and why it makes sense."*

The other major theme of the strategy process agenda is the importance of fitting strategy to "context"—that what should best be done depends on the situation in which the enterprise finds itself. Not only the *content* of strategy but also the *process* by which it is developed, adapted, and communicated differ widely for start-ups, growth firms, mature businesses, nonprofit cases, and so on.

We have gone further, however. Earlier chapters have repeatedly emphasized that, while strategic architectures of different firms might exhibit considerable similarity, the facts of every case will be unique, and must be treated as such. This implies that, within broad *classes* of context (entrepreneurial, growth, maturity, and so on), the nature, scale, and trajectory of the resources and capabilities within each firm will be quite distinctive. So too will be those resources and capabilities of rivals, as well as the important asset stocks in the external environment.

Further opportunities from a resource-system approach—corporate-level strategy

We should end with a brief note on some further potential offered by the resource-system perspective. This book has restricted itself to a focus on *business-level* strategy (i.e., the concerns facing management within a relatively well-defined, single-activity firm or division). In the process, it has also dealt with certain implications for *functional-level* strategy, notably in human resources, sales and marketing, and product development.

We have not attempted to cover issues of *corporate* strategy (i.e., the concerns facing management of the multi-business firm). This agenda includes the following concerns of corporate management, as well as many more:

- *Diversification.* Sooner or later, single-business firms use up the opportunity offered by a particular market, or else management identifies additional sectors where they think they could build business. The assessment of which opportunities to pursue, and whether and how to enter them is a major issue in strategy, and has a rather checkered history. So-called "portfolio" approaches of the 1960s and 1970s were largely disastrous, probably accounting for a greater destruction of shareholder value, in real terms, than any other management method in history. The diversified conglomerates that resulted have now largely been broken up, and the parts absorbed into more focused firms. These have tended to follow a more "related" approach to diversification, pursuing growth in new sectors where synergies were expected to arise. Synergies are readily recognized as the transfer or sharing of resources and capabilities. The process of developing an additional business unit is well captured by the resource-system framework, but now enhanced by the availability of pre-existing potential resources from the original core business.

- *Acquisition and merger.* A faster route to growth than build-it-yourself diversification is to search for opportunities to acquire or merge with firms that operate in either your own or a closely-related sector. If it's an identical business being acquired, two resource systems are being crashed together—two customer-bases will be served as one, offered a product range rationalized from those previously offered by the two firms, served by a larger salesforce featuring the best people and systems from those available, and so on (at least, that's the intention!). In practise, of course, much can go wrong; in particular, the shock of the merger can trigger vast changes in the rate of resource losses. Once again, the track record of such strategic initiatives is one of persistent disappointment—shareholders in acquiring firms typically lose value, often due to system failures. Key staff resign, major customers switch to rivals, investor confidence collapses, and hiring and sales success are devastated. A resource-system perspective both provides substance to the "before vs. after" comparison, as well as illuminating the transition process that must be navigated if the merger is to succeed. Where the acquisition is into a non-identical business, the resource-system analysis can highlight the nature and scale of change that the acquirer can expect to make to the "system" they are buying. In both cases, then, we can add assessment of the strategic architecture to the generally financial focus of the due-diligence process.

- *Alliances and business webs.* We have previously remarked that the strategic architecture of an enterprise is not restricted to the boundaries implied by legal ownership, but encompasses asset stocks outside the firm that are nevertheless a continuing component of its system. This enables us to capture entire systems that comprise more than one firm. At a basic level, we can treat a two-firm alliance as a simple linkage between two architectures, brought together precisely because each has certain specific resources or capabilities to offer to the combined system. A sound alliance will be able to outperform the prior achievements of the two separate entities, not just qualitatively but also in the quantified, financial terms referred to in Chapter 10. The combined architecture will clarify exactly the nature of the system that the new leadership team must manage, and alert both sides to any dangers of system failure. The same principle can be extended to managing the development of wider business webs comprising many firms like those clustered around enterprise resource-planning (ERP) systems.

- *Internationalization and multinational strategy.* Like diversification, acquisition, and merger, the process of geographic expansion is fraught with dangers. Resource systems that seem to function perfectly in one context either cannot be assembled in new territory, or fail to develop. In certain sectors such as retailing and professional services, failures and disappointments are numerous. Successes, too, are evident, though, and a resource-system appraisal offers a means to anticipate whether success will be likely in a particular case. Is the "potential customer" stock in a new territory similar in nature, and of viable scale, for the home country business model to stand a good chance of success? Can other system components be identified and assembled to a scale and within a timescale to achieve a self-sustaining system? Is the home-country enterprise spinning off sufficient managerial resource to deploy in the new territory and make this happen? Do there exist local partners with access to resources and capabilities of sufficient scale and quality to substitute for those the firm provides itself in its home territory? For established multinational corporations, similar questions arise, though extended across multiple geographic and product markets. Generally, though, questions of strategy development for such firms will divide into those that address the broad issues of corporate architecture and others concerned with specific developments in specific parts of the empire.

- *Corporate strategic control.* Approaches to corporate strategy control already exist that build on, but differ from, the policy questions relevant for the single-business firm. Corporate control too must take account of the trajectory of performance throughout the system of interrelated businesses. Again, this consideration will divide into questions concerning the direction in which the entire corporation is developing vs. more local questions of policy that impinge on particular parts of the group.

These issues and others such as questions concerning the evolution of industrial clusters and national industrial strategy will have to await further work.

Summary

Although SWOT analysis is an obsolete and inadequate approach to Strategy, it is still in widespread use among managers. It can be substantially improved by a sound comparison between the firm's resource base and those either offered by its rivals or required by its industry opportunities. The major contribution of the resource-system approach arises from going beyond this static appraisal of resources and capabilities, in capturing both their accumulation and interdependence.

Some form of value chain analysis is the most common tool of strategy analysis to be applied at the firm level. This essentially financial perspective often loses any connection with the underlying business resources or, crucially, with their gains and losses that are so essential. However, components of the value chain *can* be populated with cost streams based on sound, dynamic appraisal of resources, thus reducing the widespread risk that arises when strategy takes insufficient account of important interdependencies. One further tool of firm strategy, the experience curve, can be better understood in terms of the underlying resource dynamics.

Any appraisal of strategy dynamics will soon need to go beyond what can comfortably be handled on paper, or whiteboard, and will become increasingly complex. Inevitably, then, management will either need to develop modeling expertise within the firm or rely on outside advisors. It is vital, in such cases, for management to keep control of the process and avoid either being led into abstraction and excessive complexity, or bemused by seductive computer simulations that are poorly grounded in their business reality.

Most strategy insight over the last 20 years arises from industry-level analysis. The development of entire industry structures, though, is an evolving struggle between the resource systems of participating firms. Furthermore, the development, maturity, and decline of entire sectors depend on the relative strength of those sector systems, as compared with those of rival sectors offering substitute goods and services. The interaction of the five generic forces exerting pressure on industry margins are readily understood in terms of management's boundedly rational assessment of earnings opportunities offered by the industry structure as it develops through time.

These processes of industry evolution are unavoidably dynamic, so the static strategy guidelines derived from traditional, correlation-based research among large samples of firms are fundamentally and inescapably flawed.

The strategic architecture of both individual firms and entire sectors can take account of the most influential exogenous forces traditionally dealt with by PEST analysis. By doing so, management can construct fact-based, internally consistent, and quantitative scenarios, against which to assess their strategic options.

Although primarily concerned with the substance of firm strategy, the resource system also offers contributions to the strategy *process*. A crystal-clear, fact-based picture of the firm's strategic performance, prospects, and direction both eases the negotiation of strategic choices among the top team, and offers clarity of purpose and direction to others in the organization.

Beyond the concerns of those who lead focused businesses, there is considerable further scope to improve matters by applying a rigorously dynamic approach to corporate-level strategy: diversification, mergers, acquisitions, alliances, business webs, multinational strategy, regional and national strategic advantage.

Appendix

Theory Underlying the Strategy Dynamics Method

The principal quest of strategic management research is to explain firm performance, usually expressed in financial terms. Since investors value expected future cash flows, however, instantaneous explanations are not sufficient. Any useful explanation of strategic performance must also account for the stream of earnings through time.

The resource-based view (RBV) asserts that performance is a function of firm resources (Barney, 2001, chapter 5). Earnings at any moment are quite accurately calculated in the P&L account and cash-flow statements, calculations that rely merely on a subset of resources (customers, staff, capacity, etc.), and certain attributes of those resources (customers' purchase rates, employee costs, production costs, etc.). In addition, certain discretionary management choices impact immediately on current earnings, notably expenditure rates and price. Exogenous influences are also involved, like the impact of economic conditions on typical customer demand, in addition to discretionary choices by rivals, such as their price. Attributes will be shown also to be resources, so RBV can be expressed mathematically as ... *the performance of the firm* Π *at time T depends on the levels of strategic resources* R_1 *to* R_n, *on discretionary management choices M, and on exogenous factors at that time E* (Equation 1):

$$\Pi(T) = f[R_1(T), \ldots, R_n(T), M(T), E(T)] \tag{1}$$

This leaves unexplained the role of the many other resources that clearly affect future performance, but which are not involved in this current calculation of earnings. Such non-P&L resources include, for example, the current range of products, stock of technologies, and intangible factors such as staff morale and market reputation.

Furthermore, it is not possible that any *other* variables, either internal or external to the firm, can be involved in explaining current profitability such as clarity of leaders' vision, reward systems, number or size of rivals, market growth rate, entry barriers to the industry, and so on. Since all these items are clearly important, their influence must arise through giving rise, somehow, to the current quantity of each resource that is involved in the calculation of earnings.

If current earnings can be calculated directly from the limited set of items above, then that is true not only at this precise moment but also at all other times in the firm's past or future. An adequate explanation for performance over time must therefore explain the trajectory over which the levels of these resources vary through time.

Resources as accumulating asset stocks

Amit and Schoemaker (1993, A&S) define resources as "... *stocks of available factors that are owned or controlled by the firm* ..." However, firms commonly use stocks of items that they do *not* own or control, but to which they merely have somewhat reliable access. If "reliable" means the likelihood that a resource unit available today will still be available in the future, then customers and distributors can be more reliable resources than employees. The definition of "resources" therefore needs extending to "... *stocks of items that the firm owns or controls, or to which it has somewhat reliable access*". Two important positions are taken here:

- We follow A&S in distinguishing resources from capabilities—both categories are asset stocks, but resources do *not* include capabilities.
- We do not distinguish so-called "strategic" resources from others. That view assumes most resources to be easily imitable or tradable, and therefore of no relevance—only certain hard-to-imitate resources can, allegedly, account for performance differences. We reject this stance. Performance reflects the effectiveness of the entire firm system, in which "nonstrategic" resources are as inextricably involved as others. A firm with one-tenth of the cash held by an otherwise identical rival will follow a different future performance trajectory, in spite of the fact that cash is an entirely available commodity.

The distinctive feature of resources is their tendency to accumulate and deplete over time (Dierickx and Cool, 1989). The level of a resource stock can *only* be changed by adding or removing a quantity during some period. The level of a resources at any moment is thus identically equal to the sum of all resources ever added to the stock, minus the sum of all resources ever lost. Accumulation and depletion are captured by the mathematics of integral calculus, so ... *the current level of resource R at time T is the sum of its net rates of accumulation r since time t = 0*, plus its initial quantity (Equation 2):

$$R_i(T) = \int_0^T r_i(t)\, dt + R_i(0) \tag{2}$$

An unavoidable consequence of resource accumulation is that no other explanation can exist for any resource level, notably any putative causality implied by statistical correlation. Marketing expenditure, for example, might encourage current customers to purchase more frequently, and therefore be expected to correlate with sales volume. But, if marketing also affects the rate at which new customers are acquired over time, then a new but *constant* spending rate results in a *changing* sales rate.

More generally, since firm performance is computed from several accumulating resources, regression methods can only achieve predictive reliability in the vanishingly rare circumstances where resource levels are unchanging. Thus, no explanation for firm performance of the form $\Pi(T) = fn[x_1(T), \ldots, x_n(T), \ldots]$ can have any causal validity (aside from the calculation captured in the P&L account).

Accumulation also invalidates attempts to explain performance as a function of time-lagged variables; for example, demand$(T) = fn[\text{Marketing}(T - n)]$. Not only is there no feasible means by which dependent variables can respond to factors separated from them in time but the accumulation process may still be occurring also. The only means for any factor to influence other items at a later time is by being stored (i.e., accumulated) or by causing other items to be stored.

Resource accumulation depends on existing resource levels

We now turn to the question of what is required for resource stocks to accumulate. It seems that no case exists in which resource accumulation can take place in the absence of finite levels of *existing* resources. This is even true for new enterprises, where cash can be raised and key staff hired, only if the entrepreneur possesses a stock of experience and credibility.

The growth rate of a resource may also depend upon the current level of that resource itself, as when existing customers recommend the firm to others. Management choices such as expenditure rates and price are strongly involved in influencing resource flow rates. Indeed, since performance is calculated from resource levels, and those levels reflect accumulated flow rates, these are the *only* places in the firm system where management can influence future earnings. Exogenous factors play a part once more (e.g., when economic recession causes customer losses). Thus ... *the current rate of accumulation r_i of resource i at time T is a function of the current level of all existing resources, including that of resource i itself, on management choices M and on exogenous factors E* (Equation 3):

$$r_i(T) = f_i[R_1(T), \ldots, R_n(T), M(T), E(T)] \tag{3}$$

Dependence of resource flows on particular levels of existing resources may be either positive or negative. A larger resource stock of salespeople may raise the rate of customer acquisition, for example, while insufficient service staff may cause customer loss rates through poor service.

Equations (1) to (3) constitute a basic model of the firm as a system of interdependent resources. The system is open, not only because its resource accumulations and depletions are partly determined by exogenous factors but also because many of the required resources must be developed from outside the firm, and defended against loss. A firm's performance over time therefore depends on its relative progress in developing these potential assets, capturing them from rivals, and retaining them.

Since the firm need only have somewhat reliable access to resources, ownership is not necessary, and the model is indifferent to the location of firm boundaries—performance can be equally captured, for example, whether the firm manufactures in its own facilities, or subcontracts production.

The interdependence implied by Equation (3) gives rise to feedback mechanisms within the firm's system. Feedback may take one of two forms. Resource changes may be self-reinforced—an increase in r_i at time T causing further changes that result in further increases (assuming no other influences). Alternatively, resource changes can be self-balancing—an increase in r_i at time T causing further changes that result in that rate of increase being reduced. In combination with stock accumulation, such feedback denies discovery of analytical solutions to the resulting firm model. Explanations and optimal solutions for any objective can only be discovered by repeated simulation, using the system dynamics method (Forrester, 1961), whose essential components, as they apply to strategic management, are given by Equations (1) to (3).

Potential resources and rivalry (see Chapter 8)

Firms must usually accumulate certain resources from "potential" stocks, outside their current control—consumers or firms who might wish to become customers, skilled people who might be hired, and so on. If stocks of these potential resources are plentiful, then the firm's resource accumulation can be rapid, whereas, if the potential stock is empty, then it will not be able to develop the resource at all. Equation (3) therefore needs to be extended, so that ... *the firm's accumulation of resource i at time T is also dependent upon the availability of potential resource at that time P(T)* (Equation 3b):

$$r_i(T) = f_i[R_1(T), \ldots, R_n(T), P_1(T), \ldots, P_n(T), M(T), E(T)] \qquad (3b)$$

For a particular firm, resource can be won not only from potential sources but also from rivals. Competitive performance thus depends on the firm's success at persuading customers, skilled staff, and other contestable resources to switch to the firm and remain with it into the future. Since each firm's ability to accumulate and retain any one resource depends upon its existing stock of resources ... *the net accumulation rate of any resource i by firm j depends on the firm's existing resource levels $R_{1-n,j}$, rivals' resource levels $R_{1-n,1-m}$, levels of potential resources P_{1-n}, managerial choices of firms 1 to m, and exogenous factors E.* Firm j is included within the array of firms $(1 - m)$ in the industry, so Equation (3b) can be extended to deal with rivalry, as given in Equation (3c):

$$r_{i,j}(T) = f_i[R_{1,1}(T), \ldots, R_{n,m}(T), P_1(T), \ldots, P_n(T), M_{1-m}(T), E(T)] \qquad (3c)$$

To complete the formulation of rivalry dynamics, it is necessary to reflect the possibility that any pool of potential resource P may itself accumulate. Increasing functionality, falling price, and firms' marketing efforts stimulate creation of potential customers. Similarly, perceived career opportunities and good salaries stimulate creation of potential staff with skills relevant to the industry, from which pool individual firms then seek to attract individual employees. Managerial choices of all firms in the industry are involved once more, either unintentionally—as when price reductions to capture customers from rivals incidentally create new potential customers—or deliberately. Thus ... *the rate p_i at which any potential industry resource P_i grows at any time T depends on the existing* *stock of resources and potential resources in the industry, the managerial choices of all firms, and exogenous factors* (Equation 4):

$$p_i(T) = f_i[R_{1,1}(T), \ldots, R_{n,m}(T), P_1(T), \ldots, P_n(T), M_{1-m}(T), E(T)] \qquad (4)$$

Competition to develop potential resources is conveniently referred to as Type 1, and is most evident in emerging industries. However, Type 1 rivalry continues to feature in mature and declining industries—new customers, staff, and channels may continue to emerge, simultaneously with the demise of established entities.

In addition to Type 1 rivalry, firms compete to steal resources from one another. The resource accumulation and depletion rates in such processes—termed Type 2 rivalry—are still dependent upon the existing resource holdings of the firms, so this mechanism is already captured by Equation (3c). That function must also include the impact of switching costs, which constrain the rate at which customers (and other resources) flow between rivals. Switching costs also obstruct firms' ability to develop potential resources. These costs will, however, differ in nature and scale from the switching costs that constrain inter-firm capture of already-developed resources.

Certain resource items may be shared—customers, suppliers, advertizers, and even employees may not be exclusively held by a single rival. Such shared resources simply feature in the resource systems of each firm that enjoys access to them, so are already dealt with by Equations (1) to (3). In these cases, a further form of rivalry (Type 3) arises as competing firms attempt to win share of access.

Resource attributes (see Chapter 7)

Individual entities within the population of a resource stock generally differ from each other in one or more attributes that may influence firm performance. This influence may be direct (e.g., customers vary in their rate of purchase from the firm, which directly determines revenue and profitability) or operate through affecting other resource-accumulation processes (e.g., sales staff differ in skill and products differ in functionality, both of which affect customer-acquisition rates, and hence future profitability).

Such attributes, like the resources that possess them, can only be changed by means of inflows or outflows. Staff skills, for example, can be raised by training, or lost through lack of practise. Attribute stocks also rise or fall, as their resource carrier is won or lost—staff skills are added to by new recruits and lost when individuals leave. This mechanism is known as a coincident flow (Forrester, 1961). This intimate connection between a resource R_i and its attributes R_i', R_i'', ... *implies that* ... *rates of change of resource attributes* r_i', $r_b' r_i''$, ... *at time T are a function of the rate of change* r_i *of resource* R_i *itself*:

$$r_i'(T) = f_i' r_i(T) \quad \text{etc.} \qquad (4)$$

Although resource attributes differ in character from resources themselves (being intimately tied to a specific resource carrier), it nevertheless remains the case that their accumulation rate depends on the firm's existing resource levels, rivals' resource levels, levels of potential resources, and exogenous factors. Equation (3c) therefore applies equally to attributes as to resources themselves.

Firm capabilities, resource building, and system performance (see Chapter 9)

The firm's success in accumulating and retaining resources is also constrained or enabled by its capabilities. Again, for consistency and clarity, this Appendix builds on Amit and Schoemaker (1993, A&E), who define organizational capabilities as ... *"a firm's capacity to deploy resources, usually in combination, using organizational processes ... that are firm-specific and are developed over time ..."* It has been shown that firm performance is directly and immediately accounted for by current resource levels. Capabilities are not used in the computation of the P&L account or cash-flow statements, so do not feature in Equation (1).[1] What, then, is the purpose served for the firm in "deploying resources" well or poorly?

A continuing puzzle in strategic management is to explain how resource-poor firms emerge to challenge dominant, resource-rich rivals. Differences in resource-system design may partly explain such dynamics, reflected in a particular firm's choice of the function given in Equation (3c). There remains the question, though, as to how one firm is able to grow a resource more quickly than rivals when it appears to have no more (or even less) of the other resources it needs. Some firms are more *capable* than rivals at building the resource—strong capabilities in product development, financial control, marketing, and training, for example, result in rapid development of product performance, cash, the customer base, and the staff skills of the organization, respectively. If this is the case, then capabilities have no meaning in isolation from the strategic resources of the firm.

To overcome this limitation of established definitions, "capability" must be redefined as relating to a specific resource-building and resource-sustaining task; that is, as ... *a firm's capacity to build and sustain a particular resource, for any given availability of the other resources needed for that task, that is, itself, developed over time.*

Note that the phrase "developed over time" in the A&S definition implies that capabilities, like resources, are asset stocks that accumulate and deplete. To some degree, resource-building performance reflects the co-flow of staff skills, as new hires bring their skills to the team, as resignations deplete that skill base, and as training efforts boost those skills. However, capability is more than simply the sum of individuals' skills since, as the A&S definition notes, it depends upon the effectiveness of organizational processes. Capability captures how well individuals operate with those processes, with available information, and with available resources to accomplish the resource-building task.

---

[1] In fact, as explained in Chapter 9, particular capabilities may, in certain cases, feature in current rates of revenue and cost, and therefore, strictly, *will* feature in Equation (1).

Capability C_i is thus a moderating factor on the existing resource-building rate r_i, given by the function in Equation (3c). The remaining challenge, therefore, is to explain the accumulation rate c_i, for capability C_i. If the firm never undertakes any activity to build resource R_i, it is unlikely to develop the corresponding capability. Conversely, the more experience it gains in this task, the more opportunities it has to develop effective organizational processes, information, and information flows to enhance its effectiveness. This implies that ... *the rate of accumulation c_i, of capability C_i, is a function of the corresponding resource-building rate r_i* (Equation 6):

$$c_i(T) = \frac{dC_i(T)}{dT} = f[r_i(T)] \tag{5}$$

Firms do not exhibit a uniform tendency to accumulate capability in any resource-building task, in spite of relatively equal opportunities to learn. In practice, therefore, Equation (5) may need to include a factor to reflect the firm's learning effectiveness. Since this learning effectiveness itself is capable of developing through time, it too will be an accumulating asset stock, and the representation of firm capabilities becomes recursive.

Note that resource-building or maintenance tasks may be focused upon particular functions or staff groups, but are often contributed to, or hindered by, others in the firm. Customer-service staff, for example, while dominating efforts to retain customers, may be undermined if order-processing or delivery departments perform poorly. An organization may thus exhibit poor resource-building rates, in spite of employing skilled people in key functions or, conversely, may exhibit strong resource-building capabilities, while operating with relatively unskilled staff.

This discussion and formulation of the nature and role of organizational capabilities leaves no option but to include their influence in the explanation for the critical variable r_i. Since capability levels, like resource levels, are constrained in their influence by their *relative* strength vs. rivals, Equation (3c) must be extended to include the influence of capability i for all firms $1, \ldots, m$. Thus ... *the rate of accumulation r_i of resource i at time T by firm j is dependent also upon the current level of capability C_i at that resource-building task possessed by firm j, relative to all firms $1, \ldots, m$* (Equation 3d):

$$r_{i,j}(T) = f_i[C_{i,1}(T), \ldots, C_{i,m}(T), R_{1,1}(T), \ldots, R_{n,m}(T), P_1(T), \ldots, P_n(T), M_{1-m}(T), E(T)] \tag{3d}$$

A pragmatic note

This appendix has established that the rate of accumulation of strategic resources is absolutely central to a sound understanding of strategic performance over time, through its unique role in Equation (2). Yet, it might appear that Equation (3d) has become so extensive and so potentially complex that no practical application would be possible. However, application of this perspective to practical cases is more encouraging.

While the general form of resource-accumulation function is indeed given by Equation (3d), the rate of accumulation for any specific resource for any specific firm at any particular moment is readily estimated from a somewhat limited number of driving forces. Customer-acquisition rates, for example, may depend most strongly on relative price and functionality of the firm's product, and on the number of salespeople, moderated by the firm's relative sales capability. Similarly, staff resignation rates at any time may be found to reflect relative pay, workload, and the availability of alternative jobs.

The research task in practical cases, then, is to discover the dominant few factors that do indeed feature in the current explanation for r_i. In spite of earlier comments about the limitation of regression methods in the search for explanations of firm performance, such approaches *are* helpful at this point. Executives or researchers may have some insight into the likely causes of customer acquisition or staff attrition, but confidence in that insight is built by quantitative research and statistical analysis. Regression is safe in this instance, since the causality being tested is neither of an accumulating nature nor confounded by the proposed cause and effect being separated in time.

Naturally, a diverse population of customers or staff may feature subgroups, for each of which a different mix of considerations motivates behavior. But, this makes sound explanations for rates of resource accumulation more achievable (if harder work!), rather than less so.

Managerial policy and control

The discussion thus far has not addressed the means by which management exercises judgment and influence over the structure and performance of the resource system. A full exposition of this issue is beyond the scope of this appendix, but certain observations can be made.

As noted earlier, if firm performance depends on strategic resource levels, and these can only be changed by resource flows, then the *only* influence management can have over strategic performance is by choices that affect each resource flow r_i. They can, of course, make certain choices regarding how to spend revenues; for example, by raising expenditure on marketing or training in preference to declaring higher profits, but this unavoidably has consequences for resource flows, and thus for resource levels and performance in the future. Hence the appearance of managerial choices, M, in both Equation (1) and Equation (3).

Executives can influence resource accumulation rates via one of two mechanisms. First, they have some discretion as to which resources $R_1, \ldots, R_n$ they deploy to drive any resource flow r_i. They might choose, for example, to deploy distributors to promote a new product, rather than a direct salesforce, or emphasize service support resource rather than product functionality in their marketing. This mechanism includes the search for, and connecting of, potential drivers to any desired resource flow. Management can choose, for example, to research the firm's reputation level with existing customers and use its findings explicitly in new-customer acquisition efforts.

The second form of managerial influence over resource flows arises in their direct discretion over influential drivers, such as price or marketing spend in the pursuit of new customers, or salaries and training budgets in the search for new staff. These choice mechanisms reflect organizational decision-making processes that may include sociological and political influences, as well as would-be rational optimization. Those choices are, at least in part, informed by information gleaned about the current state and trajectory of business performance and its components.

Management tries to remain aware of the current rate and trend of earnings, the customer base, staff morale, and so on, and makes choices designed to bring these into line with evolving goals (goals that may, of course, conflict). In effect, therefore, executives have some limited scope to define for themselves the form of each function f_i.

References

Amit, R. and Schoemaker, P. (1993) "Strategic assets and organisational rent". *Strategic Management Journal*, **14**, 38–46.

Bain & Co. (2001) *Management Tools*. www.bain.com.

Barney, J.B. (2001) *Gaining and Sustaining Competitive Advantage* (2nd edn). Reading, MA: Addison-Wesley.

Boston Consulting Group (1970) *Perspectives on Experience*. Boston: Boston Consulting Group.

Copeland, T., Koller, T. and Murrin, J. (2000) *Valuation—Measuring and Managing the Value of Companies*, Chichester, UK: John Wiley & Sons.

de Geus, A. (1988) "Planning as learning". *Harvard Business Review*, **66**(2), 70–74.

Dierickx, I. and Cool, K. (1989) "Asset stock accumulation and sustainability of competitive advantage". *Management Science*, **35**, 1504–1511.

Doman, A., Glucksman, M.A., Tu, N.-L. and Warren, K. (2000) "The talent-growth dynamic", *McKinsey Quarterly*, **1**, 106–115.

Forrester, J.W. (1961) *Industrial Dynamics*. Waltham, MA: Pegasus Communications.

Grant, R.M. (2001) *Contemporary Strategy Analysis* (4th edn). Cambridge, MA: Blackwell.

Huyett, B. and Roxburgh, C. (2000) *McKinsey on Strategy*. New York: McKinsey & Co.

Kaplan, R. and Norton, D. (1996) *The Balanced Scorecard*. Cambridge, MA: Harvard Business School Press.

Martin, J. and Petty, J. (2000) *Value Based Management*. Cambridge, MA: Harvard Business School Press.

McGahan, A. and Porter, M. (1997) "How much does industry matter, really?" *Strategic Management Journal*, **18**(Summer Special Issue), 15–30.

Mintzberg, H. and Quinn, J.B. (1997) *The Strategy Process* (2nd edn). London: *Financial Times*/Prentice-Hall.

Morecroft, J.D.W. (1985) 'The feedback view of business policy and strategy'. *System Dynamics Review*, **1**, 4–18.

Penrose, E.T. (1959) *The Theory of the Growth of the Firm*. New York: John Wiley & Sons.

Porter, M.E. (1980) *Competitive Strategy*. New York: Free Press.

Porter, M.E. (1985) *Competitive Advantage*. New York: Free Press.

Prahalad, C.K. and Hamel, G. (1990) "The core competence of the corporation". *Harvard Business Review*, **68**(3), 79–93.

Richardson, G.P. (1999) *Feedback Thought in Social Science and Systems Theory*. Waltham, MA: Pegasus Communications.

Rumelt, R.P. (1991) "How much does industry matter?" *Strategic Management Journal*, **12**(3), 167–185.

Senge, P.M. (1990) *The Fifth Discipline*. New York: Doubleday.

Simon, H.A. (1976) *Administrative Behavior* (3rd edn). New York: Free Press.

Sterman, J.D. (2000) *Business Dynamics*. New York: Irwin McGraw-Hill.

van der Heijden, K. (1996) *Scenarios: The Art of Strategic Conversation*. Chichester, UK: John Wiley & Sons.

Wernerfelt, B. (1984) "A resource-based view of the firm". *Strategic Management Journal*, **5**, 171–180.

Zehnder, E. (2001) "A simpler way to pay". *Harvard Business Review*, **79**(4), 53–61.

Index